D1564290

ARTISAN WORKERS

IN THE

UPPER SOUTH

ARTISAN WORKERS

IN THE

UPPER SOUTH

Petersburg, Virginia
1820–1865

L. DIANE BARNES

LOUISIANA STATE UNIVERSITY PRESS

BATON ROUGE

Published by Louisiana State University Press
Copyright © 2008 by Louisiana State University Press
All rights reserved
Manufactured in the United States of America
First printing

Designer: Laura Roubique Gleason
Typeface: Whitman
Printer and binder: Thomson-Shore, Inc.

LIBRARY OF CONGRESS CATALOGING-IN-PUBLICATION DATA

Barnes, L. Diane.
  Artisan workers in the Upper South : Petersburg, Virginia, 1820–1865 / L. Diane Barnes.
    p. cm.
  Includes bibliographical references and index.
  ISBN 978-0-8071-3313-2 (cloth : alk. paper) 1. Skilled labor—Virginia—Petersburg—History—
19th century. I. Title.
  HD8085.P48B37 2008
  331.7'94—dc22

                                                                                            2007035914

The paper in this book meets the guidelines for permanence and durability of the Committee on
Production Guidelines for Book Longevity of the Council on Library Resources. ∞

This is for Ben and in memory of my best friend Reggie.

Contents

Acknowledgments

Writing and researching a book is a collective enterprise. Although only one name appears on the title page of this one, it could not have materialized without a tremendous amount of help from a variety of individuals and institutions. The research phase of this project coincided with the opening of the new and modern facility of the Library of Virginia in Richmond in 1997. This means that I have no stories of researching in the heat of summer with no air conditioning or in the winter with cold seeping around the window panes of the old building on Capitol Street. Instead, my memories are of a highly modernized library and an excellent staff of archivists and librarians. Brent Tarter stands out among those at the Library of Virginia to whom I owe a special debt. Brent's outstanding knowledge of Virginia history helped guide me in the early phases of this project, and his hospitable nature made me feel welcome at the Library and in Richmond. Others at the Library also aided my entry into Virginia history circles. Jim Watkinson shared his research on the Petersburg Benevolent Mechanic Association and pointed me in the right direction on a number of occasions. I owe a special thank you to Gregg Kimball and Sara Bearss for their assistance and camaraderie.

I also ran up a few debts across town at the Virginia Historical Society, where Frances Pollard and the library staff offered professional and cordial assistance with my research. I was very fortunate to conduct a significant part of my research in the Historical Society's world-class facility, where the most frequent concern of the librarians is whether the materials are being brought out fast enough. Two Mellon Fellowships provided by the Virginia Historical Society gave me three weeks of research that would not have been possible otherwise. I also owe a lot to Nelson Lankford, who solicited and provided an outlet for the first of my research on Petersburg artisans in the *Virginia Magazine of History and Biography.*

This project began as my dissertation at West Virginia University (WVU), where I was the beneficiary of an outstanding education. There I was lucky enough to have, not one, but two important mentors. Jack McKivigan guided the early stages of my research, beginning as a graduate research paper. He taught me how to think like a historian and how to be a workaholic. He also coaxed me into the world of documentary editing, and my work for the *Frederick Douglass Papers* provided a badly needed break from microfilm research. When Ken Fones-Wolf later became my dissertation director, the project matured under his expertise in labor history, and he taught me to remain calm in all circumstances. My historical skills grew under his guidance and I continue to value our friendship. I also owe much to Elizabeth Fones-Wolf, Ron Lewis, and Mary Lou Lustig for their able guidance during this project's development. On the administrative front, Nancy McGreevy helped me to secure two travel grants from the provost's office at WVU, allowing me to spend part of two summers in Richmond. At the WVU library, my biggest debt falls to Rhonda Donaldson, who always went out her way to make sure I had the resources I needed. During my time at WVU, my research was also supported by a Phi Alpha Theta doctoral fellowship.

The final stages of this book took shape after I began my tenure at Youngstown State University (YSU). There my history department colleagues provided encouragement to see the project through to completion. Martha Pallante, who turned out to be a good friend as well as an outstanding department chair, has offered invaluable words of support and advice. Donna DeBlasio's engaging sense of humor and camaraderie provided numerous needed diversions. Thanks also to Martin Berger for a close read in the final stage of the project. The YSU College of Graduate Studies and Research, headed by Peter Kasvinsky, provided leave in the form of a Research Professorship and financial assistance in support of my research and writing. The librarians and interlibrary loan staff at YSU's Maag Library, and most especially Ellen Banks, were very accommodating to some rather unusual loan requests. In the final editing stages of this project, my graduate research assistants, Heidi Giusto and Jarret Ruminski, each undertook a close reading of the manuscript. Maureen Wilson and the staff in Media and Academic Computing ably adapted and created maps that greatly enhance the book.

My parents, Tom and Glenda Mowrey, always encouraged my academic pursuits with both kind words and their checkbook, even when they must have privately wondered if I was planning to stay in college forever. Over the past ten years, my husband, Ben Barnes, has spent much time in the world of Petersburg artisans. He read and listened to various drafts of the manuscript, and once gave up a week of his life to act as an able-bodied research assistant. He also endured vacations in the Blandford churchyard and the Petersburg Public Library. I cannot begin to express the debt of faith and gratitude that I owe him for putting up with an historian's obsession with the past.

As often happens as part of a long-term research project, an earlier version of chapter 2 was published in 1999 as "Southern Artisans, Organization, and the Rise of a Market Economy in Antebellum Petersburg," in volume 107 of the *Virginia Magazine of History and Biography*. Parts of the manuscript also appear as a chapter titled "Fraternity and Masculine Identity: The Search for Respectability among White and Black Artisans in Petersburg, Virginia" in *Southern Manhood: Perspectives on Masculinity in the Old South*, edited by Craig Thompson Friend and Lorri Glover and published by the University of Georgia Press in 2004. I offer thanks to both the Virginia Historical Society and the University of Georgia Press for permission to reprint this material. I would also like to thank the two reviewers who offered valuable suggestions for revisions to the manuscript. I owe a special debt to Frank Towers of the University of Calgary, whose incredible review made this book a better one. Finally, my appreciation goes to the editorial staff at Louisiana State University Press, and especially to Rand Dotson for seeing the project's merit.

ARTISAN WORKERS

IN THE

UPPER SOUTH

Introduction

Visiting Petersburg, Virginia, at the beginning of the antebellum era, European traveler William Tell Harris observed that "bustle and activity are every where seen." Although the city was recovering from a recent fire, paved and level streets lined the town and "elegant brick buildings" predominated. Petersburg was already a busy commercial center, and Harris recorded its advantages: "a rich neighbouring country, and a navigable stream, the Appomattox, whose bank near the town is lined with large boats and schooners, taking in tobacco, grain, &c."[1] Between 1820 and the Civil War, Petersburg's reputation for commerce attracted significant industrial development. By 1860, five railroad links crossed the town, and tobacco factories, iron foundries, and cotton mills dotted the landscape. The town's location, just twenty-five miles south of Richmond, made it an important center of commerce and industry. Writing of his visit to America, Harris commented that "here, you know not the merchant, the lawyer, or the mechanic from each other, by their appearance; neither are any provincialisms or dialects observable; or that awkwardness of manner, which in Europe marks the difference between the higher and lower orders."[2]

This is a study about skilled white and free African American men who lived and worked within the slave economy of the antebellum Upper South, in the city of Petersburg, Virginia. These artisans, or mechanics, as they called themselves, toiled as carpenters, blacksmiths, coach makers, barbers, and in other skilled crafts in one of the most industrialized cities in the pre–Civil War South. Contrary to studies emphasizing the backwardness of southern development, the artisans of Petersburg experienced significant economic and social change as their community entered the modern industrial world.[3] In the four decades

1. William Tell Harris, *Remarks Made During a Tour of the United States of America in the Years 1817, 1818, and 1819* (London: Sherwood, Neely & Jones, 1821), 53–54.

2. Ibid., 54.

3. The pre-capitalist nature of the southern economy is most forcefully argued by Eugene

following Harris's visit, a growing class division separated the mechanic community as some masters became the merchants and entrepreneurs of an emerging middle class and other small masters and journeymen faced a reality of permanent wage labor. The class distinctions Harris found lacking were clearly evident by 1860. These changes and the natural advantages and commercial activity that attracted artisans to the town made Petersburg resemble northern cities in many respects. Class divisions and cultural change were as evident in this southern city as in any northern locale. However, Petersburg's situation in the slave economy of the Upper South complicated issues of class development and divisions with issues of race. The city's skilled white workingmen adopted a unique form of proslavery free laborism that shaped their culture and their relations with both the new middle class and area planters.

Between 1820 and the onset of the Civil War in 1861, the world of workingmen changed significantly across the United States. Many historical studies detail how the so-called market revolution influenced the lives and career paths of skilled workers in northern cities. The most elaborate studies focus on clashes between journeymen and masters, the waning of artisan republicanism, and the decline of opportunities in an advancing capitalist economy.[4] More recently, artisan studies stepped away from the paradigm of artisan republicanism and declension model to examine structural questions, including the role of evangelical religion, the involvement of mechanics in shaping urban and regional economies, and the fact that some trades actually flourished in this era of economic change.[5] Yet most of these studies still focus on communi-

---

D. Genovese in *The Political Economy of Slavery: Studies in the Economy and Society of the Slave South* (1961; reprint, New York: Vintage, 1967). See also Fred Bateman and Thomas Weiss, *A Deplorable Scarcity: The Failure of Industrialization in the Slave Economy* (Chapel Hill: University of North Carolina Press, 1981).

4. For important early studies, see Sean Wilentz, *Chants Democratic: New York City and the Rise of the American Working Class, 1788–1850* (New York: Oxford University Press, 1984); Howard B. Rock, *Artisans of the New Republic: The Tradesmen of New York City in the Age of Jefferson* (New York: New York University Press, 1979); and Charles S. Olton, *Artisans for Independence: Philadelphia Mechanics and the American Revolution* (Syracuse, N.Y.: Syracuse University Press, 1975).

5. The call for a change in artisan studies was most eloquently expressed by Richard Stott in "Artisans and Capitalist Development," in *Wages of Independence: Capitalism in the Early American Republic,* ed. Paul A. Gilje (Madison, Wis.: Madison House, 1997). Recent studies embracing his advice include William R. Sutton, *Journeymen for Jesus: Evangelical Artisans*

ties or cities in the Northeast. Examining the world of Petersburg mechanics enhances the larger body of artisanal studies by using the structure of racial slavery and location within a slave economy to explore the world of free workers, both white and African American.

This study actually began during my graduate school days while I was reading Sean Wilentz's *Chants Democratic* after just finishing Bertram Wyatt-Brown's *Southern Honor*. Wilentz's vivid portrait of New York City journeymen clashing angrily with their employers made me wonder if southern workingmen experienced similar struggles. I was certain they had not; after all, I had just learned from Wyatt-Brown that honor and deference were the key factors in maintaining the southern social order.[6] Naturally curious, I went in search of southern artisan studies, but came up largely empty-handed for the period after 1820.[7]

Among the literature detailing the early period, Charles B. Steffen's *The Mechanics of Baltimore* most convincingly details the changes artisans underwent as they grew in importance to that city's political structure. Although he does not ignore factors of race and slavery, Steffen is most concerned with the involvement of mechanics in Baltimore politics, arguing that their politicization

Confront Capitalism in Jacksonian Baltimore (University Park: Pennsylvania State University Press, 1998); and Donna J. Rilling, *Making Houses, Crafting Capitalism: Builders in Philadelphia, 1790–1850* (Philadelphia: University of Pennsylvania Press, 2001).

6. See Bertram Wyatt-Brown, *Southern Honor: Ethics and Behavior in the Old South* (New York: Oxford University Press, 1982).

7. Southern artisans of the colonial and Revolutionary period have been the subject of considerable scholarly attention. See Jean Burrell Russo, "Free Workers in a Plantation Economy: Talbot County, Maryland, 1690–1759" (Ph.D. diss., Johns Hopkins University, 1983); Jean B. Russo, "Self-sufficiency and Local Exchange: Free Craftsmen in the Rural Chesapeake Economy," in *Colonial Chesapeake Society*, ed. Lois Green Carr, Philip D. Morgan, and Jean B. Russo (Chapel Hill: University of North Carolina Press for the Institute of Early American History and Culture, 1988), 389–432; Christine Daniels, "'WANTED: A Blacksmith who Understands Plantation Work': Artisans in Maryland 1700–1810," *William and Mary Quarterly* 50 (3rd ser. October 1993): 743–767; and Johanna Miller Lewis, *Artisans in the North Carolina Backcountry* (Lexington: University Press of Kentucky, 1995). For a study focusing on the formation of class consciousness, see Mary Catherine Ferrari, "Artisans of the South: A Comparative Study of Norfolk, Charleston and Alexandria, 1763–1800" (Ph.D. diss., College of William and Mary, 1992). For the transfer of British technology, see Emma Hart, "Constructing a New World: Charleston's Artisans and the Transformation of the South Carolina Lowcountry, 1700–1800" (Ph.D. diss., Johns Hopkins University, 2002).

was the most significant change affecting the city's political structure during the Revolutionary era.[8] Following the War of 1812 the experiences of artisans in the South, indeed in the United States, diverged from those of their colonial and Revolutionary-era counterparts. As the region moved into the antebellum era, the expansion of market relations brought transportation improvements, allowing the development of market towns and cities away from traditional port cities. As a result, artisans found themselves adapting to the new and ever-changing world of the antebellum South.

To date, the antebellum-era southern artisan experience is largely uncharted territory. A fine study by Michele Gillespie, of artisans in early national and antebellum Georgia, provides the best available evidence of the struggles and triumphs of free labor in a slave economy.[9] Gillespie's white mechanics moved between the rural Georgia countryside and towns only just developing in the antebellum era, however, and are not representative of all free artisans in the Old South. Workers' experiences in the Upper South, with a larger population, more industry, and closer ties to northern states, deserve a closer look.[10] And what about skilled free African Americans in the South? How did these men fare in a slave society? My attempt to resolve these concerns and to understand the issues of class and race within the southern context forms the basis of this study.

As the largest southern state, which also claimed the biggest slave population, Virginia is a particularly interesting setting in which to examine the role of skilled free workers in a slave society.[11] Recently, Daniel W. Crofts pointed

8. Charles G. Steffen, *The Mechanics of Baltimore: Workers and Politics in the Age of Revolution, 1763–1812* (Urbana: University of Illinois Press, 1984). He expands consideration to the early republic in Charles G. Steffen, "Changes in the Organization of Artisan Production in Baltimore, 1790–1820," *William and Mary Quarterly* 36 (3rd ser. January 1978): 101–117.

9. I first encountered Gillespie's dissertation, then her monograph. See Michele Gillespie, "Artisans and Mechanics in the Political Economy of Georgia, 1790–1860" (Ph.D. diss., Princeton University, 1990); and Gillespie, *Free Labor in an Unfree World: White Artisans in Slaveholding Georgia, 1789–1860* (Athens: University of Georgia Press, 2000).

10. Although Charles Steffen examines Baltimore artisans in the early national period, he fails to go beyond the decline of economic opportunities to examine the relationship between slavery and artisan culture, and offers scant consideration of the importance of the growing free African American population in the city. See Steffen, "Changes in the Organization of Artisan Production."

11. The bulk of southern history examines the region through the plantation model. U. B.

out that despite holding the South's largest slave population, antebellum Virginia was actually representative of national trends in economic and social development. Crofts argues that Virginia's agricultural production was not in decline as often stereotyped. Instead, farming shifted from tobacco monoculture to more diversified, and less labor-intensive, crops. In the late antebellum era, the commonwealth was among leading states in production of grain, including corn and wheat. Movement toward industrial development also intensified as the annual output of manufactures grew from $30 million in 1840 to $50 million in 1850.[12] Changes in agriculture and the growth of industry linked slavery to both segments of Virginia's economy. David Goldfield was among the first to argue that slavery adapted well to both urbanization and industrial development. As grain became the major crop on many Virginia plantations, slave owners often leased their surplus laborers to skilled artisans and industrial employers.[13]

Factories and businesses in Petersburg benefited from the diversification of regional plantations. The city is located in the heart of Virginia's Southside, designating the plantation belt south of the falls of the James River that stretches to the North Carolina line. Plantations in the surrounding counties of Dinwiddie, Chesterfield, and Prince George moved from heavy tobacco cultivation early in the nineteenth century toward the production of wheat, corn, and peas. Although the focus moved toward less labor-intensive crops, the slave population of all three counties actually increased steadily after 1820.[14] Instead of selling slaves south, many area owners made a lucrative income leasing their slaves to Petersburg artisans and industries. City tobacco factories, Petersburg's

---

Phillips led the way with his *Life and Labor in the Old South* (Boston: Little, Brown, 1929), which set the agenda for examining the antebellum South through the plantation system. See also Eugene D. Genovese's books, *The Political Economy of Slavery: Studies in the Economy and Society of the Slave South* (1961; reprint, New York: Vintage, 1967); and *Roll Jordan Roll: The World the Slaves Made* (New York: Vintage, 1974).

12. Daniel W. Crofts, "Late Antebellum Virginia Reconsidered," *Virginia Magazine of History and Biography* 107 (1999): EBSCOhost, 1–2.

13. David R. Goldfield, *Urban Growth in the Age of Sectionalism: Virginia, 1847–1861* (Baton Rouge: Louisiana State University Press, 1977), 130–131.

14. Historical Census Browser, University of Virginia, Geospatial and Statistical Data Center: http://fisher.lib.virginia.edu/collections/stats/histcensus/index.html (accessed 8 August 2006). Note: there was a slight decline in the Chesterfield County slave population between 1850 and 1860.

largest employers, depended almost exclusively on slave labor before the 1850s. Many tobacconists hired their workers from plantation owners in one of the three surrounding counties.

More recently Edward L. Ayers and William A. Link expand the discussion of the connection between slavery and modern growth in late antebellum Virginia. Ayers demonstrates that Augusta County easily found use for enslaved laborers as its main town of Staunton added a rail connection, macadamized roads, and gas lighting.[15] Link demonstrates the way that the market economy broadened slaveholding into towns, cities, and industry. He argues that late antebellum "Virginians embraced national notions of business enterprise and public culture. Most were enthusiastic capitalists connected to the outside world and acutely aware of the market revolution."[16] Link could easily be describing the mindset of Petersburg's advancing middle class of master mechanics and manufacturers.

This new trend in southern studies collectively shows Virginia developing a modern capitalist economy that included slave labor. Examining the skilled workers of Petersburg will help to further bury the feudal anti-capitalist model of planter-centered political economy. As recently as 1997, Douglas R. Egerton noted that "dominant southern social relations both kept a capitalist mentality at bay and hindered the growth of precisely those market mechanisms necessary for a well-rounded capitalist economy."[17] In stark contrast to the planter-centered model, this study argues that a capitalist mentality and a strong and vibrant market economy were compatible with slavery in the Upper South.

The work of Link, Ayers, and others emphasizes changes occurring in the years following the Mexican War when economic development seemed much on the minds of many Virginians. Railroad connections reached most Virginia towns, such as Staunton, in the 1850s and led to town and city development in that decade.[18] These economic trends were evident earlier in Petersburg, mak-

---

15. Edward L. Ayers, *In the Presence of Mine Enemies: War in the Heart of America, 1859–1863* (New York: W. W. Norton, 2003), 17–20.

16. William A. Link, *Roots of Secession: Slavery and Politics in Antebellum Virginia* (Chapel Hill: University of North Carolina Press, 2003), 6–7.

17. Douglas R. Egerton, "Markets Without a Market Revolution: Southern Planters and Capitalism," in Gilje, ed., *Wages of Independence*, 51.

18. Link, *Roots of Secession*, 6–7; see also Kenneth W. Noe, *Southwest Virginia's Railroad: Modernization and the Sectional Crisis* (Urbana: University of Illinois Press, 1994).

ing an examination of the early antebellum period necessary to grasp the full measure of change. Petersburg received its first rail connection in the early 1830s, and by the mid-1850s five distinct railroads crossed in the city. On the eve of the Civil War, industry was central to the city's life and its skilled workforce.

Artisan Workers in the Upper South also bridges the gap between southern history and traditional and recent artisan studies. Despite their resemblance to northern workers, Upper South artisans were different from their northern counterparts because of their agricultural and slave-based context. But this does not mean that they lived in a pre-capitalist world. Like northern artisans, southern mechanics believed strongly in the tenets of free labor and its superiority to slave labor, although their definition of free labor extended to whites only. As studies touching on the urban working class in the South are now beginning to show, southern artisans supported, and in many cases participated directly in, the institution that was the backbone of the southern economy.[19] In Petersburg, slavery and industry were highly compatible. Many artisans, even some African Americans, saw slavery as the means toward upward mobility, a way to increase the profitability of their business establishments, and a clear symbol of their success.[20] In the 1850s, after slave prices rose beyond the means of many, slave hiring still allowed many to enter the master class. In many

19. Recent studies are bringing the issue of class to the forefront of southern history. See Jonathan Daniel Wells, *The Origins of the Southern Middle Class, 1800–1861* (Chapel Hill: University of North Carolina Press, 2004); and Frank Towers, *The Urban South and the Coming of the Civil War* (Charlottesville: University of Virginia Press, 2004). For a discussion of the free labor ideology in relation to the South, see James L. Huston, *Calculating the Value of the Union: Slavery, Property Rights and the Economic Origins of the Civil War* (Chapel Hill: University of North Carolina Press, 2003), 40–49.

20. The importance of the contrast between free and slave labor is most clearly outlined by Eric Foner in *Free Soil, Free Labor, Free Men: The Ideology of the Republican Party Before the Civil War* (1970; reprint, New York: Oxford University Press, 1995); and by David R. Roediger in *The Wages of Whiteness: Race and the Making of the American Working Class* (London and New York: Verso, 1991). Recent community studies showing the connection between southern artisans and slavery include Michael Shirley, *From Congregational Town to Industrial City: Culture and Social Change in a Southern Community* (New York: New York University Press, 1994); Steven Elliott Tripp, *Yankee Town, Southern City: Race and Class Relations in Civil War Lynchburg* (New York: New York University Press, 1997); and James Sidbury, *Ploughshares into Swords: Race, Rebellion, and Identity in Gabriel's Virginia, 1730–1810* (Cambridge: Cambridge University Press, 1997).

cases, the ability to own or lease slaves separated successful mechanics from more middling artisan workers.

In other ways, the experiences of Petersburg artisan workers closely paralleled those of their northern counterparts. Instead of a blanket displacement or "proletarianization" of the workforce, increasing competition and wider market linkages encouraged a number of artisans to adapt in creative ways by embracing the capitalistic values that the market revolution supported. Artisans possessing skills and access to investment capital often diversified their holdings into mercantile and manufacturing endeavors. Many of these successful masters moved into an emerging middle class of shopkeepers, merchants, and factory owners. Artisanal societies such as the Petersburg Benevolent Mechanic Association (PBMA), formed by successful Petersburg masters in 1825, aided these new entrepreneurs in launching their business ventures, but also provided a safety net for those less fortunate. As in the North, artisanal societies offered both benevolent assistance to mechanics displaced in the new economy and fraternity and sometimes financial support for those masters who were expanding their operations. Others adapted to new realities of wage labor by pursuing work in trades that flourished under the new system, especially those related to industry and construction, and many managed to succeed.

This rise of a market economy that brought uneven opportunities to the antebellum Upper South, and allowed some Petersburg mechanics to prosper more than others, also created a class divide within the artisan community. The increase in the importation of northern manufactured goods brought competition, and sometimes unemployment and hard times. These men struggled to get by, and many came to resent their inability to advance in the new economy. However, their animosity toward the emerging middle class rarely led Petersburg workingmen to political organization or strikes, as was common in northern cities.[21] Enterprising masters and manufacturers followed the lead of their northern counterparts by downplaying the growing differences through the continued celebration of manual labor. Jonathan A. Glickstein argues that the northern middle class sought new definitions that dignified manual labor in an effort to deemphasize the growing exploitation of labor. Others, including Eric Foner, suggest that a belief in the inherent dignity of labor has always

21. Recent works are showing that in large southern cities such as Baltimore, St. Louis, and New Orleans, artisans did gain enough power to influence the local political system. See Towers, *The Urban South*, 1–7.

existed as a part of the American culture.[22] Through speeches and celebrations Petersburg's middle-class mechanics-turned-businessmen continuously upheld the importance of skilled labor to southern society, maintaining a connection to their heritage while also aiming to pacify those less fortunate. Their expressions are analogous to those of middle-class members of many industrializing American cities who sought to reduce the "handicap in status confronting manual laborers" in the nineteenth century.[23]

Although Petersburg's workingmen shared many traits with northern artisans, their location in southern society meant that Upper South mechanics experienced economic change in a different way. Because the southern slave culture produced a clear-cut line of demarcation between whites and blacks, independent craft workers in Petersburg placed less emphasis on the protracted and political class struggle that divided masters and journeymen in the antebellum North. Although economic issues divided southern masters and journeymen, slavery provided white artisans with a psychological wage that elevated their status, created a common racial bond for all southern whites, and expanded markets for their skills. When they faced unemployment in Petersburg, many mechanics found work on plantations in the hinterland. At the same time, the importance of slavery to the southern economy prevented white workers from lashing out physically against black workers. When economic competition from blacks threatened northern workers, they waged race riots and chased African Americans from their communities. Because slavery formed the backbone of their economy, Upper South workers feeling similar pressures engaged in ineffective protests through official channels, such as filing legislative petitions.

Petersburg's white artisans understood that their livelihoods depended on an economy rooted in slavery and plantation agriculture. However, even through their participation in slaveholding or hiring, many qualified their belief in the superiority of free labor over slave labor, and found in slavery a means to enhance their wealth and status in the community. Those artisans who could not afford to own slaves were unlikely to challenge the existing order. Political and economic control at the local and state levels rested with planters and other elites who owned large numbers of slaves. Even when expressing fear and concern over competition from slave artisans and free black workers, Petersburg

22. Jonathan A. Glickstein, *Concepts of Free Labor in Antebellum America* (New Haven: Yale University Press, 1991), 4, 70–71; Foner, *Free Soil, Free Labor*, 11–12.

23. Glickstein, *Concepts of Free Labor*, 71.

mechanics were careful not to criticize slaveholders and the slave economy.[24] Artisans maintained a tenuous relationship with the area's largest slaveholders. Despite the growth of Petersburg as an urban and industrial center, in Southside Virginia planters held regional political power. Planters kept up a flourishing trade with many local artisans as needed, but generally imported most of their luxury goods from the North or Europe once rail connections secured access to those markets. Perhaps fearing the political potential of the growing working class in Petersburg, planters rarely expressed outright support for an expanded franchise and did not openly encourage skilled white labor.[25] On the other hand, Petersburg artisans who were dependent on trade with area planters found it wise not to criticize slavery or planters' stronghold on regional politics.

The primacy of agriculture and the existence of slavery in the Upper South buffered the intrusion of industrial capitalism in the form of factories and changing relations of production. Enterprising masters in the elite trades, who had the capital and desire, invested in manufacturing and other endeavors without undercutting journeymen and smaller master mechanics, who could look to the hinterland for employment. The important relationship between mechanics and plantation owners allowed some southern artisans to maintain their independence in the face of economic transformation and industrialization. Those artisans who were unable, or unwilling, to participate in the new situations that developed in the antebellum era, in many cases, still earned a living as independent producers through trade with the surrounding hinterland. Even though most area planters did not support the advancement of free labor because it represented a challenge to their political hegemony, many provided enough work to allow area artisans to make ends meet for their families. For these reasons, the experiences of southern artisans merit attention separate from that given mechanics in the North.

When William Tell Harris visited in the 1810s, Petersburg was on the verge of a market revolution. The "bustle and activity" he observed were the beginnings of a capitalist transformation that resulted in significant growth of indus-

24. For examples, see "Meeting of Mechanics," *The Republican* (Petersburg), 24 January 1849; and "The Mechanics' Meeting Saturday Night," *Daily Southside Democrat* (Petersburg), 19 August 1857.

25. For an example of the clash between working-class activists and planter political power, see Towers, *The Urban South*, esp. 7–9.

try and trade. Toward the end of the antebellum era, the factories, commerce, social attitudes, and class relations made visitors from up North feel right at home. However, the Civil War irrevocably changed the world of free workers in the Upper South. Petersburg voters overwhelmingly supported the Union and voted heavily for Constitutional Union presidential candidate John Bell in 1860. As Edward L. Ayers argues for Staunton, during the sectional crisis of the 1850s, Petersburg remained staunchly pro-Union.[26] William W. Freehling recently suggested that urban areas generally lacked in support for the Confederate cause, and formed one of the factors that led to southern defeat.[27] Yet once Virginia seceded in April 1861, Petersburg residents overwhelmingly supported the Confederate war effort. The skilled workers of the city constituted a significant force in favor of Virginia and the southern cause as they rushed to join newly forming regiments.

During the war, the industries of Petersburg churned out artillery and ordnance, railroad cars, cotton sheeting, and flour to feed the troops of the Confederacy. The city acted as a staging ground for troops and supplies moving in and out of Richmond and prospered until late in the war. Coming under siege of the Union Army from June 1864 until April 1865, Petersburg formed the last stronghold preventing the demise of Richmond. When Petersburg fell on 2 April 1865, Richmond soon followed, ending both a long, bloody war and the institution of slavery. The end of the Civil War ushered in a new era of class and race relations, including all the hallmarks of social division that Harris would easily recognize.

26. Ayers, *In the Presence of Mine Enemies*, 98–101.

27. William W. Freehling, *The South vs. The South: How Anti-Confederate Southerners Shaped the Course of the Civil War* (New York: Oxford University Press, 2001), xi–xiv, 17–32. Petersburg's support for the war effort is more akin to that described in Gary W. Gallagher's *The Confederate War* (Cambridge, Mass.: Harvard University Press, 1997).

1

"A Great Deal of Enterprise, and a Great Deal of Dirt"

THE RISE OF A SOUTHERN INDUSTRIAL TOWN

When northern book peddlers Sarah Mendell and Charlotte Hosmer came to Petersburg in the early 1850s, they found a bustling city. Boasting twenty tobacco factories, six substantial cotton mills, two iron foundries, and a host of independent artisan shops, it is no wonder that these women remarked that "Petersburg has something the appearance of a Northern town." Commerce and industry were central elements in the lives of many Petersburg residents and these northern visitors readily observed that "every one here seems to be engaged in active business, and for its size, there seems to be a great deal of enterprise, and a great deal of dirt."[1] Tracing the economic development of Petersburg offers a glimpse at a town that embraced capitalism as readily as any city in the North, yet at the same time, remained distinctly southern by making slavery and the values of the plantation hinterland important elements in its identity.[2]

Petersburg, carved from parts of Chesterfield, Prince George, and Dinwiddie counties, stands at the falls of the Appomattox River, some twenty-five miles south of Richmond and twelve miles from the river's confluence with the James River at City Point, now called Hopewell. The first European settlement at the falls was Fort Henry, a focus of trade and exploration as early as 1641. At that site English settlers met to exchange guns, knives, and other goods for the furs trapped by local Indians. When Europeans began to outnumber the

1. [Sarah] Mendell and [Charlotte] Hosmer, *Notes of Travel and Life* (New York: Authors, 1854), 165.

2. For the purposes of this study capitalism is defined as a system of economics in which individuals invest capital with the anticipation of receiving a return on their investment that will provide additional capital. Plantation agriculture as well as slave labor may be variables in the capitalist economy. See the discussion in William Kauffman Scarborough, *Masters of the Big House: Elite Slaveholders of the Mid-Nineteenth-Century South* (Baton Rouge: Louisiana State University Press, 2003), 407–411.

Indians, the falls location became something of a commercial marketplace that attracted traders from the Southside of Virginia and the northern regions of North Carolina. This pattern of trade established the usual direction of Petersburg's commercial connections. At the turn of the eighteenth century, European parish settlements dotted the area and a rudimentary system of primitive roads followed the trade routes.

Commerce continued to be important throughout the eighteenth century, but significant industrial and economic growth occurred after the War of 1812, escalating in the decade of the 1820s. The confluence of several factors makes that decade a logical starting point for an examination of this Upper South city. Petersburg's location in Virginia's Southside region made it an early locus for the trade and inspection of tobacco beginning in the colonial era. In the 1820s, the fledgling town capitalized on its central location to expand its business through transportation improvements and the establishment of tobacco manufacture. The industrial development that followed set Petersburg on a particular path of industrial growth and modernization. Although the town was located in the center of an agricultural region, its residents pushed for capital investments and transportation improvements that made Petersburg into a shining example of the industrializing South. Tobacco inspection warehouses and manufacturing facilities were soon accompanied by cotton textile mills, iron works, and a host of small and medium size artisan shops producing for the local market. This unique development attracted a diverse population of both skilled and unskilled workers. In Petersburg, Virginia-born white artisans worked alongside immigrants from Europe, enslaved men and women, and skilled and unskilled free African Americans. As the largest town in the region, Petersburg attracted a significant population of free African Americans, who came to dominate the unskilled workforce, lending the city a demographic makeup more akin to the Upper South city of Baltimore than might be expected considering its location in the center of the Southside plantation belt. To better understand how Petersburg developed into an industrial and commercial city, these factors deserve a closer examination.

Before the establishment of Petersburg as a town, in 1730 a tobacco warehouse and inspection point occupied part of prominent planter Robert Bolling's land. Before long, that warehouse stood at the heart of a growing commercial town. In 1733, William Byrd, the renowned planter from Westover, surveyed the foundation of Petersburg at the "uppermost Landing" of the Appomattox on the same expedition that created the city of Richmond on the James River. Convinced of the importance of both locations, Byrd declared "these two places . . . are naturally intended for marts, where the traffic of the outer inhabitants must center. Thus we did not build castles only, but also cities in the air."[3] Although local historians are unclear on his exact identity, the town's namesake is believed to be Peter Jones, who may have been the son-in-law of Abraham Wood, an early explorer in the region.

The area gained enough population by the mid-eighteenth century to be carved into counties, with Chesterfield created in 1749 and Dinwiddie designated in 1752.[4] The earliest map of the town that grew up on the banks of the Appomattox is a 1738 rendering that depicts a few lots extending along the river with a single main street, but by 1784, the nearby villages of Pocahontas, Ravenscroft, and Blandford were consolidated into Petersburg and incorporated under that name by the Virginia General Assembly. At the turn of the nineteenth century, Petersburg's population included around three thousand inhabitants, and the town was a well-established commercial hub.[5] The heart of that activity centered around the sale, processing, and manufacturing of tobacco. Southern Virginia increased in population because it was well suited for the cultivation of tobacco, and Petersburg grew into an important commercial and manufacturing city because its location made it the natural choice as a marketing locus for that crop.

Processing and marketing tobacco was responsible for the early growth of Petersburg. The supremacy of staple crop production in the region created an unusual pattern of urban development. Whereas conventional wisdom holds that hinterlands prosper because of their location near a city, Petersburg flourished because it was centrally located and convenient for planters in the outlying rural area.[6] Plantation agriculture created this pattern of development in other areas of the Upper South as well. Even Richmond, the urban and in-

3. William Byrd, *Journey to the Land of Eden and other Papers by William Byrd* (New York: Vanguard, 1928), 275.

4. James G. Scott and Edward A. Wyatt, *Petersburg's Story: A History* (Petersburg, Va.: Titmus Optical, 1960), 12–13.

5. Ibid., 43.

6. For an important discussion of the relationship between cities and their hinterlands, see William Cronon, *Nature's Metropolis: Chicago and the Great West* (New York: W. W. Norton, 1991), 264–268.

dustrial stronghold of the region, matured along this path. Virginia's capital city developed tobacco processing, flour milling, and iron works in an ever-tightening relationship between city and plantation.[7] David Goldfield asserts that "without commercial agriculture, southern cities would have been dusty outposts in the backwaters of American civilization."[8] Industrial development, even in such well-developed places as Petersburg and Richmond, was secondary to plantation agriculture.

More than twenty plantations of significant size and varied prosperity surrounded Petersburg. Among the most prominent were the City Point operations of the Eppes family, which included the main house known as Appomattox Manor and at least two other local plantations. Settled as early as 1635, the plantation followed a more traditional relationship between city and hinterland as it looked to Petersburg as its marketing center throughout the antebellum era. Although tobacco was the crop of choice for most Southside planters, by the early nineteenth century, the Eppes family had diversified their holdings to concentrate on wheat, corn, and peas, other regional crops that also went to market in Petersburg. To the west of the Eppes estate, Weston Manor was another City Point plantation that looked toward Petersburg for trade and the sale of its agricultural products. Created from land that originally belonged to the Eppes family, it was operated in the antebellum years by the Gilliam family, who had familial ties to the Eppes. Flowerdew Hundred, among the earliest of the famous James River plantations, was a thriving tobacco plantation that conducted business in Petersburg. Run by the Wilcox family in the nineteenth century, the plantation depended on Petersburg as the most significant source for goods needed to maintain operations.[9] Hogsheads of tobacco and other agricultural products from these great plantations floated upriver to warehouses in

7. Gregg D. Kimball, *American City, Southern Place: A Cultural History of Antebellum Richmond* (Athens: University of Georgia Press, 2000), 15–21.

8. Lynda J. Morgan, *Emancipation in Virginia's Tobacco Belt, 1850–1870* (Athens: University of Georgia Press, 1992), 18; and David R. Goldfield, "Pursuing the American Urban Dream: Cities in the Old South," in *The City in Southern History: The Growth of Urban Civilization in the South*, ed. Blaine A. Brownwell and David R. Goldfield (Port Washington, N.Y.: Kennikat, 1977), 54.

9. Bruce Roberts, *Plantation Homes of the James River* (Chapel Hill: University of North Carolina Press, 1990), 67–79; and Edward A. Wyatt, *Plantation Houses Around Petersburg in the Counties of Prince George, Chesterfield, and Dinwiddie, Virginia* (Petersburg, Va.: Reprinted from the Petersburg *Progress-Index*, 1955), 1–2.

Petersburg to await auction sales by local and distant commission merchants.

The important role Petersburg played in the marketing of tobacco gave the southern town a hinterland that stretched far beyond that of most fledgling towns, to encompass much more than the local plantation community. Petersburg is located at the edge of the Piedmont tobacco region of southern Virginia and northern North Carolina. This area between the Appalachian Mountains and the coastal plane of the Tidewater, known as the Virginia District, was the center of tobacco growing in antebellum America. For most tobacco producers in the southern part of the District, early land and water routes led directly to Petersburg. From North Carolina, where there were no significant marketing places, the heavy hogsheads of tobacco were either transported overland in carts or wagons or moved by boat up the Roanoke River to Weldon and then carted to Petersburg. By 1820, a local canal allowed boats to circumvent the falls at Weldon, offering a more advantageous route to Petersburg. At the end of the antebellum era, these connections figured strongly in the town's position as the second largest center for the marketing of tobacco in the region, with only Richmond processing more of the crop. By 1860, one-fifth of the tobacco produced in the Virginia District passed through Petersburg warehouses.[10]

In order of importance, the three major locations for the inspection and sale of tobacco in the first half of the nineteenth century were Richmond, Petersburg, and Lynchburg. By 1810, Virginia could count fifty-four tobacco inspection warehouses, but as much as 90 percent of the crop from the Virginia District was inspected in those three cities. Although Danville later competed with the big three in the manufacture of tobacco, it was never a major inspection place in the region. Once Richmond, Petersburg, and Lynchburg gained reputations as the best and most convenient inspection places, the construction of warehousing facilities in each of those locations enhanced their dominance. This concentration of tobacco commerce led to the discontinuance of inspections in other towns, giving the big three a near-monopoly on the trade.[11]

10. Joseph Clarke Robert, *The Tobacco Kingdom: Plantation, Market, and Factory in Virginia and North Carolina, 1800–1860* (1938; reprint, Gloucester, Mass.: Peter Smith, 1965), 16–17, 62, 72.

11. Robert, *Tobacco Kingdom*, 77–79. Important recent studies detail the tobacco economy in each of these towns. For Richmond, see Kimball, *American City, Southern Place*; for Lynchburg, see Steven Elliott Tripp, *Yankee Town, Southern City: Race and Class Relations in Civil War Lynchburg* (New York: New York University Press, 1997); and for Danville, see Frederick F.

After 1820, most tobacco in the District was sold at auction. Producers carted, floated, or hauled their precious leaf compressed into hogsheads, molded in rectangular wooden casks, weighing roughly 1,400 pounds each, to the nearest auction warehouse for inspection and sale. The Commonwealth of Virginia regulated the weight of the hogsheads, and collected taxes based on the number of hogsheads a producer brought to auction. Despite the attempt to standardize the weight of units to be sold, many planters ignored the weight regulations, and inspectors often overlooked oversized or obviously bulging casks.[12] Some farmers turned their tobacco crop into its own means of transportation. An English visitor to Petersburg in 1820 observed this unusual spectacle with interest and amusement: "The streets of Petersburgh [sic] were crowded with hogsheads of tobacco; and on the road we continually met with single hogsheads, drawn by two horses, coming eighty or a hundred miles from the interior. Two circular rims, like the circumference of a wheel, are fastened to them, and they turn on two pivots driven into the ends."[13]

Businessmen and planters erected as many as nineteen tobacco warehouses of various sizes in Petersburg between 1730 and 1842, but four enduring auction houses dominated the locus of inspection and tobacco sales. Founded in 1770, Moore's Auction House on North Market Street in the north end of town remained active throughout the antebellum era. West Hill Warehouse, founded in 1789, and owned by members of the locally prominent Bolling family who founded the earliest warehouse, operated on East Tabb Street, a short distance from the Bolling's home, also named West Hill. The early nineteenth century brought Oak's Tobacco Warehouse in 1806 or 1807, and the larger Centre Hill Warehouse was constructed in 1842.[14] Once the hogsheads reached the warehouse, laborers broke them open, inspected the weed for quality, and weighed it

Siegel, *The Roots of Southern Distinctiveness: Tobacco and Society in Danville, Virginia, 1780–1865* (Chapel Hill: University of North Carolina Press, 1987).

12. Robert, *Tobacco Kingdom*, 235–237.

13. Adam Hodgson, *Remarks During a Journey Through North America in the Years 1819, 1820, and 1821 in a Series of Letters* (1823; reprint, Westport, Conn.: Negro Universities Press, 1970), 107.

14. Scott and Wyatt, *Petersburg's Story*, 68; William D. Henderson, *Petersburg in the Civil War: War at the Door* (Lynchburg, Va.: H. E. Howard, 1998), 9; and Edward A. Wyatt, *Along Petersburg Streets: Historic Sites and Buildings of Petersburg, Virginia* (Richmond: Dietz, 1943), 27.

for sale. Distinctive types of buyers attended the auction sales of tobacco. Early in the century most sales were to agents for foreign merchant and shipping houses who purchased unprocessed tobacco to fill orders from manufacturers abroad. Independent shippers sometimes invested in tobacco for speculation, hoping to find a buyer and make a profit on their own. Local manufacturers provided another outlet, and after 1840 tobacco factories in the Virginia District became the largest buyers of tobacco leaf.[15]

Tobacco storage and inspection evolved into a significant business in manufacturing. In fact, the processing of tobacco into a consumable product, primarily in the form of twisted and flavored plugs for chewing, was the most important industry in pre–Civil War Petersburg. Tobacco manufacturing allowed investors to enter into the modern world of industry without the significant adoption of machines or new technology. Since it was produced by hand and raw materials were available locally in abundance, tobacco proved to be a logical step in the capitalist development of the town. By 1820, factories in Petersburg consumed 638,250 pounds of tobacco leaf annually and employed more than a hundred men, women, and children. In 1836 Joseph Martin's *Gazetteer* counted six tobacco factories, and by 1840 two of those had an annual production valued at more than $100,000.[16] Unlike some forms of manufacture in antebellum America, the processing and manufacturing of tobacco remained a manual operation and was not subject to mechanization until after the Civil War. Because tobacco factories had no machinery that required waterpower or steam power, factory owners could locate anywhere they chose. This distinction brought many tobacco factories into the center of town, where their two- and three-story brick buildings intermingled with the smaller storefronts of independent artisans, hotels and taverns, and homes that lined the main streets of downtown Petersburg.

Individuals or partnerships operated the tobacco factories, which were free from the incorporation requirements of the Virginia General Assembly. Because the operations were private, little exists in the public record to determine their ownership or profitability. Many factory owners were Scottish immigrants who came to the United States as commission merchants or agents for British merchants. Their expansion and capital investment in manufacturing

15. Robert, *Tobacco Kingdom*, 109, 118.

16. Ibid., 163, 166; and Joseph Martin, *A New and Comprehensive Gazetteer of Virginia, and the District of Columbia* (Charlottesville, Va.: Joseph Martin, 1836), 162.

was a crucial step in the economic development that characterized Petersburg after the War of 1812. Quite a few of the manufacturers were linked by kinship ties or other association. Among the most prominent was Robert Leslie, who established a factory in 1818. Declaring his intent to become a citizen of the United States in 1822, Leslie entered partnership with David Brydon, another Petersburg tobacconist. In the late antebellum era, Leslie brought his nephews into the business, and in 1857 he built a new four-story factory on Washington Street. Leslie retained close ties with his Scottish homeland, exporting most of his factory's production to Great Britain.[17]

James Dunlop, another Scotsman, built a large factory in 1820. Two of his relatives, Robert and David Dunlop, were also well established in the industry. Beginning in 1843 they joined in partnership with David B. Tennant, nephew of David Brydon. Tennant, also of Scotland, proved to be one of the most successful tobacconists of the antebellum era. By 1860 he manufactured tobacco under his own name, producing 400 tons of lump and twist tobacco worth $150,000 annually. His factory employed 80 male and 30 female operatives, most of whom were hired slaves. Tennant's former partner, David Dunlop, experienced even more financial success on his own. In 1860, his factory employed 300 operatives and produced 450 tons of lump and twist tobacco worth over $180,000. But both Dunlop and Tennant were outdone by James Chieves, the most prosperous tobacconist in Petersburg. Although he employed only 275 operatives, in 1860 the native Virginian produced 480 tons of tobacco plug worth over $200,000.[18]

In the early nineteenth century, slave labor was almost exclusively used to manufacture Petersburg tobacco. Some tobacconists owned their workforce, but the majority leased slaves from businessmen in Petersburg or planters in the hinterland. In 1825, Henry O. McEnery advertised in the *Intelligencer* his need to hire 20 to 30 slaves to work as tobacco twisters, assuring owners concerned about the welfare of their slaves that tobacco twisting was "very healthful employment." By 1833, Robert Leslie employed 60 slaves, typical of the small early

17. Petersburg, Va., Hustings Court Minute Book 1820–1822, Library of Virginia, Richmond (microfilm), 368 (hereafter cited as Vi); Robert, *Tobacco Kingdom*, 186; Edward A. Wyatt, "Rise of Industry in Ante-Bellum Petersburg," *William and Mary Quarterly* 17 (2nd ser. January 1937): 13; and Henderson, *Petersburg in the Civil War*, 28.

18. Robert, *Tobacco Kingdom*, 186–187; and Bureau of the Census, 1860 Census, Schedule 5, Products of Industry during the Year Ending June 1, 1860, Petersburg, Va. (microfilm).

factories in town. As the tobacco industry grew, so did the scale of production and the number of slaves employed. During the early 1850s, the 20 tobacco factories of Petersburg employed a total of 2,400 slaves, or an average of 120 per factory.[19]

When the cost of leasing slave labor grew prohibitive in the mid-1850s, tobacconists sought alternative sources of labor.[20] Many Petersburg factories employed free black men and women for the first time in that decade. Although no free blacks are listed as tobacco twisters in the 1850 census, the 1860 enumeration reveals that tobacco factories employed a significant number of free blacks in Petersburg. Young white women offered another source of inexpensive labor for tobacco factories. Factories across the antebellum South employed white women and children—the cheapest available labor source. Young girls and single women often supplemented their family's income with manual labor employment, especially in southern textile mills.[21] Although tobacco factories typically made use of exclusively African American labor, at least one Petersburg tobacconist employed white females by 1858. When G. V. Rambaut expanded his factory at the corner of Bank and High streets, he employed a combination of slaves, free blacks, and white girls. Because southern gender and race conventions demanded that attention be paid to the southern lady ideal, industrialists added special accommodations.[22] Rambaut built an addition to the factory, with curtained windows, and designated it as separate workspace for the girls who fashioned tobacco into lumps for consumption. He boasted to

19. Advertisement, *Intelligencer and Petersburg Commercial Advertiser*, 22 November 1825 (hereafter cited as *Intelligencer*); and Robert Starobin, *Industrial Slavery in the Old South* (Oxford: Oxford University Press, 1970), 16–17.

20. The boom in cotton production in the Lower South increased the demand for slave labor, and Virginia slaveholders gained substantial profits through the sale of their bondspersons. The demand for slaves increased the Petersburg average annual hire rate for adult enslaved men from $60 to $70 per year in 1834 to $150 in 1858. See Luther Porter Jackson, *Free Negro Labor and Property Holding in Virginia, 1830–1860* (New York: D. Appleton Century, 1942), 64–65; and Michael Tadman, *Speculators and Slaves: Masters, Traders, and Slaves in the Old South* (Madison: University of Wisconsin Press, 1989), 6–8, 289–290.

21. Michele Gillespie, "To Harden a Lady's Hand: Gender Politics, Racial Realities, and Women Millworkers in Antebellum Georgia," in *Neither Lady nor Slave: Working Women of the Old South*, ed. Susanna Delfino and Michele Gillespie (Chapel Hill: University of North Carolina Press, 2002), 273–275.

22. Ibid., 261.

a local newspaper editor that his new female employees were "vastly superior to the blacks," as they were more industrious, faster learners, and moral and temperate workers. His female employees earned as much as $1 per day, and lived in some sort of dormitory with special arrangements made for them to have ice water, soap, and clean white towels. The girls also entered the factory through a separate entrance, "thus preventing any contact whatever with the slaves employed in a portion of the building."[23] The employment of white female workers in Rambaut's tobacco factory offers an early example of whites crossing over the color line into a racially stereotyped occupation. More commonly associated with the late nineteenth- or early twentieth-century South, this pattern began much earlier in Petersburg.[24]

Tobacco marketing and manufacture formed the backbone of the economy in Petersburg, but were not the only commercial and industrial activities in town. As more modern labor practices came to characterize the workforce, transportation improvements became critical for the town to continue on its path of economic development. Internal improvements offered opportunity for investment in Petersburg's growth and followed a common path of development. First, locals looked to make the town more accessible via the Appomattox River. As Petersburg became more than a commercial center, river improvements were a natural concern of local residents and business interests. River improvements in the first three decades of the nineteenth century helped to strengthen Petersburg's position as a commercial center. In this era before railroads much rested on river commerce; by the late 1820s the annual export business of Petersburg exceeded $2 million to foreign ports, with another $1 million in domestic goods traded along the east coast.[25] This development in trade and profits helped spur investment in additional activities and was crucial to the town's industrialization. The exceptional possibilities for water-powered operations on the Appomattox River sparked even more interest in river improvements. In 1795 the Upper Appomattox Company formed to build a canal and oversee river improvements. Reflecting the town's tie to the tobacco

23. "An Excellent Move," *Daily Express*, 26 May 1858.

24. For discussion of African American women's work and racially stigmatized occupations, see Tera W. Hunter, *To 'Joy My Freedom: Southern Black Women's Lives and Labors After the Civil War* (Cambridge, Mass.: Harvard University Press, 1997), esp. 119–120.

25. "Lower Appomattox Improvements," *Intelligencer*, 3 April 1827; and Scott and Wyatt, *Petersburg's Story*, 83–85.

trade, the initial goal of canal advocates was to allow for the passage of flat-boats carrying up to eight hogsheads of tobacco. The most ambitious project of the company was operational by 1807: the Appomattox Canal was a seven-mile conduit around the falls of the river. Costing almost $60,000 to construct, the canal was initially sixteen feet wide and three feet deep. Estimates suggested an additional $10,000 might be incurred before the project was deep enough to carry all river traffic. When fully operational, the project provided a navigation system stretching a hundred miles from Petersburg to Farmville in Prince Edward County.[26]

The Appomattox was an essential trade route, but the waterpower offered by the river proved even more beneficial to a number of mills and businesses. At the same time that river improvements made it easier for commercial traffic to reach Petersburg, Niles' Weekly Register, the national commercial weekly, noted the town's potential for water-powered operations. Calling the waterpower at Petersburg "exceptional," the newspaper pointed out what local businessmen had known for a number of years. In the five miles above Petersburg, the Appomattox River drops 120 feet, giving it the strength to produce as much as 3,000 horsepower.[27] From the mid-eighteenth century, flour and grist mills naturally located on the Appomattox and served both the local population and a wider market for flour.

Petersburg's waterpower and its proximity to Richmond ensured the prosperity of commercial grist milling. Virginia's capital city became one of the nation's most important processing centers for wheat and grain in the antebellum era. When planters surrounding Richmond to the north, east, and west needed to diversify their cultivation practices, tobacco-exhausted farms gave way to fields of golden wheat and corn. Richmond businessmen met the challenge by constructing commercial milling operations. Scottish merchant David Ross built the Columbia Mills in the early 1790s, to be followed in rapid succession by competitors such as Spaniard Joseph Gallego and French national Jean Auguste Marie Chevallie, who partnered to found the Gallego Mills in 1796. By the turn of the nineteenth century another group of local businessmen formed the Haxall Mills. Richmond's economic growth from 1800 to 1810 was tied to

26. Scott and Wyatt, Petersburg's Story, 87.

27. William D. Henderson, "'A Great Deal of Enterprise': The Petersburg Cotton Mills in the Nineteenth Century," Virginia Cavalcade 30 (September 1981): 177; "Water Power," Niles' Weekly Register, 23 June 1827.

these powerful new mills as cooperages, tanneries, and wagon-constructing businesses flourished in supportive roles. By the 1850s the city's mills were the largest in the world, exporting large quantities of fine-quality flour as far as California and Brazil.[28]

Although Richmond gained a reputation as the most significant processing market for flour in the South, Petersburg mills also exported and processed grain products; the town could count six commercial mills by 1836. Large flour mills were operated by prominent businessmen who gained wealth and distinction in the community. Richard F. Hannon, who originally hailed from Pennsylvania, owned a large flour milling operation, operated a tavern for locals, and served as flour inspector from the late 1820s through the mid-1840s. His business success included owning as many as eight slaves and holding property worth $5,000 in 1850.[29] Jabez Smith, another local flour manufacturer, came to Petersburg from New London, Connecticut, sometime before 1825, and established his milling operations, which included an office building, on Old Street. Smith became a well-connected member of the community who owned as many as seven slaves and served as a school commissioner in the 1840s.[30] In 1850 Smith received permission from the General Assembly to incorporate an expanded milling operation on the turnpike road just outside the town of Petersburg in Chesterfield County. The Swift Creek Manufacturing Company was granted leave to issue between $10,000 and $50,000 in stock at $100 per share. In addition to grain processing, the new mill produced cotton, wool, hemp, and flax.[31]

The waterpower harnessed for flour and grist mills was also suitable for larger operations. Beginning in 1828, the town attracted factory owners seek-

28. Thomas S. Berry, "The Rise of Flour Milling in Richmond," *Virginia Magazine of History and Biography* 78 (October 1970): 387–392, 393–395; Werner H. Steger, "'United to Support, But Not Combined to Injure': Free Workers and Immigrants in Richmond, Virginia, During the Era of Sectionalism, 1847–1865" (Ph.D. diss., George Washington University, 1999), 36–37; Kimball, *American City, Southern Place*, 15–16.

29. Bureau of the Census, Population Schedules, Petersburg, Va., 1850, microfilm; Hustings Court Minute Book 1827–1832, n.p. (19 June 1828); Hustings Court Minute Book 1846–1847, 86; and Petersburg, Va. Personal Property Tax List, 1847 (microfilm) Vi.

30. Hustings Court Minute Book 1820, 104; and Personal Property Tax List, 1843.

31. "An Act to Incorporate the Swift Creek Manufacturing Company in the County of Chesterfield, and for Other Purposes," *Acts of the General Assembly* (Richmond: Samuel Shepherd, 1850), 162 (hereafter cited as *Acts*).

ing access to markets and waterpower. Petersburg businessmen began to look toward taking advantage of a recent boom in cotton production. By 1825, a number of planters in southern Virginia grew between twenty and a hundred acres of cotton, in addition to their other staple crops. Much of the cotton grown in the Southside found its way into the markets at Petersburg and eventually to cotton mills in the town.[32] The rapid growth of cotton textile production soon earned Petersburg a reputation as one of the major textile-producing towns in the antebellum South.[33]

Economic diversification into the manufacturing sector was not a complete anomaly in the antebellum South. Cotton milling near the source of raw materials, in fact, is good business sense. Textile production rose to become the fourth most important industry in the region by 1860, although southern cotton textiles always lagged far behind those from the New England region. In 1850, textile mills were among the top five manufacturing firms in the states of Alabama, Arkansas, Florida, North Carolina, and South Carolina.[34] The largest and most well-known southern textile mill operations were those of the Graniteville Manufacturing Company in South Carolina. The company's founder, Charleston businessman William Gregg, who incidentally apprenticed as a watchmaker and silversmith in Petersburg in his youth, began the Graniteville operations in 1849. This mill employed more than three hundred, and produced cloth valued around $275,000 annually. Although Gregg's mill complex is often cited among the most important examples of antebellum southern industrialization, Petersburg's cotton mills were established earlier and came close to competing with the Graniteville mills in both output and number of hands employed.[35]

The first of 6 important cotton textile mills incorporated as the Petersburg Manufacturing Company in 1826, and began operating with 500 spindles in 1828. When Joseph Martin prepared his statistical gazetteer of the state in 1836,

32. Wyatt, "Rise of Industry," 14–15.

33. Henderson, "'A Great Deal of Enterprise,'" 177.

34. Fred Bateman and Thomas Weiss, *A Deplorable Scarcity: The Failure of Industrialization in the Slave Economy* (Chapel Hill: University of North Carolina Press, 1981), 8–16, 186–192.

35. Tom Downey, "Riparian Rights and Manufacturing in Antebellum South Carolina: William Gregg and the Origins of the 'Industrial Mind,'" *Journal of Southern History* 65 (February 1999): 93–95; Broadus Mitchell, *William Gregg: Factory Master of the Old South* (1928; reprint, New York: Octagon, 1966), 5; Bateman and Weiss, *Deplorable Scarcity*, 190.

this mill operated 2,500 spindles and produced 1,200 pounds of cotton yarn a day, a total of 360,000 pounds annually. On his visit to Petersburg, Martin also encountered a second mill, the Merchant's Manufacturing Company, incorporated in 1832. This operation was really 2 separate factories, one of which was significantly smaller in scale. Combined operations of the company included 3,500 spindles for yarn as well as a number of looms for weaving cotton cloth. These produced 1,500 to 2,000 yards of cloth daily, and the entire operation employed 200 workers.[36]

The outstanding waterpower led some operators of independent flour and grist mills to seek out new ways to expand their operations. For several, incorporation and expansion into textiles was a viable and profitable option. The Matoaca Manufacturing Company was one such operation that diversified and prospered in the 1830s. This operation evolved out of a grist mill owned by Mordecai Barbour to an incorporated venture that processed grain and manufactured paper as well as cotton. In 1836, the company increased its capitalization to $500,000. With increased funding, Matoaca Manufacturing built 2 new 3-story mills, a machine shop, and other work buildings. The new cotton mill planned to operate 4,000 spindles and 170 looms when complete. Because of its location 4 miles outside Petersburg, the company also constructed a small village of 15 to 20 tenement houses that aimed to house a workforce of 400 to 500.[37]

That same year, the General Assembly authorized 2 additional milling operations. The Ettrick Manufacturing Company incorporated to produce cotton, wool, hemp, flax, metals, and wood along the Appomattox River just outside Petersburg in Chesterfield County. The site was originally a flour mill owned by Jabez Smith. In exchange for turning over his property and waterpower rights to the corporation, Smith received stock as compensation. It was a lucrative investment. In 2 years' time the company operated 4,000 spindles and 146 looms, and its 200 mill hands wove a million yards of cloth annually. At the end of the 1850s, the Ettrick cotton mill employed 300 workers, mostly women, who operated 212 looms. The company was also one of the first to incorporate steam-powered engines so that production time was not lost due to low water.

36. Martin, *Gazetteer*, 163.

37. Wyatt, "Rise of Industry," 22–23; and "An Act Concerning the Matoaca Manufacturing Company," *Acts*, 1836, 332.

The 5 steam engines installed by the company could dispense 100 horsepower each.[38]

Another cotton mill that grew out of a small-scale milling operation was the Mechanics Manufacturing Company, incorporated in February 1836. This corporation, authorized to issue capital stock of $30,000 to $100,000, expanded the Swift Creek mill site belonging to Robert Shanks. Construction was complete in October 1838, when the mill opened for business with 4,000 spindles and 154 looms. The 180 mill hands made nearly $1 million worth of cotton cloth each year. The sixth important mill was the Battersea Manufacturing Company, incorporated in 1839 and operating by 1840. It was located in the edge of Chesterfield County on the south side of the Appomattox, opposite the mill and village at Ettrick. Smaller than the other operations, this mill employed 80 female and 50 male hands and produced 863,000 yards of cotton sheeting worth $52,000 in 1849.[39]

The cotton mill operators of Petersburg learned much from those established in northern towns. The leading mills first operated in the Rhode Island–style developed by Samuel Slater. This type of mill, also known as the family-style factory, concentrated production in cottages rather than in one large central building.[40] The mills attracted mainly poorer white families from the surrounding countryside and hinterland through an offer of housing. Interested in employing mostly white girls, the mill owners built small villages immediately surrounding the mill site. The Mechanics Manufacturing Company created the village of Mechanicsville near the factory, and it soon became one of the largest company villages in the Petersburg area. The Ettrick Manufacturing Company built so much housing for its employees that a permanent village arose near the mill. At the end of the antebellum era, in 1859, Ettrick had a population of 830, including 460 women who formed the mainstay of the workforce for the

38. "An Act to Incorporate the Ettrick Manufacturing Company," *Acts*, 1836, 327–329; and Wyatt, "Rise of Industry," 23.

39. "An Act Incorporating the Battersea Manufacturing Company . . . ," *Acts*, 1839, 152; Wyatt, "Rise of Industry," 25–25; and Bureau of the Census, 1850 U.S. Census, Schedule 5 Products of Industry, Fiscal Year 1849–1850, Chesterfield County, Va. (microfilm).

40. Jonathan Prude, *The Coming of Industrial Order: Town and Factory Life in Rural Massachusetts, 1810–1860* (London: Cambridge University Press, 1983), 51–52, 78–79; Ernest McPherson Lander, *The Textile Industry in Antebellum South Carolina* (Baton Rouge: Louisiana State University Press, 1969), 60–62.

cotton mill. Although the Ettrick cotton mill was destroyed by fire in 1865, the community the company created continued to flourish and still exists today.[41]

River improvements and the construction of the Appomattox Canal significantly enhanced the capitalist growth of Petersburg. While waterpower and river navigability were central to the earliest industries, the commercial and manufacturing economy of Petersburg received a tremendous boost with the coming of railroads in the 1830s. Before the end of the 1850s, five rail lines crossed the city, allowing Petersburg to develop in unique ways for a southern city. The General Assembly authorized the town's first link, the Petersburg Railroad, in February 1830 to connect Petersburg with its tobacco hinterland in North Carolina. The railroad was one of the first in the nation, and was Virginia's first interstate rail link. Construction began almost immediately, with sections of the line put into operation as soon as they were complete. Three years after construction began, the sixty-mile line was open to Weldon, North Carolina, and served to strengthen the trading relationship between the tobacco-producing Piedmont and the commerce at Petersburg. Before the railroad was built, it took planters and traders two days to reach the auction houses at Petersburg. Once the line was complete, the journey took a mere four hours.[42]

The opening of the Petersburg Railroad tied commerce from the upper Piedmont region of North Carolina even more closely to Petersburg. Tobacco and cotton markets received a boost, and property values increased. The railroad made Petersburg the natural market for the Southside Virginia trade as well. Improvements on the Roanoke River about 1833 combined with the railroad to siphon much of the trade from the Pittsylvania County plantations surrounding Danville into Petersburg. Goods floated south along the Roanoke River and across the North Carolina border to Weldon, where they were loaded onto the cars of the Petersburg Railroad. Having the only rail link in the Southside and upper Piedmont was an early and important advantage for the growing town.[43]

The rail link also allowed Petersburg business interests to get the upper

41. Wyatt, "Rise of Industry," 24.

42. Peter C. Stewart, "Railroads and Urban Rivalries in Antebellum Eastern Virginia," *Virginia Magazine of History and Biography* 81(1973): 5; and Scott and Wyatt, *Petersburg's Story,* 94–95.

43. Siegel, *Roots of Southern Distinctiveness,* 51–52; and Robert, *Tobacco Kingdom,* 64–66.

hand, at least temporarily, in their rivalry with the port city of Norfolk. Norfolk residents had bitterly opposed the chartering of the Petersburg Railroad. The introduction of the railroad did shift the commercial balance toward Petersburg, and led to a Norfolk campaign for that city's own rail link with the North Carolina Piedmont.[44] But not all Petersburg residents were pleased with the introduction of the iron horse to their town, and not all businesses benefited. The railroad was a blow to some employed in the carrying trade, where horses and wagons were still the standard mode of transporting goods.

The success of the Petersburg Railroad sparked interest in building other lines. Although the actions of the Upper and Lower Appomattox companies made traffic on the river flow easier, the shallowness of the river meant that dredging was a constant and never-ending process. In 1836, residents sought to incorporate a new short-line railroad that linked the town with the plantation community of City Point at the confluence of the Appomattox and James rivers, some seven miles east of Petersburg. Completed in September 1838, the road allowed access from such important James River plantations as Appomattox Manor and Flowerdew Hundred. Travel time on the City Point Railroad from the plantations to Petersburg was less than an hour, which improved communications and commerce between Petersburg and its immediate hinterland. Planters and farmers welcomed the connection that allowed them to conduct business with Petersburg's growing retail and manufacturing districts. Planters such as Richard Eppes of Appomattox Manor could travel to the town on the morning train and return in time to enjoy a noonday meal. After observing the workings of the steam engine *Powhatan*, built in Philadelphia for the City Point Railroad, one local resident believed the railroad allowed Petersburg "to enjoy the full fruition of those great fruits, to which her unexampled enterprise and public spirit justly entitle her." Although the line was of great benefit to planters in the City Point area and commercial interests in Petersburg, the railroad was never a financial success. While it provided valuable service to the few residents of City Point, the line did not attract additional settlement that might have made it fiscally sound. The town of Petersburg purchased the line in 1847 to save it from financial ruin, and sold it to the Southside Railroad Company in 1854.[45]

44. Stewart, "Railroads and Urban Rivalries," 5.

45. Scott and Wyatt, *Petersburg's Story,* 96; and letter to the editor, *American Constellation* (Petersburg, Va.), 3 August 1838.

Local investors chartered a third railroad in 1836 to connect Petersburg with Richmond, approximately twenty-five miles to the north. The Richmond and Petersburg Railroad opened for business in 1838, but did not initially receive wide support in Petersburg. Many local business interests closely guarded their town's commercial position in the region and were conscious of Petersburg's secondary status in the state. A number worried that easing the connection with Richmond might siphon trade to the larger capital city that would otherwise naturally be conducted in Petersburg. Known as the "dammers," these opponents of the Richmond and Petersburg line failed to stop the road's construction, but managed to prevent the new line from making a direct connection with the existing Petersburg Railroad. By so doing, all southern-bound freight reaching Petersburg from Richmond had to be unloaded, placed on carts and wagons, and hauled to the Petersburg Railroad depot for reloading. The process considerably slowed the progress of travel, but workingmen employed in Petersburg's carrying trade welcomed the diversion. Throughout the antebellum era, wagoners and draymen conducted a brisk business ferrying passengers and goods between the railroad depots of Petersburg.[46]

The new railroads were the subject of much fascination for residents in the region who came out to "see what the monster steam [could] do." The Richmond and Petersburg Railroad significantly shortened the trip between the two cities. The road opened to much fanfare with a special excursion beginning in Richmond. Along the way passengers received special refreshments, and when the train arrived in Petersburg a crowd of onlookers and music from a local band met the train. Passengers enjoyed a banquet at the Powell Hotel. Describing his excursion on the newly opened road, a Richmond newspaper editor remarked, "Steam is revolutionizing everything."[47]

With connections secured to the north and the south, the circumference of Petersburg's hinterland widened with a railroad to the west in the following decade. Incorporated in 1846, the Southside Railroad Company provided a connection with Lynchburg by 1854. The western line also eventually absorbed the City Point Railroad into its system. The opening of this railroad boosted the trade of the entire southern Piedmont region because before its construction, commerce relied on poorly constructed turnpike and plank road systems that

46. Scott and Wyatt, *Petersburg's Story*, 96.
47. "Trip on the Railroad," *American Constellation*, 25 May 1838.

were unreliable in spring and fall wet seasons. This east-west connection also allowed Petersburg traders to take advantage of their position south of Richmond to pull some commerce away from the capital city.[48]

The fifth and final railroad to cross Petersburg opened in the decade before the Civil War, and was unpopular with boosters in the town. Chartered in 1851, the Norfolk and Petersburg Railroad connected those two cities by September 1858. The strong rivalry that Norfolk and Petersburg shared intensified with the proposal for a rail connection. The suggestion for a rail connection between the two cites was first broached in 1849, but failed to pass the General Assembly. In fact, Petersburg businessmen were so put off by the notion of making a rail connection with Norfolk that when the line did secure a charter in 1851, they refused to purchase stock in the project. Although prominent tobacconists, mill owners, and prosperous artisans invested heavily in all other internal improvement projects in the antebellum era, not one subscription was sold at Petersburg to the Norfolk and Petersburg Railroad.[49]

Encouraged by the town's growing status as a rail hub, the iron and forging industry became another significant factor in the industrial development of antebellum Petersburg and marked it as a significant site of southern industrialization. Iron production was important to the economy of the South. Just to the north of Petersburg, in Richmond, the Tredegar Iron Works began operating a rolling mill and foundry in the 1830s with a combination of enslaved and free skilled labor, and by the end of the antebellum era it was one of the most important iron-producers in the nation. Most southern iron mills were not so expansive as Tredegar, and often combined with other functions. Daniel Pratt's Alabama industrial village included iron founding, cotton ginning, saw and grist milling, as well as cotton cloth production. In many cases iron forging emerged to fill the needs of area planters and manufacturers. By the end of the antebellum era, iron forging was among the top industries in Alabama, Arkansas, Tennessee, and Virginia. Even South Carolina, the least industrialized

48. Stewart, "Railroads and Urban Rivalries," 12–13.

49. Ledger, 1853–1857, and Stockholders' Minutes, 6 April 1853–21 November 1861, Norfolk and Petersburg Railroad Papers, 1853–1869, Norfolk and Western Railway Archives, Special Collections, Virginia Polytechnic Institute and State University, Blacksburg, Va.; Thomas J. Wertenbaker, *Norfolk: Historic Southern Port* (1931; reprint, Durham, N.C.: Duke University Press, 1962), 182–184; and E. F. Pat Striplin, *The Norfolk and Western: A History* (Roanoke, Va.: The Norfolk and Western Railway Company, 1981), 16–23.

southern state, could claim significant iron manufacture in Charleston and the northwestern part of the state.[50]

In the 1840s, demand from tobacco, cotton, and flour manufacturers for machines and equipment led to the establishment of two important iron foundries in Petersburg. The iron industry was one of a limited number that allowed enterprising traditional skilled artisans to transform their blacksmithing shops into significant industrial operations. The earliest was the Petersburg Iron, Bell, and Brass Foundry operated by master blacksmith Uriah Wells. In 1847 Wells's foundry advertised its manufacture of mill gearing, water-wheels, steam engines, tobacco presses, both cast and wrought iron railing, and plows. The foundry employed forty-five to fifty workingmen in the original building located at the corner of Old and Market streets.[51] In 1854 Wells expanded his operation from two buildings to include a third plant near the Appomattox River. A growing business with the railroad company allowed Wells to employ as many as two hundred individuals in the manufacture of iron goods, and to expand into the manufacture of steam locomotives and railroad cars. By 1851, the Petersburg Iron, Bell, and Brass Foundry manufactured cars for the railroads. In that year the foundry produced two locomotives for the Southside Railroad Company. One carried construction materials for the project and the other served as a temporary passenger car to carry workers and others with business on the rail line construction site.[52] The foundry also fabricated steam engines for several of the cotton mills in Petersburg, including a stationary steam engine constructed in 1858 for the Ettrick Manufacturing Company, which eliminated stoppage of the cotton mill in times of low water.[53]

German immigrant and blacksmith William H. Tappey began operating another important foundry in Petersburg about 1840. His operation, the Southern Foundry, was also called the Tappey and Lumsden Foundry when he later joined in a partnership with Petersburg founder George L. Lumsden. Tappey, the more prominent of the two partners, came to Petersburg about 1840 after

50. Bateman and Weiss, *Deplorable Scarcity,* 12–14, 186–192; Charles B. Dew, *Ironmaker to the Confederacy: Joseph R. Anderson and the Tredegar Iron Works* (New Haven: Yale University Press, 1966), 26–32; and Kimball, *American City, Southern Place,* 160–161.

51. Advertisement, *Republican,* 15 February 1847.

52. "An Hour in a Foundry," *Daily Southside Democrat,* 26 July 1854; and Striplin, *Norfolk and Western,* 26.

53. Wyatt, "Rise of Industry," 23.

working in a Richmond foundry for some four years. He operated successfully as an individual for several years, even returning temporarily to a small general blacksmith works after fire destroyed his foundry in 1848.[54] By 1853 he was in partnership with Lumsden and the firm advertised its manufacture of engines, railroad cars, saw and grist mills, and fancy cast and wrought iron railing. That year the foundry cast the first fashionable iron store front in Petersburg for John B. Ege's book bindery. In 1860 Tappey and Lumsden foundry employed seventy individuals and produced engines and iron goods worth $70,000.[55]

In the late antebellum era other foundries grew out of the need to service the five railroads in the region. In 1854 the Appomattox Iron Works located on Old Street and began to manufacture boilers and other machinery. The Southside Railroad also began its own machine shop and foundry in the 1850s. Located on Bath Island in the Appomattox, the shop manufactured locomotives for the railroad and passenger coaches, some of which reportedly cost as much as $2,500 to build.[56] The manufacture of locomotives and railroad cars was a lucrative and growing industry in Petersburg, and was expanding even on the eve of the Civil War. In February 1860, the General Assembly approved the incorporation of the Petersburg Locomotive, Car, and Agricultural Implement Manufactory. Had this venture by a group of wealthy Petersburg merchants not been dashed by the coming war, it might have served to further increase the industrial reputation of the town.[57]

The flourish of industrial and internal improvements in Petersburg encouraged a healthy population growth. Indeed, the unique mix of skilled and unskilled labor in the town was intimately tied to its economic development. The growth in industrial development and transportation improvements is mirrored in the town's demographics. Petersburg began the nineteenth century as a small town with 3,521 inhabitants. (See appendix table 1, A–B.) On the eve of the Civil War in 1860, it had evolved into an important industrial and commercial city of 18,266, and ranked as the fiftieth most populous city in the United States. But as a southern city, that population was divided between free and unfree, and white and black. In 1860 the white residents of Petersburg made up

54. "Never Surrenders," *Republican*, 10 January 1849.
55. Bureau of the Census, 1860 Census Schedule 5, Petersburg.
56. Wyatt, "The Rise of Industry," 35.
57. "An Act Incorporating the Petersburg Locomotive, Car and Agricultural Implement Manufactory," *Acts* 1860, 588–589.

slightly more than half of the total population. Petersburg also counted 3,244 free black residents and 5,680 slaves.

In 1860, the census recorded that Petersburg businesses invested $1.1 million in manufacturing and produced goods worth more than $3.5 million annually, ranking it sixth among southern cities in manufactures.[58] The trade and industry of the town attracted a large and diversified population of free blacks, slaves, artisans, laborers, merchants, and immigrants. The years between 1820 and 1860 brought an additional 11,576 individuals to Petersburg.[59] Many came from the countryside, other areas of the South, and even northern cities and foreign countries. At the turn of the nineteenth century, the population of the town was heavily weighted toward men, but gender ratios balanced out by the 1840s, when textile mills became an important source of employment for women. The emphasis on manufacturing is reflected in the employment patterns of Petersburg residents. When the federal census first enumerated occupations in 1850, nearly one-quarter of the free male residents of the city recorded artisanal trades as their main way of earning a living. Enslaved men, who made up just over one-third of the male population, filled most of the industrial and general labor jobs. A scant one in ten free men worked as unskilled laborers in a variety of industrial capacities. Another one in ten were merchants or toiled in professional occupations, such as lawyers and clerks.[60]

The most unique aspect of the demography of antebellum Petersburg is the large concentration of free blacks. As early as 1810, there were slightly more than a thousand free blacks in Petersburg, accounting for about one-fifth of the total free population. As the central trading place in the Southside region, Petersburg was a natural destination for recently manumitted slaves from the surrounding counties of Dinwiddie, Chesterfield, and Prince George. In the era between 1782 and 1806, manumissions in Virginia increased because of a 1782 Virginia law granting slaveholders permission to easily free their slaves. Many slaveholders, influenced by the doctrine of natural rights and the spirit of the American Revolution, took advantage of the new law and set their bondspersons free. Between 1784 and 1806, they manumitted 120 slaves through

58. Bureau of the Census, *Statistical View of the United States, Compendium of the Seventh Census* (Washington, D.C.: Beverley Tucker, Senate Printer, 1854), 192; and Bureau of the Census, *Statistics of the United States in 1860* (Washington, D.C.: GPO, 1866), xviii.

59. Bureau of the Census, *Compendium of the Seventh Census*, 192.

60. Bureau of the Census, Population Schedules, Petersburg, Va., 1850.

deeds, and many slaves freed from plantations in the hinterland chose to make the town their home.[61] In 1806, alarm over the increasingly large population of free blacks in the state led the Virginia General Assembly to curtail the tide of manumissions. Setting the standard for emancipations for the remainder of the antebellum era, the 1806 law required that all emancipated slaves leave Virginia within twelve months of gaining their freedom.[62]

Despite the statewide restriction, the number of free blacks in Petersburg continued to grow. In fact, as the demand for cheap labor grew, pressure led to the loosening of regulations. In 1816, the legislature recognized the impracticality of forcing all recently manumitted slaves to leave the Commonwealth and passed a law to allow free blacks to petition county courts for permission to remain.[63] As a result, the free black population increased exponentially. In 1830, the free black population of Petersburg rose to 2,032, slightly less than half of the total black population and one-quarter of the free total.[64] In the two decades after 1810, Petersburg's free African American population nearly tripled. In the years following the War of 1812, the town grew into a thriving city with an overall increase in population of 38 percent, and free African Americans were central to its economic development. In the 1840s and 1850s, the free black population of Petersburg surpassed that of any other Virginia city, including Richmond. In the 1840s and 1850s, Petersburg free blacks accounted for about 19 percent of the total population. At the same time, free blacks made up less than 9 percent of Richmond's population. When compared proportionally, Petersburg could claim the distinction of having the largest free black population in the South. Even in Baltimore and New Orleans, the American cities with the largest free black populations in 1850, free blacks made up only 15 and 7.7 percent of the total population, respectively.[65]

While free African Americans were central to Petersburg's economy, another large segment of the population was enslaved. By the 1840s and 1850s, about one-third of the residents of Petersburg were not free. As was the case

61. Luther P. Jackson, "Manumission in Certain Virginia Cities," *Journal of Negro History* 15 (1930): 280–281.

62. Joseph Tate, *A Digest of the Laws of Virginia* (Richmond: Shepherd and Pollard, 1823), 502.

63. Ibid., 502–503.

64. Jackson, "Manumission in Certain Virginia Cities," 279.

65. Bureau of the Census, *Compendium of the Seventh Census*, 397–398.

in Richmond, urban slavery found a home in antebellum Petersburg.[66] Contrary to studies that argue against the compatibility of slavery and city life, the concentration of tobacco production in the surrounding hinterland and the location of tobacco manufacture in Petersburg made urban slavery work.[67] A significant number of slaves worked in tobacco factories, artisans' shops, and other industries. Some were owned by industrialists or other residents of Petersburg, but many were leased to businesses and factories from plantations in the hinterland. A number of Petersburg slaves were self-hires, that is, they hired their own time and paid their owners part or all of their earnings. Although the practice of self-hire was illegal in Virginia, it was generally accepted in Petersburg because of the need for slave labor in local industry.[68]

The white population of Petersburg was mostly made up of those born in Virginia, although some residents relocated to the town from other areas of the South. Because of the economic opportunities available, the town also attracted a number of immigrants from western Europe. By 1850, roughly 8 percent of adult men in Petersburg had been born outside the United States.[69] A considerable proportion of tobacco manufacturers and industrialists were from Scotland and England, and immigrants from those countries as well as Ireland and Germany, were not uncommon among Petersburg's skilled workers. Less than 4 percent of the merchants and artisans hailed from northern states, especially from the industrializing areas of New York and New England.

The distinctive population of Petersburg and the assortment of opportunities available to some residents, as well as barriers raised against others, created a varied and stratified economy in the antebellum era. Demographics, regional economic development, and capital investment in industrial pursuits and internal improvements all came together after 1820 to shape Petersburg into a modernizing southern city. In her study of Petersburg women, Suzanne

66. Midori Takagi, *"Rearing Wolves to Our Own Destruction": Slavery in Richmond, Virginia, 1782–1865* (Charlottesville: University Press of Virginia, 1999), 4–5.

67. For arguments concerning the incompatibility of slavery in cities, see Richard C. Wade, *Slavery in the Cities: The South 1820–1860* (London: Oxford University Press, 1964), 3–4; and Barbara Jeanne Fields, *Slavery and Freedom on the Middle Ground: Maryland during the Nineteenth Century* (New Haven: Yale University Press, 1985), 55–58.

68. Tate, *A Digest of the Laws,* 504.

69. This figure is based on the actual number of men reporting an occupation to census enumerators in 1850.

Lebsock notes that at the turn of the nineteenth century, the top 10 percent of Petersburg taxpayers controlled better than half of the town's property. At the same time, the upper half could claim 90 percent of the taxable wealth.[70] This disparity continued throughout the era as the rich got richer and the poor got poorer. These inequalities made class distinctions readily evident to residents and to visitors. Between 1820 and 1860 the income gap intensified the differences between the wealthiest and poorest residents. Opportunities for achieving independence in business withered, and concomitantly rising slave prices restricted slave ownership to those with significant means. As a result, free labor, white and black, became even more central to Petersburg's economy. In this climate, white businessmen—and some African Americans—gained significant amounts of property and wealth, while others fell upon hard times. In fact, the complex urban society that Sarah Mendell and Charlotte Hosmer readily compared to a northern town was one with economic and racial relations as intricate as any in the North. During their extended stay in Petersburg, these book peddlers noticed, in addition to the dirt and industry, that the town fostered "much knowledge and elevation of feeling among many of the mechanics." Much of this feeling was no doubt expressed by the prosperous and wealthy members of the Petersburg Benevolent Mechanic Association (PBMA), many of whom found meaningful prospects for advancement available in a southern town.[71] Members of the PBMA were among those succeeding in the changing economy. The following chapters, in turn, examine the groups competing in this modernizing southern city: the upwardly mobile master mechanics, the struggling skilled white workers, free African Americans, and the enslaved.

70. Suzanne Lebsock, *The Free Women of Petersburg: Status and Culture in a Southern Town, 1784–1860* (New York: W. W. Norton, 1984), 7.

71. Mendell and Hosmer, *Notes of Travel and Life*, 179.

2

"All of One Family; Like Brethren"

THE PETERSBURG BENEVOLENT MECHANIC
ASSOCIATION

On the chilly morning of 2 December 1826, a group of Virginia artisan workers gathered in the Blandford churchyard to pay their respects to Sceva Thayer, a fellow mechanic and Petersburg blacksmith. Two days earlier someone passing had discovered his body on Old Street in Petersburg's market district. At an impromptu meeting called in the churchyard following the funeral, his fellow mechanics resolved to offer a reward of $250 for the apprehension of the murderer. Each man present vowed to pay his share.[1] The men who pledged to bring Thayer's killer to justice were members of the Petersburg Benevolent Mechanic Association (PBMA), an organization of elite craft workers that aimed to promote solidarity among artisans and to offer benevolent assistance to its members and their dependents. The surviving records of the organization offer a rare glimpse at the upwardly mobile master mechanic in the Upper South. This group of skilled workers represents the emerging middle class in the antebellum South. Examining their experiences sheds particular light on the industrialization and modernization process that began to shape Petersburg in the 1820s.

The busy nature of Petersburg attracted many settlers, including a number of artisans or mechanics from the North and even Europe. Skilled workers consistently accounted for 10 to 15 percent of the town's total population. They set up shop as independent masters or sought wage employment as journeymen until they could raise enough capital to establish an independent business.[2] From the late eighteenth century, Petersburg could boast mills, bakehouses, tanneries, coach makers, saddlers, blacksmiths, soap and candle makers, as

1. Minutes, 2 December 1826, Petersburg Benevolent Mechanic Association Papers, 1825–1921, University of Virginia Library, Charlottesville, Va. (hereafter cited as ViU).

2. A total of 2,626 artisans have been identified as residing in Petersburg between 1820 and 1860. This figure includes 293 free African American artisans.

well as a growing trade in building and boat manufacture.[3] Among the artisans attracted to Petersburg was Joseph C. Swan, a bookbinder from Londonderry, Ireland. Swan's entrepreneurial skills allowed him to prosper in the expanding economy, so that by his death in 1874 he owned two houses in Petersburg and a substantial amount of property in the states of Florida and Mississippi.[4] Cordwainer Samuel Stevens hailed from New Haven, Connecticut, sometime around 1825, and prospered in a shoemaking partnership situated on High Street. Thomas Wallace, a tanner and currier, came to Petersburg from Yorkville, South Carolina, at about the same time, but was less successful in his business operations than either Swan or Stevens. Upon his untimely death in 1833, Wallace's worldly possessions included only a small selection of household goods and his tanning equipment; the entire estate was worth less than $200.[5] All of these men found promise in the developing Petersburg economy.

As in other southern towns, the trade of local artisans was tied closely to the needs of the plantations in the surrounding region. The ability of mechanics to survive in business also depended upon the available market for their products, and hence, to the plantation economy. A primary task of southern artisans was to supply the surrounding plantations with the tools, furniture, and household items required to maintain independent operation. A number of artisan trades also processed the crops produced on plantations, and in the Petersburg region, this meant tobacco. Petersburg craftsmen who processed and exported tobacco products were among the wealthiest men in the town, and were clearly separated from mechanics who relied on trade with the agricultural hinterland. In years that brought a low yield to area plantations, artisans' bills remained unpaid and goods lay in shops awaiting purchase. Local artisans often experienced hard times and occasionally defaulted on taxes and other debts. In some areas of the South, artisans fled the region to escape debt, traveling to northern cities or southern seaports in search of work.[6]

---

3. Edward A. Wyatt, "Rise of Industry in Ante-Bellum Petersburg," *William and Mary Quarterly* 17 (2nd ser. January 1937): 2.

4. Membership list, n.d., PBMA Papers, ViU; and Petersburg, Va., Hustings Court Will Book 6: 92, Library of Virginia, Richmond (microfilm) (hereafter cited as Vi).

5. Membership list, n.d. PBMA Papers, ViU; and Hustings Court Will Book 3: 68, 142.

6. Michele K. Gillespie, "Artisans and Mechanics in the Political Economy of Georgia, 1790–1860" (Ph.D. diss., Princeton University, 1990), 15, 39, 133; and Johanna Miller Lewis, *Artisans in the North Carolina Backcountry* (Lexington: University Press of Kentucky, 1995), 7–

To protect their interests and skills in the local economy mechanics often organized institutes or benevolent organizations. These institutes or associations were based on a tradition of mutual aid and were sometimes connected to political organizations such as the Working Men's and other labor parties that formed in the 1820s and 1830s. With or without involvement in labor radicalism, mechanics' institutes and societies offered independent artisan masters and journeymen a collective vehicle to express their political ideas, including their republican ideology, and to create a tenuous safety net that offered a small measure of assistance to members or their families who found themselves in an impecunious situation. In light of increasing changes in the relationship of mechanics in the economy and the competition from mass-produced manufactured goods, this type of organization was vital to artisan survival in many areas of the nation. For those fortunate artisans who were advancing in a modernizing economy, mechanics' associations offered fraternal support and acknowledgment of their success in the business world.

Some mechanics' organizations stretched across geographical regions, such as the upstate New York Mechanics' Mutual Protective Association, which formed in 1841 and gained a broad membership from New York to the Midwest by 1845. Others, including the Mechanical Society of Philadelphia, were politically active, campaigning for higher tariffs and supporting the national bank. Southern artisan organizations were sometimes concerned with members' political rights, but had the unique agenda of protecting the place of white workers in a slave society. In Georgia, the Savannah Mechanics Association expressed concerns particular to the coexistence of artisan workers in a plantation economy. That organization stressed the importance of maintaining the training, skill, and dedication required in craft making, and made plans to offer benevolent relief to needy members.[7] The Charleston Mechanic Society, first

8. Citations in this chapter are from Gillespie's dissertation, which was later published as *Free Labor in an Unfree World: White Artisans in Slaveholding Georgia, 1789–1860* (Athens: University of Georgia Press, 2000). Since the dissertation contains broader information than is available in the monograph, citations have not been adjusted.

7. Bruce Laurie, *Artisans into Workers: Labor in Nineteenth-Century America* (New York: Noonday, 1989), 98; Charles S. Olton, *Artisans for Independence: Philadelphia Mechanics and the American Revolution* (Syracuse, N.Y.: Syracuse University Press, 1975), 99–105; Gillespie, "Artisans and Mechanics," 95; Ronald Schultz, *The Republic of Labor: Philadelphia Artisans and the Politics of Class, 1720–1830* (New York: Oxford University Press, 1993), 228–229.

incorporated in the 1790s, aimed to "promote the interests of the Mechanic," but made clear that membership would be extended to white men only.[8]

In the antebellum era, as industrialization altered relationships between masters and journeymen, the composition and goals of mechanic associations shifted as well. Masters' associations became concerned with mutual aid and fraternity, and with supporting their members' upward shift into new roles as entrepreneurs. Also occupied with benevolence and mutual aid, journeymen's societies recognized the growing disparity of interests in the craft system and often became trade unions as well as fraternal associations.[9] Howard B. Rock explains that even as masters became entrepreneurs and strict bosses, through their associations they still collectively viewed themselves as "protectors of all followers of their craft." In this role they could find justification for their opposition to the complaints and protests of journeymen.[10]

Studies of organizations in northern cities show that masters-turned-businessmen often used mechanics' associations and institutes to proclaim their middle-class status and to foster their bourgeois economic ideas. It was not uncommon for these masters to continue to identify themselves as mechanics and remain concerned with the status of their trades. Upwardly mobile masters had consequential reasons for portraying themselves as "progressive businessmen who improved the trade and increased its value to society by making it more productive." Most important was their aim to encourage harmony in their workshop or factory in an era when journeymen increasingly protested over withering opportunities for their own advancement to master status. Continuing to call themselves mechanics allowed masters to quell some debate and labor unrest by setting themselves apart from merchant capitalists through emphasizing a more harmonious and common past.[11]

8. The Constitution of the Charleston Mechanic Society, Instituted at Charleston, South-Carolina, 1794 (Charleston, S.C.: James and Williams, Printers, 1858), 17.

9. Sean Wilentz, Chants Democratic: New York City and the Rise of the American Working Class, 1788–1850 (New York: Oxford University Press, 1984), 56–57.

10. Howard B. Rock, "'All Her Sons Join as One Social Band': New York City's Artisanal Societies in the Early Republic," in American Artisans: Crafting Social Identity, 1750–1850, ed. Howard B. Rock, Paul A. Gilje, and Robert Asher (Baltimore: Johns Hopkins University Press, 1995), 174–175.

11. Stuart M. Blumin, The Emergence of the Middle Class: Social Experience in the American City, 1760–1900 (Cambridge: Cambridge University Press, 1989), 134–136 (quote p. 135); Gary J. Kornblith, "From Artisans to Businessmen: Master Mechanics in New England, 1789–

Examinations of nineteenth-century male fraternal organizations similarly suggest that such groups denied the significance of class differences and instead used gender and race to support a collective identity. Fraternal organizations, such as the Freemasons, Odd Fellows, and mechanics' associations, attracted individuals who wanted to assert or preserve a symbolic relationship with the productive artisan. Fraternalism glorified skilled labor, but at the same time justified social inequality by presenting the artisan system as one open to all who were talented and worked hard. However, through the promise of mutual aid, mechanics' associations recognized the growing inequalities and displacement of individuals in the market economy.[12] The first mechanics' association in Petersburg reflected these trends. The association served as fraternal, and sometimes financial, support for upwardly mobile masters as they moved from mere mechanic status into an emerging middle class. Although dominated by masters and entrepreneurs who no longer engaged in productive labor themselves, the organization remained concerned with the status of mechanic trades in the changing economy of the antebellum South.

On 4 January 1825, a group of Petersburg master mechanics gathered in Richard F. Hannon's tavern and founded the PBMA. By the third meeting of the group on 15 January the association included twenty-five local artisans; after twenty-two months, membership rose to ninety-eight. The group prepared a constitution, and the organization formally incorporated through an act of the General Assembly in February 1826.[13] Charter members of the association represented a wide spectrum of craft occupations, including tailors, blacksmiths, carpenters, cabinet makers, tanners, printers, weavers, bakers, and coppersmiths. Prominent crafts in the association also included tobacconists, bricklayers and masons, coach makers, shoemakers, millers, surgeons, and machinists. All believed organization necessary because they feared a "too

1850" (Ph.D. diss., Princeton University, 1983), 219, 224–225, 497–501; and John S. Gilkeson Jr., *Middle-Class Providence, 1820–1940* (Princeton, N.J.: Princeton University Press, 1986), 14–17, 95.

12. Mary Ann Clawson, *Constructing Brotherhood: Class, Gender, and Fraternalism* (Princeton, N.J.: Princeton University Press, 1989), 14–15.

13. Minutes, 4 January 1825, 15 January 1825, PBMA Papers, ViU; Membership List, Petersburg Benevolent Mechanic Association, Petersburg, Va., Records 1825–1836, Virginia Historical Society, Richmond, Va. (hereafter cited as ViHi); and "An act incorporating the Petersburg Benevolent Mechanic Association Virginia," *Acts of the General Assembly* (Richmond: Thomas Ritchie, 1826), 80–82 (hereafter cited as *Acts*).

general neglect which prevails among persons exercising the various mechanic arts, especially as respects the young and inexperienced, apprenticed to those arts." The organization aimed to provide mutual aid to members in the Petersburg area. The group placed special attention on aiding unemployed mechanics and their families. Association founders recognized the interdependence of mechanics in different trades and believed that the PBMA fostered the growth of all manufactures. In creating the association, they believed they would be "better [able] to effect these benevolent and useful objects" and to "remedy such evils, and to promote the improvement of the mechanic arts generally."[14] From its inception the dual aims of providing fellowship and support to enterprising masters who found success in new opportunities and offering a small measure of relief to artisans struggling in a changing economy concerned members. As the antebellum era progressed, the association transformed into a fraternal society for successful masters and businessmen, and became one of the wealthiest organizations in Petersburg.

The association limited membership to those "who have been or are now engaged in any kind of Mechanical or Manufacturing business." Other requirements limited membership to those twenty-one years old, and "of good moral character" with at least six months' residence in the Petersburg area. Each applicant had to produce a certificate from his master or a diploma from another mechanics' association. As might be expected in the antebellum South, the association excluded African American artisans, enslaved or free, from membership, but readily accepted most European immigrants who met the other requirements.[15] Although the group sometimes granted honorary membership to local lawyers, ministers, and politicians, the PBMA maintained these criteria through the Civil War. When an agent for a manufacturing company applied for membership in 1839, the group discussed his application and after "mature

14. "Act of incorporation," *Acts* 1826, 81 (quotations); and preamble to the constitution, n.d., PBMA Papers ViU.

15. PBMA constitution, Article II, 1826, PBMA Records, 63, ViHi. The organization maintained its ban on African American members during the entire ninety-four years of its existence. When the PBMA dissolved in 1919, the contents of the association's library were given over to the Petersburg School Board with the explicit instruction that the materials were "for the use of white people only" (minutes, 12 June 1919, PBMA Papers, ViU; *Charter, Constitution and By-Laws of the Petersburg Benevolent Mechanic Association . . . Revised October, 1900* (Petersburg, Va.: Fenn & Owen, 1900), 9.

deliberation," denied his request "by a very large majority."[16] The member lists reveal that a key component of membership eligibility was the physical activity involved in an occupation. Surgeons and dentists, who worked with their hands, enjoyed full membership privileges in the PBMA, but the few attorneys affiliated with the group were accorded honorary membership with limited benefits. In the decades before the Civil War membership in the organization swelled to include more than 350 masters, journeymen, and other independent producers who worked with their hands, representing approximately 10 percent of the free white men in the city.[17]

The occupational distribution of the PBMA represented most traditional nineteenth-century artisanal occupations. (See table 2.) Ninety-one artisans in the construction and woodworking trades, which included carpenters, bricklayers, stonemasons, and coach makers, dominated the association. Next in membership were craftsmen concerned with food and tobacco processing. These tobacconists, millers, confectioners, and others contributed 64 members to the PBMA. Tied for third were the forging craftsmen, dominated by blacksmiths, machinists, and gunsmiths, with 45 members; and tailors and hatters were most prominent among the 45 members in the clothing crafts. Then followed 26 printing and paper workers, and 19 artisans, including tanners, shoemakers, and saddlers working in leather. Other significant trades represented were clock and jewelry crafts, 12 members; furniture making and repair, 10 members; service occupations including surgeons, plumbers, and engineers, 10 members; and boiling crafts and rope making, 3 members.[18]

At the time of the organization's establishment, its members formed the core of an emerging middle class of master mechanics, businessmen, and small merchants in Petersburg. Although never as wealthy as the planters in the surrounding hinterland or large commission merchants, the master mechanics of

16. Minutes, 23 April 1839, PBMA Papers, ViU.

17. This figure is approximated from the total of 3,177 white males enumerated in the city of Petersburg in the 1850 census and includes males of all ages. The data are not broken down by age groups for urban areas in the antebellum census aggregates. See Bureau of the Census, *The Seventh Census of the United States, 1850* (Washington, D.C.: Robert Armstrong, 1853), 258.

18. Membership list, n.d., PBMA Papers, ViU. Craft categories are adapted from Howard B. Rock, *Artisans of the New Republic: The Tradesmen of New York City in the Age of Jefferson* (New York: New York University Press, 1979), 13.

the PBMA gained moderate amounts of property and experienced considerable business success. They were status-conscious men concerned with their image in the community and in southern society. Because many retained ties to their heritage in the manual arts, they had a vested interest in elevating the status of mechanics in the eyes of the community. As individuals who straddled the social division between manual and non-manual labor, PBMA members found their organization to be a means to promote their own success and to elevate the status of artisans in the South. Although the association remained committed to providing benevolent aid to needy members, most PBMA members found the fraternal benefits of membership increasingly important.[19] Through the association's constitution they proclaimed that "Mechanics are all of one family; like brethren, they should live together in harmony, be governed by the same rules: then, like the members of a well-ordered household, they will advance upon the stage, and become 'useful in their day and generation.'"[20]

In some respects, the attitudes of PBMA members presaged those of post–Civil War labor activists, particularly the Knights of Labor. Leon Fink argues that the most skilled and successful workers of the late nineteenth century offered their ideals and used their economic clout to protect struggling workers. The Knights of Labor managed to unite skilled and unskilled workers to push for a common cause that celebrated the role of the producer in society. Statements and actions of PBMA members reflect a similar attempt by the "aristocrats of labor" to uphold the importance of manual labor in the antebellum South.[21] Through continuing to lionize manual labor and uphold their place in southern society, PBMA members were able to accomplish two things. Preserving the reputation of skilled workers fostered a special relationship with more middling artisans and offered renewed hope that they too could advance economically. Keeping the peace with the men who were increasingly becoming lifelong wage employees made life on the shop floor easier for PBMA master artisans-turned-employers. Upholding manual labor and especially skilled me-

---

19. Wilentz, *Chants Democratic*, 36–37.

20. Blumin, *Emergence of the Middle Class*, 126–127; and PBMA constitution, preamble, 1826, PBMA Records, ViHi.

21. Leon Fink, *Workingmen's Democracy: The Knights of Labor and American Politics* (Urbana: University of Illinois Press, 1983), 13–14. In fact, at the height of its strength in 1886, the Knights of Labor could claim 576 members in Petersburg. See Melton Alonza McLaurin, *The Knights of Labor in the South* (Westport, Conn.: Greenwood, 1978), 49–50.

chanics' trades also allowed PBMA members to firmly discount those in the South who denigrated such work as befitting only slaves.[22] Their rising status as middle-class merchants, manufacturers, and contractors could not hide their origins in the laboring class. Celebrating the artisan tradition aimed at boosting their own status as well as at pacifying their employees. As Gordon S. Wood argues for other areas, the changes separating the artisan class into employers and employees occurred over time in Petersburg. In the antebellum era, both PBMA members and middling mechanics "still shared a common resentment of a genteel world that had humiliated them and scorned their 'laboring' status from the beginning of time."[23]

But members of the PBMA were not merely brethren to the middling mechanics who struggled in the changing economy. The widespread ownership of slaves among members set them apart from less successful masters, journeymen, and especially their northern counterparts. The association's roster included many of the most prominent men in the town, and in sharp contrast to the free labor ideology of northern artisans, most members owned or leased one or more slaves.[24] According to James Oakes, the middle class held the majority of all slaves in the antebellum South. The use of slave labor in artisan shops and factories proved to be profitable for master mechanics and entrepreneurs. Tobacco processing, iron forging, and other industrial pursuits of PBMA members adapted easily to the use of slave labor. The number of middle-class slaveholders in the South generally increased from the 1830s through the 1860s. In fact, Oakes points out that by 1850 half of all slaveholders owned five or fewer slaves, and at least twenty thousand of these small slaveholders were in artisan occupations.[25] Most PBMA members held slaves and many employed them

22. For a discussion of negative attitudes toward manual labor, see Gordon S. Wood, "The Enemy is Us: Democratic Capitalism in the Early Republic," in *Wages of Independence: Capitalism in the Early American Republic*, ed. Paul A. Gilje (Madison, Wis.: Madison House, 1997), 143–144. For a contemporary account, see Frederick Law Olmsted, *The Slave States before the Civil War*, ed. Harvey Wish (New York: Capricorn, 1959), 69–71.

23. Wood, "The Enemy is Us," 143–144.

24. For a discussion of the inclusion of slave property in the free labor ideology, see James L. Huston, *Calculating the Value of the Union: Slavery, Property Rights and the Economic Origins of the Civil War* (Chapel Hill: University of North Carolina Press, 2003), 40–49.

25. James Oakes, *The Ruling Race: A History of American Slaveholders* (1982; reprint, London: W. W. Norton, 1998), 39–41, 58–59, 67–68; Richard C. Wade, *Slavery in the Cities: The South 1820–1860* (New York: Oxford University Press, 1964), 33–36; Robert S. Starobin, *Indus-*

in their workshops and factories in increasing numbers before the Civil War.

From the founding of the organization in 1825, slave ownership defined success for PBMA members. As Charles Steffen has shown for Baltimore, the wealthiest mechanics were most likely to own slaves, and PBMA members were at the top of Petersburg's artisan hierarchy. Among Baltimore's wealthiest mechanics in 1800, about two-thirds owned at least one slave.[26] A survey of the 1823 personal property tax records of seventy-nine future members of the PBMA revealed that 96 percent were slaveholders. The ledgers show tax paid on slaves for all but three association members located in the 1823 assessment.[27] As startling as these figures seem, the actual slave ownership rate among early members may have been as high as 99 percent. It seems likely that the tax assessor missed recording the bondspersons of Herbert B. Elder, who was taxed for eight slaves in 1820. An atypical slaveholder, Elder owned a thriving coach-making establishment. Following his death in 1826, Elder's will offered his slaves the option of emigrating to the colony of Liberia, provided that the local chapter of the colonization society paid their transport.[28] Tobacconist Thomas N. Lee, who emigrated to Petersburg from Yorkshire, England, also probably held slaves in 1823, as he held thirty or more slaves in the tax assessments for 1836 and 1838.[29] Among early PBMA members, only John M. Neal, a carpenter who later left Petersburg permanently, had no history of slave ownership.

The slave ownership rates of PBMA members decreased slightly as the antebellum era progressed, but a majority of members continued to own or lease slaves. Tax records for 1838 show that 82 percent of association members assessed held slaves, and this rate increased slightly to 85 percent the following decade.[30] Members in manufacturing trades held significant numbers of slaves, with tobacconists holding the most. In the 1830s and 1840s, Petersburg tobacconists averaged slightly more than twenty slaves each. Members practicing heavy construction trades, including bricklaying and stone masonry, and com-

---

trial *Slavery in the Old South* (New York: Oxford University Press, 1970), 14–18; and Charles B. Dew, *Bond of Iron: Master and Slave at Buffalo Forge* (New York: W. W. Norton, 1994), 30–31.

26. Charles G. Steffen, *The Mechanics of Baltimore: Workers and Politics in the Age of Revolution, 1763–1812* (Urbana: University of Illinois Press, 1984), 38–39.

27. Petersburg, Va., Personal Property Tax List, 1823, Vi.

28. Hustings Court Will Book 2: 227–228.

29. Petersburg, Va., Personal Property Tax Lists, 1836, 1838.

30. Petersburg, Va., Personal Property Tax Lists, 1838, 1847.

mercial grain milling, also tended to own more slaves. (See table 3.) With the exception of tobacconists and hat manufacturer Joseph L. Moore, who owned forty-eight slaves in 1838, PBMA members averaged between one and five slaves.[31]

The increase in slave prices in the 1850s did not significantly affect the ability of PBMA mechanics to employ slave labor. In 1860, Allen Archer, a prominent bricklayer and officer in the association, owned as many as 16 slaves, including 6 men between the ages of 18 and 50 likely employed in his masonry business.[32] Most members owned fewer slaves than Archer, and reflect Oakes's finding that most slaveholders held 5 or fewer bondspersons. More typical was master cabinetmaker William Badger who owned 3, and tobacconist James Dunlop, whose personal property included 5 slaves.[33] Some PBMA members found leasing slaves on an annual basis an effective way to circumvent the rising cost of slave ownership in the 1850s. Daniel Lyon, another Petersburg bricklayer and president of the PBMA in the 1850s, leased a slave from tobacconist Charles F. Osborne each year from 1852 through 1858. The prosperity of Lyon's building business meant he could afford the increasing annual cost of leasing, which jumped from $87.50 in 1852 to $125 the next year and to $135 in 1857.[34] For most PBMA members, slave ownership was just one of several factors that bound them together. The benefits of fraternity included assuring that members supported and patronized each other's businesses. The group also recognized its responsibility to the younger generation of workers by establishing a school for apprentices.

The constitution of the PBMA notes that the organization's principal goal was mutual aid, but of equal importance was the recognition of the interrelation and interdependence of artisan occupations. In this way it fits the mold of other nineteenth-century fraternal organizations Mary Ann Clawson described

31. Petersburg, Va., Personal Property Tax Lists, 1838; and Oakes, *The Ruling Race,* 58–60.

32. Bureau of the Census, Population Schedules of the Eighth Census of the United States, 1860, roll 1389, Virginia, Slave Schedules, vol. 2 (Washington, D.C., 1860).

33. Petersburg, Va., Personal Property Tax Lists, 1859.

34. Slave hiring, 1852–1854, auction sales record book, 1847–1854, slave hiring, 1855–1859, auction sales record book, 1854–1867, Branch & Company, Richmond Va., Records, 1837–1976, ViHi. In 1859 Bragg was hired out to the Southside Railroad for $140. Bragg's owner, Charles F. Osborne, was also a member of the PBMA.

in her study of class, gender, and fraternalism. According to Clawson, it was common for organizations such as the PBMA to simultaneously recognize "the dislocations of capitalist development through its promise of mutual aid."[35] Curiously, the group did not express attachment to political ideology in its records of quarterly or annual meetings, and in 1860, as the sectional crisis roiled, the group amended the constitution to expressly forbid political discussion.[36] The founding members of the group recognized that in order for small businessmen to compete in the marketplace, they must organize and work collectively to achieve their goals. In accepting membership in the association, mechanics pledged to "give preference to members of [the] Association in employing them and recommending them to the patronage of others." Members also agreed to avoid disputes with each other that might "disturb the harmony which ought to subsist between the members of such an institution."[37] At a special meeting of the PBMA called on 30 March 1830, the association's board of officers proved that they were serious on this last point. The board ordered coach maker Jedediah T. Atkinson and blacksmith Peyton Lynch each to pay $10 into the PBMA treasury unless they dropped charges and suits filed against one another in a dispute over a bond.[38] These actions suggest that the artisans of Petersburg were experiencing some economic pressure from the changes that the market economy brought to antebellum America and that the mechanics' association helped temper the effects that those changes had on the lives of Petersburg master mechanics.

Nineteenth-century mechanics upheld a producer ideology celebrating the contribution of artisans in the community and the economy. Their rhetoric, often adapted from the republicanism of the Revolutionary era, placed independent mechanics and artisans in a strong position as the backbone of the community. When economic pressure and dislocation seemed imminent, they organized to protect against disaster.[39] The adoption of egalitarian language

35. Clawson, *Constructing Brotherhood*, 14.

36. This amendment, which read "no subject of a religious or political nature shall be discussed at the meetings of this association," was passed 9 April 1860, but earlier minutes show no record of political discussions or debates (minutes, PBMA, 9 April 1860, ViU).

37. PBMA constitution, Article XIV, 1826, PBMA Records, ViHi.

38. Board of officer minutes, 30 March 1830, PBMA Records, ViHi.

39. Wilentz, *Chants Democratic*, 87–97; and Robert H. Babcock, "Decline of Artisan Republicanism in Portland, Maine, 1825–1860," *New England Quarterly* 63 (1990): 12–13.

and the promotion of reform drove artisan politics in both Revolutionary and late antebellum Baltimore. In smaller cities such as Petersburg, mechanics held less sway in the city's political realm, but still spoke as citizens of the republic.[40] Master mechanics who were moving away from direct participation in manual labor still used the language of republicanism to support their success, and continued to celebrate the importance of mechanic arts in American society. At the annual meeting of the PBMA in 1826, the association's board of officers congratulated the members on the success and prosperity Petersburg mechanics and the association enjoyed during its first year of organization. Luzon Whiting, a prominent Petersburg tailor and, as first director, chairman of the board of officers, nevertheless warned members of the "necessity of using all their diligence and influence to perpetuate the same; and to sustain that character and respectability in the community which mechanics are so fully entitled to." Whiting assured the artisans that "there are no branches of productive industry deserving a more elevated standing than Mechanics."[41]

The perpetuation of the artisan system was crucial to ensuring the independence and virtue of Petersburg mechanics, as well as to maintaining their status as community leaders. Lack of education among the apprentices who would succeed them or form the mainstay of their paid workforce seriously concerned early PBMA members. This was a typical vexation of the emerging southern middle class. In a society shifting toward an industrial economy, education would be critical for a new generation of artisans. One of the first acts of the organization was to found the Mechanic and Apprentices' Library and to establish an evening school open to apprentices and the male children of members. In so doing, PBMA members mirror the emerging southern middle class both John W. Quist and Jonathan Daniel Wells describe in their examinations of class relations in the region. PBMA members and their support of a library fit the mold of southern townfolk who embraced a diversity of benevolent causes aimed at self-improvement for members of their class.[42] At the end

40. Steffen, *Mechanics of Baltimore*, 281–283; Frank Towers, *The Urban South and the Coming of the Civil War* (Charlottesville: University of Virginia Press, 2004), 86–87.

41. Minutes, 10 January 1826, PBMA Records, ViHi.

42. John W. Quist, *Restless Visionaries: The Social Roots of Antebellum Reform in Alabama and Michigan* (Baton Rouge: Louisiana State University Press, 1998), 14; Jonathan Daniel Wells, *The Origins of the Southern Middle Class, 1800–1861* (Chapel Hill: University of North Carolina Press, 2004), 89–90, 105–106.

of the association's first year, the library consisted of a "large and promiscuous collection of works" totaling more than six hundred volumes. The PBMA demonstrated its concern for the moral well-being of its youth and apprentices by giving works of theology prominence in occupying "the first and most interesting portion of the Library." Other titles reveal the association's concern that apprentices receive a grounding in some elements of a liberal education as well as the vocational training gained in the workshop. The library and school committee boasted the inclusion of Charles Rollin's massive history of the ancient world in translation, histories of Greece, Rome, and England, and many works on geography "from the pens of approved authors." The committee encouraged members to send their apprentices to the school, promising that "incalculable benefits would Result to them."[43]

The formation of a library and school also reflects the image-conscious nature of upwardly mobile masters. Education and other methods of self improvement, such as temperance reform and evangelicalism, collectively concerned the emerging middle class in antebellum America. Libraries, lyceums, and formal mechanics' and apprentice schools were common expressions of the desire to improve the position of artisans in the community and to promote middle-class values. In New York City, the Mechanics' Institute, like the PBMA, eschewed political discussion and concentrated on improvement through education. A spokesman for that group warned that if education was neglected, the laboring classes "will be doomed to an intellectual and political slavery by the better educated classes."[44] The Mechanics' Association of Providence, Rhode Island, kept its library open six nights a week, and petitioned city authorities to establish a reform school for youth lacking proper habits of industry and sobriety.[45] As early as 1796, Baltimore area carpenters advertised their desire to build a hall and library to educate members of the Carpenter's Society in the latest building techniques.[46] Striving to overcome the popular portrait of artisans as unlearned and crass, through instilling habits of industry and education, PBMA members also hoped to improve the knowledge of their workers

43. Minutes, 15 January 1825, PBMA Records, ViHi; ibid., 25 January 1825; and ibid., 10 January 1826 (quotations).

44. Gulian C. Verplanck, quoted in Wilentz, *Chants Democratic*, 272.

45. Gilkeson Jr., *Middle-Class Providence*, 72–73.

46. Steffen, *Mechanics of Baltimore*, 104–105.

as well as the status of mechanics in general. Yet as the chances for independence became slimmer, apprentices and journeymen found little time to take advantage of education and other forms of self-improvement. Similar to the shoemakers of Lynn, Massachusetts, who rarely used the Free Public Library established there, at the end of a long workday, Petersburg apprentices had little energy for education.[47]

Although never very popular with the youth of Petersburg, the mechanics' school operated throughout the antebellum period. The minutes of the association reflect the efforts of the library and school committee to convince masters and apprentices of the necessity of advancing the education of the young. The school adopted various schedules to encourage participation, but apprentices were less than enthused by the idea of spending their free evenings in the classroom. The fact that the PBMA persisted in offering schooling to apprentices suggests that some masters realized the value of education to the next generation of southern workers. The school presented a unique opportunity for the apprentices and children of mechanics, for the only other educational opportunities available in Petersburg were expensive academies that catered to the children of wealthy locals. Public schools were nonexistent in Virginia until after the Civil War.[48]

Such moves to preserve the artisan tradition were necessary in the South as the effects of industrial transformation and a growing system of factory labor entered the region. In the 1830s and 1840s, evidence of Petersburg's growing market economy included villages of company-owned houses constructed to accommodate wage laborers employed in the area's new cotton mills. The Matoaca and Ettrick cotton mills and the Petersburg Manufacturing Company harnessed the waterpower of the Appomattox River and employed large numbers of poorer whites from the region. Tobacconists also increased the scale of their enterprises, so much so that tobacco processing became the town's most important industrial activity. Because these impressive tobacco factories were not dependent on waterpower, their operations were located throughout the

47. Paul G. Faler, *Mechanics and Manufacturers in the Early Industrial Revolution: Lynn, Massachusetts, 1780–1860* (Albany: State University of New York Press, 1981), 192–193.

48. James D. Watkinson, "Reluctant Scholars: Apprentices and the Petersburg (Virginia) Benevolent Mechanics' Association's School," *History of Education Quarterly* 36 (1996): 434–435.

artisan and business districts of Petersburg and provided a visible symbol of change.[49] The rapid advancement of mechanics-turned-industrialists over more middling members of the community also served as a harbinger of a new order in an advancing market economy. By the Civil War, the PBMA became an organization of prominent masters and businessmen, many of whom no longer engaged in actual productive labor.

The mechanics of Petersburg found that these structural changes of industrial capitalism affected their lives as well as their livelihoods. Although most PBMA members escaped the economic effects of competition, their role as the city's elite craftsmen required that they recognize the struggle more middling mechanics faced. As early as 1830 the board of officers of the PBMA reported that although the cooperative spirit among Petersburg mechanics was strong, many members complained that "much work Executed in foreign [and northern] workshops has been introduced and sold in this Town, where the Public would have been as well served had their Patronage been given to the Mechanics of this place." The board maintained that competition from imported goods was so strong that some masters' shops experienced a 50 percent reduction in the number of journeymen and apprentices employed. John Paterson, a baker, reminded members that the only way to advance the "workshops from any state of depression" was to "give a Preference to a Member of this Association, and recommend him to the Patronage of others."[50]

In the 1830s, nature, as well as northern imported goods, threatened the mechanics of Petersburg with economic hard times. An 1835 outbreak of cholera in the region meant that "considerable mortality prevailed," and although no workshops in the town closed, the epidemic proved to be "highly prejudicial to trade with the neighboring country," including the surrounding tobacco plantations that many mechanics depended on for survival. The economic crisis impelled a reiteration of the importance of promoting local mechanics. In a speech given at the 1835 annual meeting, buhrstone maker James Davidson commended PBMA members for upholding the pledge to urge others to buy locally manufactured goods. He asserted that through encouraging patronization of local shops "we prevent the fluctuations which produce distress and create sources of future prosperity for our members."[51]

49. Wyatt, "Rise of Industry," 6–7, 9–10, 12–14, 18–19.
50. Minutes, 11 January 1830, PBMA Records, ViHi.
51. Ibid., 12 January 1835; and ibid., 8 January 1838 (quotations).

Another crisis came with the Panic of 1837 and the "great pecuniary distress" that followed the suspension of specie payments at Petersburg banks. Davidson and fellow PBMA directors John Pollard and Allen P. Lee, both successful saddlers, maintained that the industrious employment of mechanics in either "manual or automatic" labor was still of great value to the wealth of the individual as well as the country. Yet recent changes in the nation's economy meant that labor could not command a price equal to the "price of former days when the necessaries of life could be cheaply procured when rents were low and the currency unimpaired."[52]

The master mechanics of the PBMA were interested in protecting and promoting the interests of commerce and internal improvements as well as the patronage of local artisan establishments. Protecting their new status as middle-class businessmen meant supporting the industrial development of the South as well as celebrating the importance of manual labor to the modernization process. When the southern commercial convention movement took shape in the 1840s and 1850s, members of the association used their fraternity to support southern industrial development. When a convention was held at Charlotte Court House, North Carolina, in the summer of 1846, 40 percent of the fifty Petersburg delegates were members of the PBMA. Designated to explore new transportation and trade opportunities for the Roanoke River watershed, Petersburg delegates supported only those river improvements that would not take away from the commerce created by the already established Petersburg Railroad.[53] PBMA members were designated as representatives to larger commercial conventions in the 1850s. Founder Uriah Wells, tobacconists Robert Leslie and John Rowlett, as well as honorary members Thomas Wallace and D'Arcy Paul were among those selected to represent Petersburg at a Charleston, South Carolina convention in 1854.[54] Wallace was selected as the lone Petersburg representative to a Richmond convention held in January 1856. He was also among fifteen PBMA members who represented Petersburg at a Savannah, Georgia meeting in December 1856.[55]

Many PBMA members had personal reasons for supporting the economic

52. Minutes, 8 January 1838, PBMA Records, ViHi.

53. "Town Meeting," *Republican*, 29 July 1846; and "The Charlotte Convention," ibid., 12 August 1846.

54. "The Meeting," *Daily Southside Democrat*, 20 March 1854.

55. "Delegates from the State to the Southern Com. Convention," *Daily Southside Demo-*

and industrial development of the Upper South. A number of master mechanics in Petersburg found that the market revolution offered opportunities for enterprising artisans to advance in the new capitalist economy. In line with the actions of mechanics in other areas of the South, PBMA members were often involved in a diverse range of business ventures, including merchant shops, investment banking, manufacturing, and transportation schemes. A small number also enjoyed careers as local and state politicians. Several held such offices as mayor of Petersburg or alderman, sat on the Hustings Court, or served in the state legislature. In response to market pressures, a number of southern mechanics transformed themselves into merchants and retailers. Especially true in the luxury crafts, such as furniture making and silversmithing, many converted mechanics continued to call themselves artisans in their advertisements long after they stopped producing goods in their shops.[56]

The dearth of local election records and the self-imposed ban on political discussion make it difficult to trace the political leanings of many individual PBMA members.[57] As William G. Shade suggests for Virginia towns and cities in the antebellum era, it is likely that a lively two-party system operated among the elites of Petersburg.[58] Urban areas in Virginia tended to be strongholds for the Whig Party, but the Southside region below the James River (including Petersburg) may have been an exception. A case study of Prince Edward County, located in Southside Virginia, found Democrats to be in the majority, although a well-defined Whig faction operated there after 1840. Southside Whigs tended to own twice as many town lots and were more likely than Democrats to own slaves. Artisan workers were inclined to be evenly divided between political

crat, 18 January 1856; and "The Mayor has appointed . . ." ibid., 28 November 1856. Thirty percent of Petersburg delegates to the Savannah convention were PBMA members.

56. Gillespie, "Artisans and Mechanics," 74–75; 176; and Wilentz, *Chants Democratic*, 35–36.

57. In-depth political analysis at the local level requires access to a unique collection of voting records. For two excellent studies in this vein, see Daniel W. Crofts, *Old Southampton: Politics and Society in a Virginia County, 1834–1869* (Charlottesville: University Press of Virginia, 1992); and Paul Bourke and Donald DeBats, *Washington County: Politics and Community in Antebellum America* (Baltimore: Johns Hopkins University Press, 1995).

58. William G. Shade, *Democratizing the Old Dominion: Virginia and the Second Party System, 1824–1861* (Charlottesville: University Press of Virginia, 1996), 119–121; and William D. Henderson, *Petersburg in the Civil War: War at the Door* (Lynchburg, Va.: H. E. Howard, 1998), 13.

parties, with the exception of carpenters, who held a strong allegiance to the Democratic Party. Southside Whigs may have had a slightly stronger proclivity to invest in internal improvement projects and other corporate ventures, but elite Democrats in Prince Edward County also supported local enterprise and industry, including a local branch of a state-incorporated bank.[59] With the collapse of the national Whig Party in the early 1850s, most Virginians supported the Democratic Party.

Petersburg generally followed this pattern, and while the Whig Party maintained a following, city voters tended to support the Democrats for state and national office. In 1855 Petersburg elected local physician and PBMA member John Herbert Claiborne as their Democratic representative to the Virginia General Assembly.[60] An exception to Petersburg's Democratic inclinations occurred in the 1859 gubernatorial election, when city voters overwhelmingly supported the unsuccessful Whig candidate W. L. Goggin.[61] Despite the Democratic leanings of Petersburg voters as a whole, evidence for political diversity among PBMA members can be found in the control members held over the local press. In the 1840s and 1850s, PBMA members, all printers by trade, claimed the editorship of three of the city's four newspapers, each with a different political position. Printer J. M. H. Brunet edited the Democratic Petersburg *Republican,* and Andrew F. Crutchfield held the reins of the long-running independent *Daily Express.* A succession of PBMA members, including Francis G. Yancey, Richard Birchett, and John Y. Syme, edited the Petersburg *Intelligencer,* which evolved into the local Whig organ.[62] Partisanship emerged in statewide or national elections, but was largely absent from city mayoral or common council

59. William G. Shade, "Society and Politics in Antebellum Virginia's Southside," *Journal of Southern History* 53 (1987): 170–173, 179–180, 182–183.

60. John Herbert Claiborne, *Seventy-Five Years in Old Virginia* (New York: Neale, 1904), 132–134.

61. "State Elections," *Daily Express,* 27 May 1859. This anomaly may be explained by the controversy surrounding Democrat John Letcher, whose opponents accused him of antislavery leanings. Petersburg voters supported Democratic candidates for the other statewide races. See W. G. Bean, "John Letcher and the Slavery Issue in Virginia's Gubernatorial Contest of 1858–59," *Journal of Southern History* 20 (1954): 22–49; and William S. Hitchcock, "The Limits of Southern Unionism: Virginia Conservatives and the Gubernatorial Election of 1859," *Journal of Southern History* 47 (1981): 57–72.

62. Lester J. Cappon, *Virginia Newspapers, 1821–1935: A Bibliography with Historical Introduction and Notes* (New York: D. Appleton-Century, 1936), 149–153.

races. With the exception of city elections of 1855, in which a slate of Know-Nothing candidates were pitted against mostly incumbent Democrats, party affiliation is not mentioned in newspaper accounts of city election results.[63]

North or South, Democrat or Whig, antebellum mechanics who enjoyed economic mobility shared some experiences. These individuals relied on a combination of family connections, access to capital, a high level of skill at their craft, sensitivity to changing markets, and the shrewdness to invest wisely in manufacturing. These advantages are at the root of the distinctions between most PBMA members and middling artisans. Mechanics who could draw on several of these resources were likely to be involved in mercantile, manufacturing, and internal improvement projects.[64] As Frank Towers argues for larger southern cities, the antebellum era witnessed the emergence of a new class of industrialists who no longer shared the economic goals of most mechanics. Although they occasionally gave lip service to a republican equality among workers, they no longer claimed a real social equality with manual workers in skilled trades.[65] For these individuals artisanal organizations became a source of fraternal, and at times economic, support for their endeavors.[66] Enterprising members of the PBMA were as likely to obtain a business loan from the association as poverty-stricken members were to receive small sums of aid in times of financial crisis. Many successful PBMA members also used the fraternity they found with fellow members to guide their future investments.

Tobacconist John Rolwett was one such ambitious mechanic. Rowlett was a moderately successful artisan when he joined the PBMA in April 1829, but in a decade's time began to diversify his interests. In 1839 he and fellow association member Pierce Ryan invested in the Petersburg Towing Company, a partnership that moved goods on the Appomattox and James rivers to link with transport ships in the Atlantic trade in southern cash crops. Although no longer a mere mechanic, Rowlett likely found the fraternity with other upwardly mobile association members helpful to his business. He maintained his con-

63. See, for example, "The Approaching Elections," *Republican*, 17 April 1843; "Common Councilmen," ibid., 5 May 1848; and "The Municipal Election," *Daily Southside Democrat*, 5 May 1857.

64. Gillespie, "Artisans and Mechanics," 191–199; Wilentz, *Chants Democratic*, 35–37; and Olton, *Artisans for Independence*, 10–12.

65. Towers, *Urban South*, 38–39.

66. Rock, "'All Her Sons Join as One Social Band,'" 162–164.

nections with the PBMA and in 1841 paid $40 to become a life member. Later that decade, he was among six PBMA members the General Assembly authorized to accept stock subscriptions in the Petersburg Fire and Life Association, which offered investors the promise of a dividend and provided the town with a private fire department. By 1851, Rowlett advertised in a mercantile directory that reached four states and the District of Columbia. Instead of supporting his trade as a tobacconist, his ad touted his experience as a commission merchant and forwarding agent, and asserted his ability to "attend to the sale of all kinds of produce."[67]

Petersburg gunsmith William Morgan took advantage of changing economic opportunities to incorporate his skilled manufacture of guns, pistols, and rifles into a mercantile establishment he called the Petersburg Gun and Sporting Store. Morgan's ambition matched that of northern masters whose response to the prod of the market was to join the ranks of the commercial bourgeoisie.[68] His store was located on the busy commercial center of Sycamore Street, and in 1851 the establishment earned enough to allow Morgan to purchase a full-page advertisement in *Thomson's Mercantile and Professional Directory*. Morgan's business boasted a variety of imported goods, including cutlery, three brands of razors and scissors, and a "full assortment of fishing tackle." Gun making was also conducted "in the *manufacturing* branch, [where] they have the *most experienced workmen employed*." The Petersburg mechanic-turned-merchant retained his ties with the PBMA from his initial membership in 1837; he became a life member in January 1858.[69]

Morgan and Rowlett took advantage of structural changes in the local economy to expand their traditional crafts into mercantile establishments. Other enterprising Petersburg mechanics found a similar fraternity as they invested in new manufacturing endeavors that developed in the antebellum period. By the 1840s the town was a transport hub and a burgeoning manufacturing center. Incorporated internal improvement projects provided lucrative investment possibilities for those in search of a large return. Funding for Virginia railroads

67. Minutes, 13 April 1829, PBMA Records, ViHi; "An Act incorporating the Potomac coal and iron company, and the Petersburg towing company," *Acts* 1839, 148; "An Act to incorporate the Petersburg fire and life association," *Acts* 1848, 292–294; and *Thomson's Mercantile and Professional Directory* (Baltimore: William Thomson, 1851), 215.

68. Wilentz, *Chants Democratic,* 116.

69. Membership list, n.d. PBMA Papers, ViU; and *Thomson's Mercantile,* 213 (quotations).

came from a combination of private and public investment, including stock sold to individuals and municipalities along the proposed line. On occasion the state Board of Public Works authorized state investment in projects of vital interest to the Commonwealth.

In addition to the Petersburg Railroad with its southern connection, investors chartered the Richmond and Petersburg Railroad in 1836, and in 1849 the Southside Railroad Company, linked with Lynchburg after 1854. In the decade before the Civil War, the Norfolk and Petersburg Railroad formed the fifth rail connection. These transportation links, coupled with the Appomattox River, which was navigable to the James River, allowed Petersburg to develop in ways unique for a southern city. Between 1830 and 1840 Petersburg's population grew from 8,322 to 11,136. Manufactures expanded along with population, and in the mid-1840s mechanics seeking to invest in new and larger projects could choose from eight cotton factories, three flour mills, a paper mill, and a woolen factory.[70]

Chartered in 1826, the Petersburg Manufacturing Company operated the first textile mill in Petersburg. Two PBMA members were among those authorized to receive stock subscriptions for the project. Jabez Smith, a flour mill operator, came to Petersburg from New London, Connecticut. He joined the PBMA in February 1826, becoming a life member five years later. In addition to his investment in the textile mill, in the 1820s and 1830s Smith bought stock in a turnpike company that intended to connect Petersburg with Clarksville, Virginia, and in the Petersburg and South West Railroad project. Edward Pescud, publisher of two successive Petersburg newspapers in the 1820s, was another authorized subscription receiver. After joining the PBMA in 1825, Pescud served a term as Petersburg mayor, and stayed involved in a number of community activities.[71]

The textile mill was so successful that in 1831 *Niles' Weekly Register* reported

---

70. James G. Scott and Edward A. Wyatt, *Petersburg's Story: A History* (Petersburg, Va.: Titmus Optical, 1960), 75, 94–97; and Wyatt, "Rise of Industry," 3–5.

71. Membership list, n.d., PBMA Papers, ViU.; "An act to incorporate the Petersburg Manufacturing Company," *Acts* 1826, 82–83; "An act incorporating a company to construct a turnpike road from Petersburg to Clarkesville, in the county of Mecklenburg," *Acts* 1828, 65–66; "An Act to incorporate the Petersburg South-western rail-road company," *Acts* 1837, 121–122; and Edward A. Wyatt IV, *Preliminary Checklist for Petersburg, 1786–1876, Virginia Imprint Series, No. 9* (Richmond: Virginia State Library, 1949), 228–230.

that the Petersburg Manufacturing Company operated 2,500 spindles and 15 power looms. The establishment employed 100 white operatives "who are of good moral character and seem pleased with their occupation." The mill consumed up to 1,000 bales of cotton each year. When the mill expanded operations and issued additional stock in 1833, investors such as Smith and Pescud benefited; the $120,000 stock offering was sold out in 2 hours' time.[72]

Mechanics trained in elite crafts were most likely to subscribe to manufacturing ventures. The PBMA's tobacconists invested most frequently. By 1820, Petersburg was emerging as one of four centers of tobacco manufacture in Virginia.[73] Because tobacco was the most important plantation crop in the region surrounding Petersburg, it is not surprising that mechanics who processed tobacco into a consumable product were among the most prominent craft workers in the city.[74] Tobacconists ranged from independent masters to owners of manufactories employing more than a hundred men and women. Six PBMA members, including four tobacconists, were among the charter members of the Petersburg Savings Institution, which opened in 1836 to offer financial and loan opportunities to area residents and businessmen. Two of the tobacconists, Charles F. Osborne and James McFarland Jr., also invested in textile mills and internal improvement projects.[75] In all, ten, or 40 percent, of the Petersburg tobacconists holding membership in the PBMA held enough capital to invest in projects outside their workshops.

Tobacconists and other PBMA mechanics also figured prominently in two artisan-related ventures, the Mechanics Manufacturing Company and the Mechanics Savings Society, each founded in the mid-1830s. Authorized to process cotton, hemp, flax, metals, and wood, the Mechanics Manufacturing Company operated a water-powered textile mill on Swift Creek in Petersburg. Stock subscriptions were expensive; investors pledged up to $100,000 at $100 per share.

72. "Scraps Relating to Manufactures, Internal Improvements, Foreign Commerce &c.," *Niles' Weekly Register,* 18 June 1831(quotation); and "Scraps Relating to Manufactures," *Niles' Weekly Register,* 5 October 1833.

73. Joseph Clarke Robert, *The Tobacco Kingdom: Plantation, Market, and Factory in Virginia and North Carolina, 1800–1860* (1938; reprint, Gloucester, Mass.: Duke University Press, 1965), 163–167.

74. Wyatt, "Rise of Industry," 8–10.

75. Membership list, n.d., PBMA Papers, ViU.; and "An Act incorporating the Petersburg and Norfolk savings institutions," *Acts* 1836, 256–258.

PBMA members involved in this project included muslin manufacturer Robert Ritchie, who had emigrated from Scotland some time before 1825, tobacconist-turned-commission merchant John Rowlett, druggist Joseph Bragg, and tobacconist James McFarland Jr. In 1850 the mill employed 200 individuals, reported invested capital of $145,000, and produced $80,000 worth of cotton shirting.[76]

Ten members of the PBMA, including Petersburg printer and future-southern-nationalist Edmund Ruffin, were among the twenty-seven charter members of the Mechanics Savings Society, which organized as a savings and loan corporation in 1837. If three honorary PBMA members involved in the venture are counted as well, 48 percent of the incorporating members were affiliated with the local artisan organization. In fact, throughout the antebellum period PBMA members participated or invested in more than a dozen of Petersburg businesses or internal improvement projects authorized by the General Assembly. Only the Petersburg Navigation Company, incorporated in 1836 to establish "a line or lines of coasting packets to ply between Petersburg and New York and other northern ports in the United States," and the Norfolk and Petersburg Railroad, chartered in Virginia in 1851, did not number PBMA members among their backers.[77]

With only a few exceptions, these PBMA investors were skilled in trades that offered significant opportunity for capital gain. The response of these upwardly mobile-mechanics to a shifting economy is easy to trace through the public record of their investments. More difficult to discern are the ways that middling or average mechanics responded to increased competition from northern manufactured goods and to the changes that occurred in their own region as Petersburg evolved into a manufacturing and transportation center.

Evidence available for successful members of the PBMA suggests that most

76. Membership list, n.d., PBMA Papers, ViU.; "An Act to incorporate the Mechanics manufacturing company," Acts 1834–1835, 332–333; and Bureau of the Census, 1850 U.S. Census, Schedule 5, Products of Industry During the Year Ending June 1, 1850, vol. 1 (Washington, D.C., 1850).

77. "An Act to incorporate the Mechanics savings society of Petersburg," Acts 1837, 184–186; "An Act to incorporate the Petersburg navigation company," Acts 1835–1836, 281–283 (quotation); stock ledger, Norfolk and Petersburg Railroad, 1853–1869, Norfolk and Western Railway Archives, Special Collections, Virginia Polytechnic Institute and State University, Blacksburg, Va.; and register of stockholders, 1796–1910, register of stockholders, 1836–1926, Upper Appomattox Company Records, box 5, ViHi.

trades did not experience a full-blown displacement of the craft system before the Civil War. For these above-average Petersburg artisans, economic transformations in the nineteenth century meant adjusting to new opportunities. The increase in the number of railroads and factories led to employment for mechanics who were willing to adapt and pursue industrial work. The textile mills and iron forges and locomotive manufactory that served the railroads near Petersburg required skilled mechanics to work in the foundries and machine shops and to repair facilities. Factories needed carpenters and other skilled men to build them and machinists and gaugers to keep them operational. The tobacco manufactories supported a number of skilled mechanics to construct presses and screws, druggists to prepare the oils and spices that flavored the tobacco, and coopers and box makers to provide containers for marketing the finished product.[78]

Despite the successes of many PBMA members, prosperity and growth was not guaranteed to all southern mechanics. Artisan workers who were not at the top of their craft or who lacked access to capital often had a different experience in the industrializing economy. If member mechanics failed in their investments, or were unable to find a place in the changing business climate of the city, the PBMA offered temporary relief. The preamble to the PBMA constitution articulated the association's desire "to alleviate the wants of the unfortunate, [and] prevent poverty, by furnishing the means of employment to those who are becoming idle and poor for the want of those means."[79] One of the original purposes of the organization was to provide a safety net of mutual aid for Petersburg mechanics and their families. In an era that offered little government assistance for the widowed or the unemployed, benevolent societies were essential to artisans. In recording incidences of mutual aid bestowed on members and the relatives of deceased members, the minutes of the PBMA offer a glimpse at the economic well-being of less successful mechanics in antebellum Virginia.

In a detailed accounting of the expenses for the PBMA in its first year of organization, treasurer Thomas Jordan reported that only $15.77 out of total expenditures of $267 was expended to support needy members. In 1829 the board of officers noted that from the beginning of the association there had

78. Robert, *Tobacco Kingdom*, 212; and Wyatt, "Rise of Industry," 14–24, 32–35.

79. Preamble to the constitution, 1826, PBMA Records, ViHi (quotation); *Charter, Constitution and By-Laws* (PBMA), 7.

been only "two or three calls for pecuniary aid" from members or the families of deceased members. An atypical incident involved Luzon Whiting, one of the association's directors, who died unexpectedly in August 1828. The PBMA took complete charge of his care, and "from the time the Board was acquainted with his Situation to the time of his decease, he was under their charge[.] T[he] expenses of Medicine, Nursing and interment was defrayed by draft on the Treasurer."[80]

Although the 1830s brought complaints of competition from northern industrial goods, there was little increase in direct calls for financial assistance from the PBMA. At the 1832 annual meeting, the organization reported only two offers of relief for the previous year, one for $5 and another for $10. Clearly, these master mechanics were separating themselves economically from the ranks of middling artisans and laborers, for whom permanent wage labor was becoming a reality. Despite their success, PBMA members continued to identify with, and to glorify, manual labor and the mechanic arts. In 1834 president and carpenter Beverly Drinkard boasted of the fact that artisans and their families required such little amounts of pecuniary aid. He believed this self-reliance indicated the supremacy of mechanics and noted that "the time is not remote when the Southern artisan will vie for intelligence and wealth with any in the world."[81]

The years following the Panic of 1837 witnessed a rise in the amount and frequency of relief payments. Expenditures to assist members and dependents for 1839 were $130, an all-time high for the benevolent association, and in 1843 payments topped $200 for the first time. Yet records indicate that widows and orphans of deceased members received the bulk of relief. Rarely were payments made to mechanics active in the association. For example, Mrs. Francis G. Yancey, widow of the first president of the PBMA, received regular quarterly payments of $5 to $10 for more than a decade, and the association paid the funeral expenses of her daughter, Louisa Yancey, in 1857.[82]

Mechanics in need of money because of unemployment, or seeking a limited amount of capital to finance investments, could obtain a different type of

80. Minutes, 10 January 1826, PBMA Records, ViHi ; and ibid., 12 January 1829 (quotations).

81. Minutes, 9 January 1832 PBMA Records, ViHi; and minutes, 13 January 1834 (quotations), PBMA Papers, ViU.

82. Minutes, 13 January 1840, 8 January 1844, 14 October 1847, 16 July 1857, PBMA Papers, ViU.

assistance from the PBMA. Until the authorization of free banking in 1851, Virginia businessmen in need of bank loans could only look to a few large "mother banks that spawned branches in satellite cities." Eventually, Petersburg gained a branch of each of Virginia's three state-chartered banks, two savings and loans, and at least two private banks.[83] However, in the antebellum era, the policies of chartered banks moved away from granting short-term loans as borrowers increasingly demanded longer terms. Younger men and those just starting to expand their business also dreaded the prospect of seeking credit without much collateral or an established reputation. For these reasons, mechanics and businessmen seeking a loan on good terms often looked to private lenders and commission merchants.[84] Members of the PBMA also looked to their fraternal association.

Loans at low interest formed the base of mutual aid that the association offered its members. A state-approved lottery fund, through which the General Assembly allowed the organization to raise up to $10,000, and membership dues, funded the loan program. Dues for PBMA members were quite expensive. In 1827 the fee was $4, but in the late antebellum era, the cost for belonging to the PBMA was $10 for annual membership; life membership meant an investment of $40. Payment of dues was a serious matter, and any mechanic who fell behind was first given notice from the treasurer of the debt owed. If still unable to pay, suspension from the group followed until the back-dues were repaid. Failing that, he was expelled and his name placed on a list of withdrawn members. In October 1828, the PBMA suspended Radford Blankenship, Edwin H. Badger, Thomas Alley, and Charles Delano for failing to pay their regular quarterly dues. Blankenship and Alley were likely itinerant artisans because after that date their names disappear from association and city records. Badger remained in Petersburg and even prospered in his cabinetmaking establishment, but he never regained membership in the PBMA. Only Delano made good on his back-dues and was reinstated to full status. Membership in the association proved to be to his benefit after the Petersburg painter fell on hard times in 1831. The board appointed a committee to review Delano's family situ-

83. Shade, *Democratizing the Old Dominion*, 40–41 (quotation p. 41); and Howard Bodenhorn, "Private Banking in Antebellum Virginia: Thomas Branch & Sons of Petersburg," *Business History Review* 71 (1997): 522–523.

84. Bodenhorn, "Private Banking in Antebellum Virginia," 528–529, 534–535.

ation and authorized a relief payment of up to $10. Delano retained ties with the association, becoming a life member in 1841.[85]

Loans from the association also aided members in temporary need of cash for personal or household concerns. Carpenter Jacob Crowder received such a loan when he borrowed $20 in January 1830 on his own signature, with no security required. Assistance with capital for business needs was also available. Bricklayer Allen Archer applied for and received an extension on a loan of $200 in May 1826, and in November of that same year buhrstone maker James Davidson borrowed $100, to be repaid in ninety days' time. Prominent miller Richard F. Hannon, whose tavern was the site of the association's formation, received a more substantial business loan from the PBMA in 1835. His request to borrow $1,000 for six months required that he enter into a deed of trust, find two endorsers, and put up eighty-three acres in Blandford as security.[86] Most loans made to members fell somewhere in between those made to Crowder and Hannon, but on the eve of the Civil War, the treasurer of the PBMA reported that more than $4,000 was on loan to members, a sum that left the association with just over $400 on hand for emergency expenditures.[87]

From its inception, the PBMA was a master mechanics' organization formed to sustain and protect the interests of upwardly mobile businessmen. Membership in the group, although technically open to all engaged in "manual" labor, tended toward those artisanal masters who had already transformed themselves into employers and capitalists. Through belonging to the PBMA, members hoped to find a sense of fraternity with others succeeding in the changing economy of the nineteenth-century South. The group helped to cement the personal connections that promoted business prosperity and affirmed their roles as community leaders. Remaining committed to its foundation as a benevolent organization, the PBMA conferred small amounts of financial aid to mem-

85. "An act to authorise a lottery for the benefit of the Petersburg Benevolent Mechanic Association," *Acts* 1829–1830, 114–115; minutes, 13 October 1828, PBMA Records, ViHi; board of officers minutes, 9 June 1831, PBMA Records, ViHi; and membership list, n.d., PBMA Papers, ViU.

86. Board of officer minutes, 20 January 1830, 17 May 1826, 17 November 1826, 23 April 1835, PBMA Records, ViHi.

87. Minutes, 8 January 1827, PBMA Records, ViHi; minutes, 12 January 1846, 11 January 1858, 11 April 1860, PBMA Papers, ViU; and withdrawals, n.d., PBMA Papers, ViU.

bers and their families who fell on hard times. However, the focus of mutual aid turned toward support for business as the antebellum era progressed, and members were most likely to seek a short-term loan for investment or expansion in their businesses.

Although the masters of the PBMA were generally employers who no longer engaged in manual labor, they continued to identify with their crafts. PBMA members took pride in celebrating manual labor and spoke favorably on behalf of working mechanics in their private meetings and at public events. Perhaps, as historian Howard B. Rock suggests, they were interested in promoting harmony in their own workshops and clung to an obsolete artisanal republicanism to quiet the complaints of journeymen.[88] More likely, PBMA members were eager to retain ties to the artisanal past in an ever-changing economy and society. Because they were part of an emerging middle class in the South and could not shake their manual labor past, PBMA members sought to elevate all skilled southern workers. Resembling the fraternal orders that flourished in all corners of the nineteenth-century United States, PBMA members celebrated manual labor to elevate their own status and that of practicing mechanics. As such, the fraternal association was a means of organizing the social and cultural life of its members.[89]

Throughout the antebellum period this important sense of fraternity allowed the members of the PBMA to maintain the solidarity and sense of benevolent duty they felt as they stood at Sceva Thayer's grave in December 1826. The historical record is silent on the identity of Thayer's murderer, but the blacksmith's importance to his fellow mechanics as a founding member of the PBMA and as a drafter of its constitution can be demonstrated. Before the members of the association left the Blandford churchyard, they placed a sealed phial in Thayer's grave. Enclosed in the tube was a certificate inscribed with his age and other personal information. Authorized by the PBMA, this symbol of their fellowship rests there still.[90]

88. Rock, "'All Her Sons Join as One Social Band,'" 174.
89. Clawson, *Constructing Brotherhood*, 14–15.
90. Minutes, 1 December 1826, PBMA Records, ViHi.

3

Artisans Caught in the Middle

WHITE WORKERS IN PETERSBURG

The Petersburg Benevolent Mechanic Association (PBMA) represented, for the most part, those masters succeeding in an expanding market economy. Although a significant segment of Petersburg artisans found membership in the elite artisan organization beneficial to their career goals, many more skilled workers either could not afford to, or chose not to, join the PBMA. In February 1848, Petersburg carpenter Monroe L. Birchett came before the Hustings Court on order of the town's Overseers of the Poor. Birchett faced complaints for sending his children begging around the town. At a subsequent hearing on 16 March, Birchett argued before the court that his children should not be bound out as indentured apprentices. He was only partly successful, for the court ordered his son, Albert Birchett, bound out to learn a trade until he reached age twenty-one. Although he continued to try to eke out a living in Petersburg, Birchett and his family always lived in poverty and membership in the PBMA was beyond his reach. By 1856 he was described as a "poor laboring man," who lived with his wife and seventeen-year-old daughter "in a miserable shanty in that wretched place called Donough's alley"; in 1860 he still struggled, and owned no property other than a small personal estate valued at $25.[1] Birchett's example may be extreme, but his struggle to survive in a changing economy is illustrative of many southern artisans who found themselves facing an expanding industrial world in antebellum Virginia. In the antebellum era, economic and cultural changes created a gap that split the Petersburg artisan community and led to a significant class divide. White Petersburg artisans caught in the

1. Petersburg, Va., Hustings Court Minute Book 1848–1851, Library of Virginia, Richmond (hereafter cited as Vi), 17–18, 27–28; "The Slave Edmund and the Monroe Birchett Family," *Daily Southside Democrat*, 25 September 1856; and Bureau of the Census, Population Schedules, Petersburg, Va. (Washington, D.C.,1860, microfilm). The Hustings Court met monthly to administer local government; it held the power of appointment for local offices, heard small court cases, and handled will probates and all criminal and civil cases involving slaves and free blacks.

"middle" of the expanding economy lived and worked in the town, but did not gain membership in the PBMA.

As studies of artisan workers in antebellum America move their focus away from the declension model that was inherent in the artisan-republican paradigm, historians are uncovering new and more complex relationships between workers and capitalism.[2] More recent studies of artisans, and particularly those that focus on the South, are discovering a host of structural dimensions that refute the notion that all crafts experienced a decline, and that in general, the early nineteenth century was not a particularly good time to be a skilled craft worker. Although poor and unsuccessful artisans such as Birchett could be found in all areas of the country, in many places, skilled trades declined less dramatically than was once believed. In fact, some trades expanded and prospered in the antebellum era. In Petersburg, the division of labor, not mechanization, brought the biggest shift in workplace organization. Although this new division of labor saw the percentage of skilled workers decrease, it also brought an increase in production that amplified demand for skilled artisans in many trades. Occupations related to construction trades or supportive of industry actually flourished.[3]

Although some southern industries, notably iron manufacture and textiles, were significantly dependent upon machinery from an early date, most industrial growth came from a reorganization of labor in tobacco manufacturing and construction trades.[4] The precipitate growth of the city and the concomitant

2. The most prominent early studies upheld the primacy of republicanism to artisan politics and culture and argued that industrialization brought the decline of traditional artisan work cultures. See Sean Wilentz, *Chants Democratic: New York City and the Rise of the American Working Class, 1788–1850* (New York: Oxford University Press, 1984); and Howard B. Rock, *Artisans of the New Republic: The Tradesmen of New York City in the Age of Jefferson* (New York: New York University Press, 1979). For the South, see Charles G. Steffen, *The Mechanics of Baltimore: Workers in the Age of Revolution, 1763–1812* (Urbana: University of Illinois Press, 1984).

3. Richard Stott, "Artisans and Capitalist Development," in *Wages of Independence: Capitalism in the Early American Republic* ed. Paul A. Gilje (Madison, Wis.: Madison House, 1997), 105–106.

4. For important studies of mechanized industry in the antebellum South, see Charles B. Dew, *Ironmaker to the Confederacy: Joseph R. Anderson and the Tredegar Iron Works* (New Haven: Yale University Press, 1966); and Tom Downey, "Riparian Rights and Manufacturing in Antebellum South Carolina: William Gregg and the Origins of the 'Industrial Mind,'" *Journal of Southern History* 65 (February 1999): 77–108.

changing nature of opportunities available led to new experiences for Petersburg residents. One important reality for artisan workers was that the changing economy could offer a variety of opportunities for those who were willing to adapt and pursue industrial work. Some, like Monroe Birchett, failed under the new system and fell into the ranks of the general laboring class of the town. A significant number, who were more motivated (or perhaps less rooted) than Birchett, moved on to try their luck elsewhere. But an equally important number of those who adapted their pre-industrial work cultures to the new realities of an expanding market economy might hope to prosper as a new breed of master mechanic/entrepreneur. These artisans formed a "middling class," that fell somewhere between Petersburg's rising middle class of tobacconists and commission merchants and the unskilled manual laborers who filled a host of occupations on the lower social stratum.[5]

Examining these middling skilled workers and their experiences in Petersburg offers an opportunity to study both the emergence of a southern middle class and the redefinition of what it meant to be working-class and white in a slave society. Middling mechanics occupied a separate stratum in the social hierarchy of the South, below that of the emerging middle class. Because they practiced skilled trades and identified with the occupations of the upwardly mobile members of the PBMA, middling mechanics received patronage from those businessmen who once worked with their hands. PBMA members helped uplift the manual arts and sometimes sent business their way. The continued celebration of the artisan tradition by middle-class businessmen gave middling mechanics hope for their own economic advancement. Location in a slave economy also made the experiences of these middling mechanics unique. Even when their economic status fell into decline, middling southern mechanics enjoyed the privilege of being white. The racial divide within the South guaranteed middling workers social status above at least two classes in society, the enslaved and free African Americans. On racial issues, middling mechanics in

<hr>

5. Bruce Laurie, "'Spavined Ministers, Lying Toothpullers, and Buggering Priests': Third-Partyism and the Search for Security in the Antebellum North," in *American Artisans: Crafting Social Identity, 1750–1850*, ed. Howard B. Rock, Paul A. Gilje, and Robert Asher (Baltimore: Johns Hopkins University Press, 1995), 99; Frank Towers, *The Urban South and the Coming of the Civil War* (Charlottesville: University of Virginia Press, 2004), 38–39; and Jonathan Daniel Wells, *The Origins of the Southern Middle Class, 1800–1861* (Chapel Hill: University of North Carolina Press, 2004), 10–11.

Petersburg continued to identify with the emerging middle class of masters-turned-merchants in much the same way that yeoman farmers identified with southern planters.[6] Both groups accepted the benefits of their whiteness, and hoped that economic success would follow.

Most artisans never reached the ranks of the commercial bourgeoisie, but the changes brought by the market revolution and the new relations between workers and employers in the nineteenth century created a more fluid society, leading many to believe that advancement was possible. In the early republic, wealthy people continued to enjoy the most influence and political power, but democratization increasingly challenged traditional hierarchies, creating new national and regional values and an increased popular participation in politics.[7] One of the new values the nation celebrated was the ideal of the "self-made man," even though most who experienced upward mobility were personally connected to those in the elite class.[8] Nevertheless, the very definition of class altered in the antebellum era. Karen Halttunen notes that by 1830, to be middle class meant to be without a fixed social status. She argues that prior to the market revolution a middling class of people existed in a relatively static social position between a "peasantry" and an "aristocracy." In antebellum America, status-conscious "members of the middle class imagined themselves on a social escalator to greater wealth and prestige."[9] Charles Sellers similarly suggests that the emerging middle class was one constituted by ideology rather than actual physical relations of production. He and others argue that the emerging class of shopkeepers, small merchants, and manufacturers created and promoted new middle-class values to others in the community who aspired to self-improvement or advancement. Through evangelicalism, fraternal

6. For a discussion on the uneasy relationship between yeomen and planters on the issue of slaveholding, see Stephanie McCurry, *Masters of Small Worlds: Yeoman Households, Gender Relations, and Political Culture of the Antebellum South Carolina Low Country* (New York: Oxford University Press, 1995), esp. 93–129.

7. Joyce Appleby, *Inheriting the Revolution: The First Generation of Americans* (Cambridge, Mass.: The Belknap Press of Harvard University Press, 2000), 52–55.

8. Paul E. Johnson, *A Shopkeeper's Millennium: Society and Revivals in Rochester, New York, 1815–1837* (New York: Hill and Wang, 1978), 28–32; and Judith A. McGaw, *Most Wonderful Machine: Mechanization and Social Change in Berkshire Paper Making, 1801–1885* (Princeton, N.J.: Princeton University Press, 1987), 130–133.

9. Karen Halttunen, *Confidence Men and Painted Women: A Study of Middle-class Culture in America, 1830–1870* (New Haven: Yale University Press, 1982), 29.

lodges, temperance organizations, libraries, and lectures they sought to impose their new standards of work discipline and personal behavior on themselves and those who worked for them. Jonathan Daniel Wells's examination of the antebellum South finds that the southern middle class admired and emulated the northern middle class, adopting many of their cultural values.[10] Petersburg provides an excellent setting in which to observe the emergence of the southern middle class, but also for exploring those who strove for middle-class status but failed. The fascination of historians for examining the middle class should be expanded to incorporate those middling workers who never quite attained middle-class status, but formed a new working class in the antebellum South.

Members of the PBMA as a whole closely resemble this emerging middle class. They expanded their shops into merchant and contracting firms, leading to an economic and social removal from the ranks of the middling artisan. Those who joined the elite mechanics' group were for the most part not self-made men, but members of a local elite whose political, personal, and business ties aided their success. PBMA members routinely served as justices on the Petersburg Hustings Court, sat on grand juries, held local political offices and positions as militia officers, and populated the boards of educational institutions and poor relief agencies. Similar to modern-day business organizations, such as Rotary and Kiwanis, the PBMA offered its members a fraternal bond that promoted their mutual success while it celebrated and affirmed the importance of their roots in manual labor.[11] However, many artisans who were not members of the PBMA also aspired to middle-class status. Often lacking personal connections to boost their chances for success, a number of Petersburg mechanics struggled to pull themselves out of the ranks of wage labor. Although even the most successful of these middling artisans never enjoyed the offices and community positions of the PBMA elite, some did gain enough wealth so that between 1820 and 1860 clear-cut class divisions appeared in Petersburg and split the artisan community. As more middling mechanics became employers and

10. Charles Sellers, *The Market Revolution: Jacksonian America, 1815–1846* (New York: Oxford University Press, 1991), 237; McGaw, *Most Wonderful Machine,* 265–266; Patricia C. Click, *The Spirit of the Times: Amusements in Nineteenth-Century Baltimore, Norfolk, and Richmond* (Charlottesville: University Press of Virginia, 1989), 16–18; Johnson, *Shopkeeper's Millennium,* 138; and Wells, *Origins of the Southern Middle Class,* 10.

11. Mary Ann Clawson, *Constructing Brotherhood: Class, Gender, and Fraternalism* (Princeton, N.J.: Princeton University Press, 1989), 260–261.

merchants, the lines between PBMA members and other middle-class artisans began to blur. Two things became central in the lives of workers who struggled in the changing economy. Profit and the ability to earn a higher wage overshadowed the significance of their craft identity. Those who became employers and manufacturers drew upon their newfound middle-class status even while they continued to exalt the importance of manual labor. This was true whether or not they joined the PBMA. Regardless of their economic position, all white workers cherished their racial identity and free status within the slave society of antebellum Virginia. Exploring the way the craft economy changed and the shifting alliances and identities among white workers in Petersburg sets the stage for understanding the complexities of antebellum class formation in the South.

Placing focus on the makeup of this middling working class in Petersburg not only illuminates the opportunities available for skilled white workers in the expanding economy but also explains the changes the market economy brought to the South. The tobacco factories, iron foundries, railroad facilities, and cotton textile mills provided ample openings for artisans in a number of trades. Petersburg's population more than tripled in the first five decades of the nineteenth century, and by 1850 skilled white artisans made up 6 percent of the total. (See table 4.) Most were native to Virginia or other southern states, but one in ten were immigrants mainly from Scotland, Ireland, and Germany. The smallest group of skilled white workers were forty-four hailing from northern states.[12] In the 1850s, which proved prosperous for Petersburg businesses until the Panic of 1857, the skilled workforce continued to grow. During that decade, the number of skilled white workers increased 67 percent, and the workforce grew in diversity as more European immigrants entered the southern city.[13]

Most Petersburg artisans labored in crafts related to the major industrial

12. James G. Scott and Edward A. Wyatt, *Petersburg's Story: A History* (Petersburg, Va.: Titmus Optical, 1960), 43; Bureau of the Census, *The Seventh Census of the United States: 1850* (Washington, D.C.: Robert Armstrong, Public Printer, 1853), 256–258; and Bureau of the Census, Population Schedules, Petersburg, Va. (Washington, D.C., 1850, microfilm).

13. Bureau of the Census, *Population of the United States in 1860: The Eighth Census* (Washington, D.C.: GPO, 1864), 516, 519; and Bureau of the Census, Population Schedules, Petersburg, Va., 1860. For a detailed study of urban diversity, see Dennis C. Rousey, "From Whence They Came to Savannah: The Origins of an Urban Population in the Old South," *Georgia Historical Quarterly* 79 (1995): 305–336. In this case the 1860 census enumerator collected information detailing the county or city of residents' birthplace.

activities of the city. Those in construction and woodworking trades such as carpentry, bricklaying, painting, and coach making formed the bulk of the artisan community. Just over one-third of all white artisans listed employment in construction crafts. (See table 5, A–B.) Employed primarily building the cotton and tobacco factories and iron foundries that were the base of Petersburg's growth, many also constructed housing for the rising population, including that for the Matoaca and the Ettrick Manufacturing companies, the latter of which grew into a mill village with a population of 830 by 1859.[14]

The five railroads crossing Petersburg by the 1850s were a main reason for the location of iron forges and locomotive manufactories in the city. As the second largest employer of skilled labor, trades related to forging and supplemental to manufacturing employed close to one in five white artisans. Blacksmiths and machinists were the most numerous among these tradesmen—not surprising, considering the growing demand for those skills in new industry. At the beginning of industrial growth in 1820, Petersburg and the surrounding county of Dinwiddie claimed only sixty-four blacksmiths and no machinists or other iron workers.[15] Demand from the railroads and other industries led to a dramatic increase in iron workers. Blacksmith William H. Tappey's establishment grew to become one of the largest employers of artisans skilled in forging and machine manufacture. In less than twenty years, his blacksmith operations evolved from a small shop across from the Jarratt Hotel to a full-scale foundry building such complicated equipment as a steam-powered printing press for a local newspaper and railroad cars in the 1850s.[16] Tappey's success helps to illustrate the growing division between PBMA members and more middling mechanics. Association members such as Tappey often became capitalist-entrepreneurs whose ownership of the means of production set them apart from the journeymen they employed. The Petersburg Railroad also attracted a number of men skilled in forging trades. By 1854, the company was operating its

14. Edward A. Wyatt, "Rise of Industry in Ante-Bellum Petersburg," *William and Mary Quarterly* 17 (2nd ser. January 1937): 22–24.

15. Bureau of the Census, Records of the 1820 Census of Manufactures, roll 18, Schedules for Virginia, Vi (microfilm). The 1820 census combines the enumeration for Petersburg and Dinwiddie County.

16. Advertisement, *Republican*, 30 December 1846; Editorial, *Daily Southside Democrat*, 22 June 1855; and "The City Water as a Motive Power," *Daily Express*, 2 May 1859.

own locomotive and car works in the town and the railroad's president, Henry D. Bird, boasted that all the car trucks used on the line were of local manufacture.[17]

Almost tied in number with the forging and manufacturing crafts were occupations related to food and especially to tobacco manufacture. Food and tobacco workers accounted for about 17.5 percent of all skilled white workers, with more than one-third of these involved directly in the manufacture of tobacco into a consumable product. A few tobacconists owned large factories employing slave and free black workers, but others produced on a small scale. Plug and twist tobacco were the most common products made, although a small segment of the tobacco workers were skilled craftsmen who made cigars for the fancy local trade and export. An important related craft was that of apothecary or druggist. Some apothecaries served medicinal needs of individuals in Petersburg, but most were a combination of merchant and supplier for local tobacconists. Apothecaries mixed and prepared the spices and flavorings that gave each tobacco label or brand its distinct flavor and public appeal. A number of the food workers also found opportunity in filling the needs of the growing urban population, as millers, bakers, confectioners, butchers, and even bottlers were evident in the latter part of the era.

Construction, forging, and food and tobacco trades together accounted for about 70 percent of the skilled jobs in Petersburg. These expanding opportunities were tied closely to the city's growth and to the industries forming the base of the evolving local market economy. They demonstrate that artisans willing to adapt their traditional workplace notions to pursue industrial work often times could find employment in the city. Those engaged in transportation and service related occupations also found some opportunity in Petersburg. Physicians, cart and wagon drivers, and even plumbers filled important niches. Among the transportation and service workers were new occupations, including daguerreian artists who created novelty portraits for area residents, florists and gardeners who tended to the landscaping needs of the middle and upper class, and a veterinary surgeon who looked after the health of family pets and livestock.

Unfortunately, skilled workers in other crafts did not fare as well in the

17. "Car Wheels, Engines, &c.," *Daily Southside Democrat*, 6 May 1854.

changing economy, and many found that cheap imported goods manufactured in the North or Europe were a threat to their livelihoods.[18] Leather crafts and furniture making were two areas imports hit hard. Clothing crafts fared a little better, but it is hard to imagine that seventy-nine tailors could clothe a city of eighteen thousand in 1860. Most of the clothing workers were shoe and boot makers, but again, just over a hundred shoemakers would not have filled the need for footwear in the region. Southern shoemakers were especially vulnerable to competition from northern manufacturers who concentrated their product line to make crude brogans for sale to slave owners. Agents for Lynn, Massachusetts shoemakers reached Petersburg even before the turn of the nineteenth century. One Lynn shoe merchant, Major John D. Atwill, operated a wholesale trade in Petersburg and Richmond as early as 1790, and was still an active regional trader in 1820.[19] Luxury trades including watchmakers, jewelers, and silversmiths also suffered from import competition, along with less well-to-do men employed as soap makers, potters, and book binders.

When the trades of middling mechanics are compared to those of PBMA members it becomes apparent that more than half of all middling artisans worked in trades related to new industries, including construction and forging. These occupations grew along with the demand for building and machinery, but trades such as carpentry and stone cutting were those also strongly affected by a growing division of labor and permanent wage status.[20] Opportunities to achieve independence in these trades declined even as the numerical strength of their ranks grew. About 40 percent of PBMA members also clustered in these crafts, but association members tended to benefit from the labor of middling mechanics once they elevated themselves as bosses or capitalists. PBMA carpenter Beverly Drinkard was in reality a contractor whose firm employed at least three white journeymen and seven slaves as early as 1820.[21] Daniel Lyon, a bricklayer by trade, employed white journeymen, free blacks, and slaves in his contracting firm.[22] "Blacksmith" Uriah Wells employed many founders, black-

---

18. Michele Gillespie, *Free Labor in an Unfree World: White Artisans in Slaveholding Georgia, 1789–1860* (Athens: University of Georgia Press, 2000), 97.

19. Paul G. Faler, *Mechanics and Manufacturers in the Early Industrial Revolution: Lynn Massachusetts 1780–1860* (Albany: State University of New York Press, 1981), 18–19.

20. Wilentz, *Chants Democratic,* 132–134.

21. Petersburg, Va., Personal Property Tax List, 1820, Vi.

22. Personal Property Tax List, 1843.

smiths, and molders at his Southern Foundry, one of the largest iron works in Petersburg; by 1859, Wells's workmen completed such large-scale projects as forging locomotives for the railroad.[23] PBMA mechanics were also more likely to hold on to positions in luxury crafts that experienced decline because of competition from imported goods. Although the number of clockmakers and jewelers remained small, twice as many PBMA members practiced those trades than their middling counterparts. Middling artisans, on the other hand, outnumbered PBMA members in transportation and service occupations. These trades grew in number, but were also occupations that represented declining opportunities for advancement.

For the majority of middling artisans the expansion of markets, revolution in transportation, and industrialization meant a new way of life. Although some trades expanded and new ones developed, the traditional hierarchy and expectations of white journeymen and apprentices fundamentally changed in this era. Mechanics still strove to attain a "competence," but for many, the dream of working toward independence became a reality of working for wages. For a few with access to capital and personal connections, upward mobility into the ranks of the commercial bourgeoisie was possible. Some expanded their workshops into retail ventures where they imported and sold northern goods alongside their locally manufactured items. Whatever their strategy, and rate of success or failure, there can be little doubt that by the end of the 1850s, the experience of skilled white workers in Petersburg bore little resemblance to the pre-industrial artisan workshop.[24]

One departure from the pre-industrial work culture was evident in Petersburg as early as 1820. Even at that early date, few independent journeymen lived in a household headed by a master mechanic.[25] In fact, in Petersburg, little evidence suggests that "living in" was ever a common practice. Of the masters paying city personal property tax in 1820, only 24 listed additional adult white males or journeymen in their household. More significantly, successful

23. Editorial, *Daily Express*, 21 September 1859.

24. For studies of pre-industrial work culture, see Carl Bridenbaugh, *The Colonial Craftsman* (Chicago: University of Chicago Press, 1950); Herbert G. Gutman, *Work, Culture, and Society in Industrializing America: Essays in American Working-Class and Social History* (New York: Vintage, 1977); and Bruce Laurie, *Artisans into Workers: Labor in Nineteenth Century America* (New York: Noonday, 1989), esp. 35–38.

25. This was also true for northern cities. See Wilentz, *Chants Democratic*, 48.

members of the PBMA headed 21 of those households, suggesting that only the wealthiest artisans provided housing for their journeymen. Saddler William Couch had the largest shop, which included 7 white adults in addition to himself. Shoemaker Nathan Vincent employed 5, and printers Francis G. Yancey and Edward Pescud each employed 4. Only 3 middling artisans included adult workers in their household in 1820. Miller John Edwards employed 4, and carpenter William A. Cain employed 3. Wheelwright William Griffin's household employed 5 men, but the tax ledger lists him in partnership with his brother James L. Griffin, a PBMA member.[26]

Although existing records make it difficult to accurately assess the number of journeymen who "lived in," and how that changed over time, the trend toward a wage-earning workforce undoubtedly increased as the antebellum era stretched on. Masters' obligations to journeymen and apprentices shifted as some masters transformed themselves into entrepreneurs, factory operators, and merchants. The pre-industrial pattern of providing journeymen with room and board was largely absent in Petersburg by 1860, even among the wealthiest artisans. In that year, the city directory recorded twenty-eight artisans who specifically identified themselves using the title "journeyman." Of those, only two boarded with the master mechanic who employed them; most lived with relatives or at other facilities in the city. One of the two journeymen who boarded with his employer may have done so out of convenience rather than obligation. Silver plater R. E. Lambeth boarded with H. T. Alley, but was not the only journeyman employed in Alley's shop. Another journeyman, E. T. Stell, worked there but apparently lived elsewhere.[27]

The apprenticeship system was another feature of traditional artisan culture altered in the antebellum era. Designed to train future generations of craftsmen, apprenticeships sometimes became a bastardized system of indentured labor and an important provider of poor relief in the Upper South.[28] As the apprenticeship system adapted to the realities of an industrial economy, the practice actually expanded in Petersburg, peaking in the 1830s. Many middling Petersburg masters sought apprentices for their ability to provide extra labor; apprentices also became a significant measure of a master's legitimacy and

26. Personal Property Tax List, 1820.

27. W. Eugene Ferslew, comp., *Second Annual Directory for the City of Petersburg* (Petersburg, Va.: George E. Ford, 1860), 92, 122.

28. For examples from early Baltimore, see Steffen, *Mechanics of Baltimore*, 28–29.

competence as an artisan.[29] Masters sought apprentices as status symbols, and to demonstrate confidence in the future success of their shops.

In a brief column on the state of the apprentice system in Petersburg, the editor of the *Daily Express* reminded readers in 1859 that "to make a good mechanic, it is necessary to be first a good apprentice, which can only be effected through the agency of competent supervisors, and self-application on the part of the apprentice."[30] Apprentices were generally teenage boys who spent three to seven years learning the "art and mystery" of an artisanal trade. During this training period apprentices were bound to a master mechanic under an indenture contract for a specified period of time, usually until age twenty-one. In exchange for their labor, the master was to provide training, room, board, and the necessities of life. Under the traditional artisan system, apprentices graduated to journeyman status at the end of their indenture and received a suit of clothes and a set of tools appropriate to their trade.[31]

Apprentices could be legally bound in one of two ways. An apprentice's guardian or parent might negotiate a contract, which required the approval of the Hustings Court. In May 1830, tobacconist and merchant John Rowlett arranged for his ward, James T. Murphy, to be bound to Stephen Jackson to learn saddle and harnessmaking.[32] If an orphaned youth had no guardian, or his parents were unable to provide for him, the Overseers of the Poor would negotiate his contract. For example, in October 1825, the Hustings Court ordered that the Overseers of the Poor arrange an apprenticeship contract to bind the orphan Abel Bowman to John Ritchie to learn the butcher's trade.[33] Bowman completed his apprenticeship and then worked as a butcher in Petersburg, although he never prospered. City records show he accumulated no taxable property, with the exception of a single horse listed in the 1843 assessment.[34] The practice of indenture was so common that between 1820 and 1860, two hundred young boys served as indentured apprentices in Petersburg.

29. For a detailed argument on this point, see Gillespie, *Free Labor in an Unfree World*, 23.

30. "The Apprentice System," *Daily Express*, 22 August 1859.

31. Laurie, *Artisans into Workers*, 35–36; for an in-depth study of apprentices, see W. J. Rorabaugh, *The Craft Apprentice: From Franklin to the Machine Age in America* (New York: Oxford University Press, 1986).

32. Hustings Court Minute Book 1827–1832, n.p. (21 May 1830).

33. Hustings Court Minute Book 1823–1827, n.p. (22 October 1825).

34. Personal Property Tax List, 1836, 1838, 1843.

Additional evidence suggests that training by apprenticeship was even more widespread than the legal record reflects. Petersburg mechanics also practiced less formal forms of apprenticeship. Masters often passed their skills on to their sons through an apprenticeship. Boot and shoemaker Robert Penman trained his son John alongside three unrelated indentured apprentices in his shop in the 1850s.[35] Prominent coach maker Jonathan Camp trained his two sons in similar fashion. Camp's household included his son and three unrelated apprentices in 1850, although no legal contract indenture existed.[36] It seems likely that many masters negotiated private terms to train young men in their craft. Many of these arrangements occurred without benefit of record, making it difficult to accurately gauge the number of apprentices who served under Petersburg masters. For some, the apprenticeship experience was a positive avenue toward gaining the skills needed to enter the southern workforce. For others, the apprentice system bound them as laborers to less than "competent supervisors" who were more interested in exploiting their labor than passing on the secrets of their trade.

Painter Charles Anson Delano, who had a history of mental illness, fell into the category of negligent masters. In 1834 Delano's two apprentices, George W. Stephens and Robert Blick, ran away, claiming mistreatment. Delano offered a $10 reward for the return of Blick, but noted "I will give one cent reward for Stephens." His newspaper advertisement warned that he would prosecute anyone who employed the runaways or offered them shelter. Another Petersburg mechanic, John B. Jackson, defended the actions of the apprentices, especially Stephens. In the same edition of the *American Constellation*, Jackson refuted Delano's claim to Stephens, denying that the boy was an indentured apprentice in Delano's household. Instead, Jackson noted, "he has been living with that individual for some years, and would have remained until he was twenty-one, but for a course of mistreatment disgraceful to the man who practiced it."[37] Delano's mental health problems may have interfered with his ability to fulfill his obligations to Stephens and Blick. In the 1840s he was committed to the lunatic asylum at Williamsburg, but returned to his painter's trade after his release in 1850. Toward the end of the antebellum era he published a rambling account

---

35. Bureau of the Census, Population Schedules, Petersburg, Va., 1860.
36. Bureau of the Census, Population Schedules, Petersburg, Va., 1850, 1860.
37. Advertisements, *American Constellation*, 14 June 1834.

of his life and insanity in which he equated himself with Christ.[38] What happened to Blick is unclear, but George W. Stephens remained in Petersburg as a middling house painter for many years. In 1860 he claimed a modest personal estate worth $250, but had yet to gain any real property. Instead, he lived in a boardinghouse.[39]

In another case, butcher Jefferson Grimes, also known as Edward or E. J. Grimes, was brought before the mayor in 1858 for whipping his sixteen-year-old apprentice, John H. Payne. Grimes told the court he administered the punishment because the youth "acted very improperly in the family of his benefactor," and then ran away rather than face his master. The mayor warned Grimes that if the apprentice made a formal complaint, the case would be tried before the Hustings Court. If Grimes was a cruel or unsuitable master, then Payne found release the following year. Grimes died in early 1859, and after temporarily transferring Payne's indenture to his widow, the Hustings Court ordered the Overseers of the Poor to find a new and "suitable place" for the orphan Payne to finish his apprenticeship.[40]

The apprenticeship system in some Petersburg trades bore resemblance to the metropolitan industrialization occurring in northern cities. Characterized most strikingly by the division of labor, changes in some crafts meant enlarging the workplace into a "factory."[41] Some masters found that adding additional employees was a promising way to expand their fortunes as well as increase production. In antebellum Baltimore, for example, the proprietor of a foundry employing six hundred continued to accept apprentices. In 1858, 43 percent of employees in the foundry's tin shops were indentured apprentices who received no cash wages until age seventeen.[42] Because of their dependent status as indentured apprentices, the practice of expanding the workshop often led to an

38. Hustings Court Minute Book 1848–1851, 269; and Charles Anson Delano, *The Man-Child Born of the Sun, and an Exposition of the Prophecies of Daniel and the Book of Revelation* (Petersburg, Va.: Author, 1858).

39. Bureau of the Census, Population Schedules, Petersburg, Va., 1860.

40. Petersburg, Va., Hustings Court Will Book 4: 550, Vi; and Hustings Court Minute Book 1858–1861, 159, 205.

41. Wilentz, *Chants Democratic*, 32–33; and Steven J. Ross, *Workers on the Edge: Work, Leisure, and Politics in Industrializing Cincinnati, 1788–1890* (New York: Columbia University Press, 1985), 80–81. See also Jonathan Prude, "Capitalism, Industrialization, and the Factory in Post-revolutionary America," in Gilje, ed., *Wages of Independence*, 81–100.

42. Towers, *Urban South*, 64.

exploitative work environment. It also posed a threat to the livelihood of journeymen and the future of certain trades. In 1858 the Petersburg Typographical
Union attacked A. F. Crutchfield, publisher of the *Daily Express*, for degrading the printing profession by employing too many apprentices. Journeymen
printers resolved not to work in any printing shop employing more than three
apprentices. Apparently, Crutchfield was also employing young boys without
benefit of contract because the journeymen further resolved that "every boy
employed in a Printing Office, for any work, is considered an Apprentice."[43]

Crutchfield's response is indicative of the new mindset of many masters-
turned-liberal capitalists. His success as a printer and editor mirrored that of
members of the PBMA, which he joined in 1864, and his response to the labor
unrest in his workshop demonstrates the bourgeois values that set him apart
from his workers. Crutchfield was more concerned with his individual situation than the changes his printer-employees faced. He denied the accusation
of exploitation and announced that the newspaper and printing office would
"conduct our business in our own way, and would not agree to bind ourselves to
any policy with regard to apprentice[s]." Sounding eerily like the industrialists
of a later age, Crutchfield told the Typographical Union that "no businessman
who has a proper respect for himself, would ever consent to subject his business
arrangements to the dictation of any body of men." Following this announcement, all of the journeymen and a few of the apprentices employed at the *Daily
Express* office walked off the job. Resolution of the matter remains unclear, and
there was no future mention of the labor problem in the *Daily Express*. Perhaps
Crutchfield found replacements for his workers, since the economy of Petersburg was still recovering from the Panic of 1857 at the time of the strike and
jobs were scarce. In the same edition he advertised that he would give "immediate employment to five or six journeymen printers," offering monthly wages
between $15 and $18. Showing his resolve on the matter of apprentices, he also
advertised for "eight or ten smart, active, intelligent lads" to learn the printing
business, and offering to "even ordinary minds, advantages quite equivalent to
a liberal education."[44]

In addition to being the traditional means of entry into many crafts, the apprenticeship system in Virginia played an important role in poor relief. Aside

43. "To the Public," *Daily Express*, 29 June 1858.
44. Ibid; "To Jour Printers," ibid.; and "Apprentices Wanted," ibid.

from the Female Orphan Asylum, which opened its doors to white girls, Petersburg had no public institutions to provide care and education for orphans or children of impecunious parents.[45] Indentured apprenticeship formed the main method of providing for poor young white and black boys and black girls in antebellum Virginia. Each county or town designated Overseers of the Poor to find suitable positions and to negotiate contracts of indenture. For boys, terms of indenture lasted until age twenty-one; for girls, until age eighteen. Between 1820 and 1860, Petersburg records show that fifty-six girls, in addition to the two hundred boys already mentioned, were bound as indentured apprentices. With only one or two exceptions, the young girls bound out were African American. The only difference between contracts for white and black apprentices was that masters were not required to provide educational opportunities for black youth.[46]

In some cases the apprenticeship system adapted to the growth of factories and the introduction of new technologies. Once industry gained a hold in the town, Petersburg court records show that boys were apprenticed to cotton textile mills under terms similar to a traditional indenture contract. As early as 1829, Isham Eanes bound his eighteen-year-old son, William, to the Petersburg Manufacturing Company to learn the trade of a power loom weaver.[47] The practice of binding apprentices to industry was also used at the Tredegar Iron Works in Richmond and at foundries in Baltimore. In the 1840s Tredegar provided its apprentices with room, board, and clothes, usually through residence in the household of senior iron workers. By 1850 the practice of accepting apprentices ended at Tredegar, and indenture records for Petersburg indicate that the practice declined there as well.[48]

Antebellum industrial labor needs stretched outside the cities into the countryside. If skilled workers in Petersburg found opportunities shifting in the city, they could rest assured that their trades were in demand on local plantations

---

45. Suzanne Lebsock, *The Free Women of Petersburg: Status and Culture in a Southern Town, 1784–1860* (New York: W. W. Norton, 1984), 202–205.

46. Virginia, *The Revised Code of the Laws of Virginia* (Richmond: Thomas Ritchie, 1819), 268–269.

47. Hustings Court Minute Book 1827–1832, n.p. (20 August 1829).

48. Gregg D. Kimball, *American City, Southern Place: A Cultural History of Antebellum Richmond* (Athens: University of Georgia Press, 2000), 172–173; and Towers, *Urban South*, 64–65.

in the surrounding hinterland. Artisans have traditionally shared important economic relationships with farms and estates in the rural countryside. In the Beauce region of France, skilled workers, including blacksmiths, harness makers, and cartwrights, continued to flourish throughout the nineteenth century. There, static agricultural techniques helped to perpetuate some craft occupations. Other trades, including carpentry, flourished on hinterland trade, although as the century progressed, building craftsmen were more likely to be employees than independent masters.[49] In Central Europe, particularly Vienna, a specific migratory artisan system developed in the eighteenth century established the shops of small masters in large towns, but left journeymen to make a living from the surrounding rural area.[50] Up through the beginnings of industrial transformation, Hungarian urban craft workers likewise took care of the needs of the countryside and "thus played a leading role in the economic relationship between towns and their hinterlands."[51]

With more than twenty major plantations in the surrounding counties of Dinwiddie, Chesterfield, and Prince George, Petersburg artisans frequently divided their time between city and plantation jobs. In the South artisans in luxury trades, such as carriage making, silversmithing, and fancy furniture or cabinetmaking, gained a measure of security by catering to the needs of rich planters, providing them with goods that were either too expensive or too fragile to import, although after the railroad improved transportation in the late 1830s and 1840s, Petersburg area planters were more likely to rely on local artisans for repair and service of imported luxury goods, including furniture, watches, and guns.[52] Although Jean B. Russo and Christine Daniels argue that the rise of Baltimore and other factors brought a concomitant decline in the number and importance of local artisans in rural Maryland, such was not the case with Pe-

49. Jean-Claude Farcy, "Rural Artisans in the Beauce during the Nineteenth Century," in *Shopkeepers and Master Artisans in Nineteenth-Century Europe*, ed. Geoffrey Crossick and Heinz-Gerhard Haupt (London: Methuen, 1984), 225–226.

50. Josef Ehmer, "Worlds of Mobility: Migration Patterns of Viennese Artisans in the Eighteenth Century," in *The Artisan and the European Town, 1500–1900*, ed. Geoffrey Crossick (Hants, U.K.: Scholar Press, 1997), 172–175.

51. Vera Bácskai, "Artisans in Hungarian Towns on the Eve of Industrialization," in ibid., 200–201.

52. For an example from the Lower South, see Michele K. Gillespie, "Planters in the Making: Artisanal Opportunity in Georgia, 1790–1830," in Rock, Gilje, and Asher, eds., *American Artisans*, 36.

tersburg-area mechanics.[53] The most skilled regional artisans lived in the city and surviving records from a few plantations surrounding Petersburg suggest that the relationship between skilled workers and planters involved a constant interchange of goods and services and artisans of many diverse trades, not just those in luxury crafts, had meaningful economic relationships with plantation owners.

Existing receipts from the 1830s show that John Vaughan Wilcox owned more than 4,000 acres of land and 65 slaves. His Flowerdew Hundred plantation in nearby Prince George County gave Petersburg artisans a significant amount of business. Between January 1830 and October 1831 he paid prominent bricklayer Daniel Lyon $192.49 for work on brick fireplaces and chimneys at Flowerdew Hundred. In the early 1830s, he also patronized Petersburg confectioners, physicians, apothecaries, book binders, painters, and shoemakers. He paid $7 to a Petersburg shoemaker for a pair of boots, but his accounts also show the purchase of raw materials, suggesting he counted a shoemaker among his slaves. In January 1832 Wilcox paid local tanner George Zimmerman $26.53 for 3 sides of upper and 4 sides of sole leather, likely to be made into brogans for his slave community. In the era before railroads reduced the transit costs for imported or northern-made luxury goods, Wilcox patronized local cabinetmakers for his furniture needs. In 1832 he paid one local artisan $31 for a bookcase and bureau, and contracted with another cabinetmaker to build a looking-glass frame, 2 mahogany bedsteads, a pair of wash stands, and another bureau at a total cost of $95.50.[54]

Other Prince George County plantations, including the one owned by Richard Dunn, transacted regular business with Petersburg artisans. In 1848 Dunn recorded nearly two dozen transactions with the Petersburg iron foundry operated by William Birchett and an unknown partner. Dunn relied on the founders for a variety of small jobs, including making and installing bolts on the

53. Christine Daniels, "'WANTED: A Blacksmith who understands Plantation Work': Artisans in Maryland, 1700–1810," *William and Mary Quarterly* 50 (3rd ser. 1993): 766; and Jean B. Russo, "Self-sufficiency and Local Exchange: Free Craftsmen in the Rural Chesapeake Economy," in *Colonial Chesapeake Society*, ed. Lois Green Carr, Philip D. Morgan, and Jean B. Russo (Chapel Hill: University of North Carolina Press for the Institute of Early American History and Culture, 1988), 405.

54. Loose receipts, Accounts 1828–1833, John Vaughan Wilcox Papers, Virginia Historical Society, Richmond, Va. (hereafter ViHi).

plantation's wharf, forging braces and rods for scythes, and making hooks and a hasp to repair a gate.[55] Charles Friend, the owner of White Hill plantation in Prince George County, also patronized Petersburg artisans. His account book for the 1840s and 1850s includes transactions with druggists Bragg and Willson, saddler Allen P. Lee, coach maker Daniel Perkinson, shoemakers Drummond and Wyche, cabinetmaker Samuel Coldwell, butcher John Enniss, and founder Uriah Wells.[56]

The most detailed evidence of the link between skilled white workers and regional plantations is found in the ledgers and diaries of Richard Eppes, a wealthy physician and planter who owned three large plantations near City Point, approximately twelve miles southeast of Petersburg. The diaries and records Eppes kept in the 1850s show his pattern of employing middling and wealthy artisans, in luxury and common crafts, as needed. In October 1851 Eppes hired machinist and bell gauger James C. Patton to forge and hang bells at Appomattox Manor, his main City Point plantation. Patton was a middling artisan who persisted in Petersburg, but never flourished. By 1860 he owned no real property, listing a meager personal estate worth just $50.[57] Eppes also did considerable business with Uriah Wells, a PBMA member and prosperous owner of a large iron foundry. In 1855 Eppes paid Wells more than $400 for machine parts, bolts, and iron works needed to construct a wharf on the Appomattox River.[58]

Eppes occasionally patronized artisans in luxury trades, including Petersburg gunsmiths, watchmakers, and coach makers, but most of these transactions were for repairs and upkeep on luxury items imported from the North or Europe. By the mid-1850s, plantations in the Petersburg region were more closely tied to national markets and shipping methods, with railroad access that allowed for the importation of larger and more delicate items. In 1852 Eppes engaged Petersburg cabinet maker E. H. Badger to repair a bedstead, then called on him again in 1857 to clean and fix another bedstead. Around the same time Eppes recorded in his diary that he "received furniture from Philadelphia." Even though he failed to note the cost of the imported furniture,

55. Loose receipt, Accounts folder, Richard G. Dunn Papers, ViHi.

56. Account Book 1839–1869, Charles Friend Papers, ViHi.

57. Account Book 1851–1861, 1, Richard Eppes Papers, ViHi; and Bureau of the Census, Population Schedules, Petersburg, Va., 1860.

58. Account Book 1851–1861, 53, 54, 56, Eppes Papers.

which included a piano, it is certain that the northern goods cost much more than the mere $8 that Badger earned for his two calls to the plantation.[59]

Artisans in construction and forging trades found a significant amount of work on area plantations. Many planters owned slave artisans, especially carpenters and blacksmiths, whom they employed in the everyday needs of plantation operation, but most looked to highly skilled white workers for important construction and forging tasks. Eppes owned a carpenter named Ned who was responsible for basic construction projects, including fence building, but even then, Eppes gave Ned specific instructions such as "to saw off the tops of the palings & place planks at the bottom." In 1856 Eppes took his slave blacksmith, Solomon, to Petersburg to help select the supplies and tools necessary to outfit a blacksmith shop on his plantation.[60] Yet Eppes was reluctant to trust important tasks to his slave artisans. Instead, he looked to carpenter G. F. Marks to construct new housing, most likely for his growing slave population, in 1857, and to painter William H. Jarvis to apply two coats of paint to his main house at Appomattox Manor in 1858. These highly skilled craftsmen earned in excess of $300 each for their services, excluding materials.[61]

When the City Point Railroad connected the Appomattox River hinterland with Petersburg in 1838, plantation owners along the line could reach Petersburg in about an hour's travel time, increasing the frequency of business conducted in the city. Richard Eppes, like other planters in the area, came to town often to trade with Petersburg mechanics. On his 1 November 1851 trip to Petersburg he reported that he "called on Mr [L. C.] Tappey, [who] promised to come down and paper the parlor next Thursday." Exactly one year later he noted that he "visited Petersburg today . . . paid James Doherty 50 dollars for a rifle & $1 for canister of powder. Told him to put a new barrel to the stock of my old rifle." Later, in November 1852, he made another trip to Petersburg, where one of his errands was to leave "measures for negro shoes at Messrs. Drummond & Witch [sic], selecting mens at $1.25 & womens brogues at $1. Ditto boys & girls." Eppes was less than pleased with the contract at this shoemaker's shop, remarking "price high" in his diary. In November 1855 another trip recorded

59. Account Book, 16, 78, Eppes Papers; and 23 April 1852 entry, 39, Diary, 12 March–30 September 1852, Richard Eppes Papers, ViHi.

60. 16 March 1852, 9, Diary, 12 March–30 September 1852; 13 June 1856, 133, Diary, 12 March 1854 and 24 October 1855–31 December 1857, Eppes Papers.

61. Account Book, 74, 89, Eppes Papers.

that he "called at Well's foundry & left a cast wheel to be recast for cobcrusher ordered at the same time a bar of wrought iron with a steel point resembling an ax to be made to be used for cutting up stumps."[62]

The close ties area planters maintained with Petersburg mechanics helped some craftsmen to prosper even in the changing economy, but artisans who failed to find enough work in Petersburg or the surrounding hinterland often left to pursue their trade elsewhere. Geographic mobility was a common experience in the lives of many skilled journeymen and middling mechanics in the industrializing economy of antebellum America. Those who found themselves caught in between the ability to advance to master status and the possibility of a lifetime of wage labor often took to the road in search of better opportunities. Itinerant artisans were so common that a formal "tramping" system evolved in some cities. In New York City journeymen had a reciprocal structure including detailed trade tickets and labor exchanges, and even established a house of call for tramps in the carpentry trade. In the North, itinerant printers developed a similar network encompassing the New England states and Pennsylvania. Along the route boardinghouses and rooming houses catered specially to the needs of journeymen on the move with short-term leases and inexpensive lodging.[63] In Petersburg, the PBMA recognized the ubiquitous nature of itinerant mechanics through designating them a place to march with the fraternal group in parades and celebrations. When planning a ceremony to celebrate the construction of their new Mechanics' Hall the organization noted that "Transient Brother Mechanics are respectfully invited to join in the services and festivities of the day."[64]

Persistence rates for artisans depended on a variety of factors. Communities facing rapid change from mechanized industries and a growing pool of unskilled labor tended to have low persistence rates. In the rapidly mechanizing industries of Newburyport, Massachusetts, for example, about two-thirds of all unskilled workers moved on between 1850 and 1860. In Cincinnati, the persistence rate for skilled workers was just over one in five. On the other hand, skilled workers were more rooted in towns depending on a single industry, such

62. 1 November 1851, n.p., Diary, 29 September 1851–11 March 1852; 1 November 1852, 30, 30 November, 43, Diary, 1 October 1852–11 March 1854; and 26 November 1855, 36, Diary, 12 March 1854 and 24 October 1855–31 December 1857, Eppes Papers.

63. Wilentz, *Chants Democratic*, 52–53.

64. Notice, *Th' Time O' Day*, 20 August 1839.

as shoemaking.[65] Although most studies examining the geographic mobility of mechanics focus on northern cities and communities, the pattern was common in the antebellum South as well. Artisans in Georgia participated in a "tramping tour through plantation lands," comparable to the circuit northern printers made through New England and Pennsylvania. In the more rural regions of the Lower South, planters and farmers depended on roaming artisans to perform blacksmithing and to build and maintain farm equipment, such as mills and cotton gins.[66] The paths that itinerant artisans took in the Upper South are less clear, but mobility was just as prevalent among artisans who worked in Petersburg before the Civil War.

The first opportunity to study the geographic mobility patterns of Petersburg artisan workers is with the census of 1850, the first to designate occupations for those enumerated. Of 523 artisans identified and traced from the 1850 census, only 187, or 36 percent, remained in Petersburg in 1860.[67] Most of these skilled workers left Virginia before 1860 because few can be identified within the state in the following census enumeration. Their pattern of mobility or "tramping" likely led most of them to cities far beyond the Upper South, but a few were still nearby in 1860. A small handful moved to Richmond to try their trade in Virginia's capital city. Baker Richard Adams, who originally hailed from Scotland, was the most successful. He owned real estate worth $30,000 and a personal estate valued at about $5,000. Pennsylvania-born daguerreian artist George W. Minnis also prospered in Richmond, where he owned property worth $5,000 and a personal estate valued at an additional $6,000. Less successful was Canadian blacksmith Francis Gordon, who claimed property worth $800, and engineer Martin Alley, who owned a small personal estate worth $150 but no real property.[68]

Those artisans remaining in Petersburg tended to be more successful than

65. Stephen Thernstrom, *Poverty and Progress: Social Mobility in a Nineteenth Century City* (Cambridge, Mass., Harvard University Press, 1964), 97; Ross, *Workers on the Edge*, 162; and Faler, *Mechanics and Manufacturers*, 140–141.

66. Gillespie, *Free Labor in an Unfree World*, 116–121.

67. This figure refers to middling white artisans identified from the manuscript census population schedules for 1850, who did not belong to the Petersburg Benevolent Mechanic Association.

68. Bureau of the Census, Population Schedules, Richmond City and Henrico County (Washington, D.C., 1860, microfilm).

their itinerant counterparts, but not necessarily engaged in flourishing trades. Persistence patterns conflict with the trend that concentrated the bulk of Petersburg's skilled whites in construction, forging/manufacturing, and food/tobacco crafts. Persisting mechanics in the flourishing trades were actually somewhat underrepresented; only 65 percent of those remaining practiced in those three areas. (See table 6, A–B.) Construction crafts, and especially carpentry, employed nearly 40 percent of all remaining mechanics. Forging/manufacturing and food/tobacco trades accounted for 12 and 14 percent, respectively. Other trades with significant persistence levels include clothing crafts and transportation and service occupations, including physicians. The lowest persistence rates fell to luxury trades, including furniture making, leather goods, and clock and jewelry making, all hit hard by competition from imported and northern goods.[69]

Those artisans choosing to remain were often native to the area, or experienced substantial economic success after locating in Petersburg. A significant measure of economic success in the antebellum South rested in the ability to accumulate land. Many of the most successful persisters invested in urban and industrial property. Between 1850 and 1860 the property ownership rates of middling artisans increased significantly. In 1850 only one in five persisting mechanics owned real property in Petersburg, but the trend grew in the coming decade. In 1850, most property owners held a moderate amount of real estate, usually worth less than $5,000. Typical among this middling group were saddle and harnessmaker John H. Laymeyer, and cabinetmaker George F. Newsom, who owned property worth $800 and $500, respectively. A bit more successful were coach maker John J. Slaughter, with $3,600 in property, and cooper Abraham Tucker, who owned $3,000. Among the group, only six owned more than $5,000 of property in 1850 and none more than $15,000. Wealthiest among this group in 1850 was tobacconist James Chieves, whose holdings were at $14,000.[70]

A small number, about 3 percent, of the persisting artisans owned less property in 1860 than they did in 1850. Most who lost property were in crafts facing competition from imported goods. Leather worker M. D. Davidson owned property valued at $2,500 in 1850, but held only $700 worth in 1860. Shoe-

69. Bureau of the Census, Population Schedules, Petersburg, Va., 1850 and 1860.
70. Bureau of the Census, Population Schedules, Petersburg, Va., 1850.

maker Silas Pearman's real estate holdings were valued at $2,500 in 1850, but dropped to $1,700 within a decade. Others lost property when they changed occupations. John W. Walden's holdings dropped in half, from $6,000 to $3,000, when he abandoned his occupation as a metal dyer to take up the new trade of photography as a daguerreian artist. Even a few mechanics in the so-called flourishing trades were subject to a change in fortunes in the 1850s. The property holdings of master painter William P. Roach, for example, dropped from $650 to a modest $500 in 1860.[71]

Although a few middling artisans experienced a decline in property ownership, the prosperity of the early 1850s meant rising fortunes for many of these white mechanics. At the end of the decade, persisting artisans were significantly more wealthy. John H. Lahmeyer's harnessmaking business flourished so that at the end of the 1850s his property holdings rose from a modest value of $800 to include land and buildings worth $4,000. His newfound fortunes also allowed this German immigrant to purchase a slave, who probably worked as a domestic servant in his household.[72] In 1860 property ownership rates rose to just under 38 percent, and of those holding property, about one-third held title to real estate valued over $5,000. Six could even claim property worth more than $15,000. George F. Newsom's fortunes increased to allow his property holdings to rise to a value of $1,900, but the coach-making business of John J. Slaughter was even more successful in the 1850s. In 1860 he listed his occupation as a carriage manufacturer and his property holdings rose to a value of $18,000.[73] Holding title to real property made Petersburg the final stopping place for many middling mechanics, and allowed some to prosper in the last antebellum decade.

The persistence rates of middling white artisans in Petersburg, although low, were not inconsistent with patterns of artisan mobility in other antebellum cities. These men, who made up the bulk of the skilled workforce in the city, moved to search out employment situations that provided them with stability and a chance for independence. In contrast to the high mobility rate of middling white artisans, for those skilled craft workers belonging to the PBMA, Petersburg was often the final stopping place. Because the association kept detailed

71. Bureau of the Census, Population Schedules, Petersburg, Va., 1850 and 1860.
72. Personal Property Tax Lists, 1856.
73. Bureau of the Census, Population Schedules, Petersburg, Va., 1860.

membership records from its organization beginning in 1825, mobility patterns for that group of skilled workers can be traced throughout the antebellum era. Of the 340 mechanics who held membership in the PBMA between 1825 and 1860, only 22 percent left Petersburg permanently to seek their fortunes elsewhere. Another 9 percent withdrew from membership in the organization and many of these likely left the city as well. If those who permanently removed and withdrew are considered together, then the persistence rate of mechanics belonging to the PBMA nearly inverts that of the middling white artisan population. A mere 36 percent of the middling population persisted between 1850 and 1860, but nearly 69 percent of PBMA artisans remained in Petersburg until their death or retirement between 1825 and 1860.[74]

The high persistence of artisans belonging to the fraternal organization can be attributed to several factors. PBMA members were some of the most successful businessmen in Petersburg. More so than middling white artisans, these elite men tended to be rooted in the community, with access to capital and personal connections that gave them a distinct position in southern society. In response to the changes brought about as Petersburg industrialized, many of these men used their money and connections to transform themselves into entrepreneurs and merchants.[75] Miller Richard F. Hannon operated a tavern in addition to his flour milling business in the 1820s, and served as town flour inspector from 1828 until at least 1847. It was in his tavern that the PBMA originally formed in 1825. In 1832 Hannon appeared before the Hustings Court with a license to practice as an attorney, allowing him to diversify his career in ways impossible for most middling mechanics.[76] The successes of PBMA members were further reinforced as their business connections brought them prosperity and strengthened their ties to Petersburg through involvement in local politics and community organizations. Carpenter Beverly Drinkard served on the Hustings Court and qualified as second tobacco inspector at the West Hill ware-

74. Membership list, Petersburg Benevolent Mechanic Association Papers, 1825–1921, University of Virginia Library, Charlottesville, Va. (hereafter cited as ViU).

75. Gillespie, *Free Labor in an Unfree World*, 20–21; Wilentz, *Chants Democratic*, 35–38; and Clawson, *Constructing Brotherhood*, 213–221.

76. Hustings Court Minute Book 1823–1827, n.p. (16 April 1824); Hustings Court Minute Book 1827–1832, n.p. (19 June 1828); and Hustings Court Minute Book 1832–1835, 24.

house in 1857.[77] Stone worker James Davidson, who specialized in millstones, grave monuments, and headstones, was appointed town coroner in 1820, a post he held for several years. In 1831, Davidson presented the Hustings Court with a certificate of his qualifications to serve as colonel of the 39th regiment of the local militia, a post elites or planters often held in southern communities.[78] PBMA members regularly served on the Hustings Court and on the boards of local educational institutions, and held other prominent positions in the community, such as offices in the local militia.

Recently, Frank Towers demonstrates that Baltimore artisans managed to penetrate various levels of that city's antebellum political structure by forming alliances with the businessmen who monopolized the top offices.[79] PBMA artisans similarly took advantage of connections to local elites in Petersburg city government. In sharp contrast, few of the middling white artisans, even those who gained substantial amounts of property, were active in the local community or politics. Most of these mechanics were too busy trying to earn a competence and support their families to take on outside involvements. Even those who wanted to participate lacked the personal or family connections that entrance into local politics and volunteer boards often required. An exception was John R. Eckles, a Virginia-born hatter and hat merchant. Although he owned little real property ($25 worth in 1850), Eckles's manufacture and trade with Petersburg residents and country merchants must have afforded him some important personal connections. In 1858 he was appointed commissioner of the revenue, a post he still held at the time of the Civil War.[80] Nathaniel J. Blick Jr., a tobacconist and factory manager for the firm of Chieves and Osborne, was another middling artisan who gained prominence in the community. He was confirmed as second tobacco inspector at the West Hill warehouse in 1856, an appointment no doubt influenced by his father's prominence as a tobacconist

77. Hustings Court Minute Book 1856–1858, 422.

78. "Virginia & N. Carolina French Burr Mill-Stone Manufactory," Broadside, 1836, ViHi; Hustings Court Minute Book 1820–1823, 131; and Hustings Court Minute Book 1827–1832, n.p. (17 February 1831).

79. Towers, *Urban South*, 56–57.

80. Bureau of the Census, Population Schedules, Petersburg, Va., 1850 and 1860; Advertisement, *Daily Southside Democrat*, 13 October 1853; and Hustings Court Minute Book 1856–1858, 526.

and inspector as well. Although he did not belong to the PBMA, Blick probably chose not to be a member of that group, for he certainly had the wealth and connections equal to many of its members.[81]

If economic success and strong ties to the community were positive influences on the persistence rates of elite artisans belonging to the PBMA and a few others, then it would seem logical that lack of economic success and disconnection from the community were factors in the high mobility rates of middling artisans. Some historians suggest that a high transience rate explains the lack of concerted efforts of workers to organize in opposition to poor or unfair working conditions, because transient workers rarely stayed in any one place long enough to establish unions or organizations that could bring about social change.[82] Indeed, for the middling artisans of Petersburg, it was only in the late 1850s that a mechanics' organization formed to meet their needs. But beyond hindering their inability to organize collectively, mobility became both an important source of, as well as solution to, their economic distress. Middling artisans moving on in hopes of finding a better situation usually forfeited the important personal and business connections that fostered the success of elite masters and members of the PBMA. Transient artisans also were less likely to be slave owners, although slaveholding became an important part of the lives of many persisting workingmen.

For artisans remaining in Petersburg, the ownership or leasing of slaves also served as a visible symbol of their success and as a link to the dominant social order of the South. It is commonly accepted that the precarious position of northern workers in antebellum America resulted in the development of an identity based on race, specifically emphasizing the virtues of "whiteness." For example, David Roediger notes that "slavery provided white workers with a touchstone against which to weigh their fears and a yardstick to measure their reassurance."[83] In the South artisans used slavery as more than a measure of

81. In 1860 Blick owned property worth $5,000. Bureau of the Census, Population Schedules, Petersburg, Va., 1860; and Hustings Court Minute Book 1856–1858, 43, 131.

82. See, for example, Faler, *Mechanics and Manufacturers*, 139–140.

83. David R. Roediger, *The Wages of Whiteness: Race and the Making of the American Working Class* (London: Verso, 1991), 66–71 (quotation p. 66). For an important recent discussion of the meaning of whiteness, see David R. Roediger, "The Pursuit of Whiteness: Property, Terror, and Expansion, 1790–1860"; and Lacy K. Ford Jr., "Making the 'White Man's' Country White: Race, Slavery, and State-Building in the Jacksonian South," *Journal of the Early Republic* 19 (Winter 1999).

their fears and reassurance of their position in society. Through the ownership or leasing of slaves, southern mechanics counted themselves among the elite of southern society. Although the world of the southern artisan was not changing as fast as that of northern mechanics, by actively seeking inclusion in the white social order of the planter elite, southern mechanics clung to the belief that they held an important place in the social and political order of the South.[84]

Slavery was compatible with the urban lifestyle and work habits of southern mechanics. James Oakes has shown that slaveholders were a diverse class and that most owners were not paternalistic planters living an idealized pre-capitalist existence. In the antebellum era at least one of every ten slaveholders lived in urban areas, and half of all slaveholders owned five or fewer slaves. Slave owning was common among the middle class and was an aspiration of many middling mechanics. By 1850, twenty thousand skilled artisans owned slaves in the South.[85] A major goal of southern artisans was to earn enough capital to purchase an unskilled slave. The ability of a mechanic to own or lease a slave "provided a strong indication of his rising economic and social status." Purchase of a skilled slave proved even more costly and would be of more benefit in the workshop, but the ability to own any slave signaled a rise in economic status in the antebellum South.[86] In Petersburg more than half of the members of the PBMA owned or leased slaves for their personal or business use. These enterprising masters demonstrated their success and rising economic status and their commitment to the dominant white social order.

In strong contrast to the slave ownership rates of the more successful members of the PBMA, only 223, or about 12 percent, of middling white artisans owned slaves. For many middling Petersburg mechanics, slaveholding was a temporary status. As Oakes has shown, it was quite usual for owners to hold slaves only temporarily or as their economic situation would permit.[87] The ability to own slaves became a status-defining hallmark of the upwardly mobile

84. Gillespie, *Free Labor in an Unfree World*, 63–65.

85. James Oakes, *The Ruling Race: A History of American Slaveholders* (1982; reprint, New York: W. W. Norton, 1998), xviii–xix, 39, 50, 58–59. For an alternative view of slaveholders as paternalistic and pre-capitalist, see Eugene D. Genovese, *The Political Economy of Slavery: Studies in the Economy and Society of the Slave South* (New York: Vintage, 1967), esp. 28–36.

86. Gillespie, "Planters in the Making: Artisanal Opportunity in Georgia, 1790–1830," in Rock, Gilje, and Asher, eds., *American Artisans*, 40.

87. Oakes, *The Ruling Race*, 40–41.

artisan and divided the middling community. Tobacconists and physicians claimed the most slaveholders, with 25 and 27 percent, respectively. These elite occupations were usually filled by men with significant personal connections and offered the potential for making a great deal of money. Their success in the business world allowed them to distinguish themselves from more middling mechanics. These individuals were among the most stable and consistent slaveholders in Petersburg. Daniel Lyon Jr. operated as a tobacconist and apothecary and owned four slaves in 1856. Lyon came from a prominent family in Petersburg, and like many tobacconists, is not really representative of most middling artisans. His father, Daniel Lyon, was a successful bricklayer and member of the PBMA. The elder Lyon was a militia captain and served as commissioner of the revenue in Petersburg for several years. These personal connections no doubt helped the young tobacconist and apothecary to succeed in his business, which in turn provided the capital to purchase slaves.[88]

Slaveholding rates for other occupations were significantly lower among middling artisans. Most mechanics owned only one slave, frequently a female who labored as a house servant. Often, mechanics owned slaves for only a short time or a few years. Certain tradesmen, especially those flourishing in the antebellum era or those with special labor needs, were most likely to own slaves. For example, metal working occupations required the labor of an assistant who served as a striker. Twenty percent of tinners and 10 percent of blacksmiths held slaves who were probably employed in that capacity. Tinner William Davidson owned one slave under the age of sixteen in 1836, but his dwindling economic position forced him to sell his bondsperson by 1843. Davidson's personal wealth never allowed him to achieve slaveholder status again. In 1860 he owned no property and only claimed a modest personal estate worth $100.[89] Davidson most likely employed his slave as an assistant in his tin and coppersmith shop, but when blacksmith John Roberts purchased a slave he chose a female domestic to ease the burden of household chores as well as provide evidence of his rising social status.[90]

88. Personal Property Tax Lists, 1847, 1856; Hustings Court Minute Book 1827–1832, n.p. (21 March 1828) (17 February 1831); and Bureau of the Census, 1860 Census, Schedule 5, Products of Industry during the Year Ending June 1, 1860, microfilm.

89. Personal Property Tax Lists, 1836, 1843; and Bureau of the Census, Population Schedules, Petersburg, Va., 1860.

90. Personal Property Tax Lists, 1838, 1847.

Artisans in prospering and elite trades also tended to hold slaves. Twelve percent of coach makers, 11 percent of millers, and 18 percent of butchers held slaves. Coach maker John J. Slaughter's slaveholdings increased as his business prospered. When he first appeared in city tax records in 1838, Slaughter owned no taxable personal property. By 1843, he made his first slave purchase, a female domestic to ease the workload of the women in his family. Four years later Slaughter owned 4 slaves, 2 adult males he likely used in his business and 2 adult females to take care of the domestic household. By 1850, his coach making establishment employed 8 white men in addition to the slaves and produced carriages and buggies worth $3,000.[91]

Men in trades facing stiff competition from factory goods and imports held fewer slaves. Only 6 percent of printers, 5 percent of watchmakers, and 8 percent of gunsmiths attained slave ownership. Occupations adapting to industrial work or wage labor also had a low rate of slave ownership. Less than 1 percent of middling white carpenters, the most numerous artisan occupation in Petersburg, were able to elevate their social status by owning slaves. James Doherty was more typical of middling artisans struggling to earn a competency in the changing economy and yearning for inclusion among the elite of southern society. The competition his gunsmith shop faced from imported northern goods affected his fortunes. Doherty first came to Petersburg from Ireland in the mid-1830s, and in 1847 finally accumulated enough capital to purchase a young slave, although it is not clear whether his bondsperson was male or female. For many immigrants, becoming slaveholders was just as important as it was for native whites. For immigrant artisans slave ownership symbolized not only their elevation in white southern society but also their success in the New World.[92] However, Doherty's elevation to slaveholder status lasted less than ten years. By 1856, he owned no slaves or real property, but he did manage to accumulate other goods worth $3,000. Carpenters Samuel Watson and George Summers were immigrants who had more success in becoming slaveholders. Hailing from Ireland in the late 1830s or early 1840s, Watson managed to become a slave owner even before he became a citizen of the United States. By 1847, he still owned the slave that was his one hallmark of success, and his

91. Personal Property Tax Lists, 1838, 1843, 1847; and Bureau of the Census, 1850 Census, Schedule 5.

92. Oakes, *The Ruling Race*, 42–43.

son, Samuel Watson Jr., managed to purchase three slaves of his own.[93] George Summers, a carpenter and English immigrant also purchased a slave before becoming a citizen. In 1843, he owned a female domestic, and by 1847 he added an adult male slave who probably assisted in his carpentry work.[94]

Slave ownership became a fleeting aspiration for many middling artisans in the 1850s. The boom in the cotton economy of the Lower South led to rising prices for both the purchase and lease of slaves. Until prices rose in the 1850s, slave leasing was the easiest means for an artisan to advance to the master class.[95] According to one account, the cost of leasing a slave on an annual basis averaged $100 between 1833 and 1852. After 1852, the average annual lease was closer to $150. When the costs of annual maintenance, including food, clothing, and board, are added, after 1852 a middling mechanic would need a surplus of nearly $250 to lease a slave.[96] In the 1850s, only the most successful artisans reached the ranks of slaveholders. This distinction served to increase the divide between middling mechanics and the successful masters who were moving into the southern middle class. The price for purchasing an enslaved worker for either the workshop or the home also grew prohibitive. In the nearby Richmond market, a strong male slave between the ages of 19 and 25 cost between $500 and $725 in 1846, but by 1859 the price doubled to more than $1,400. A young woman, aged 16 to 20, cost $425 to $550 in 1846, but more than $1,200 in 1859.[97] These inflationary prices left many Petersburg artisans unable to realize their goal of inclusion in the elite of southern society by becoming a slaveholder. It was just one more change in the industrializing reality of the antebellum era. A shifting ethnic composition, brought about by a large influx of European immigrants, also altered the workplace and culture of the southern city.

As slaveholding records demonstrate, a substantial number of the white ar-

93. Personal Property Tax Lists, 1843, 1847; Hustings Court Minute Book 1841–1842, 157; and Hustings Court Minute Book 1846–1847, 127.

94. Personal Property Tax Lists, 1843, 1847; and Hustings Court Minute Book 1846–1847, 147.

95. However, it is impossible to trace most slave leasing by artisans because property taxes were assessed on both slaves owned and slaves leased.

96. Robert S. Starobin, *Industrial Slavery in the Old South* (New York: Oxford University Press, 1970), 162.

97. Michael Tadman, *Speculators and Slaves: Masters, Traders, and Slaves in the Old South* (Madison: University of Wisconsin Press, 1989), 289–290.

tisans in Petersburg were immigrants from Europe or migrants from northern states. Immigrants and northerners played an important role in the antebellum South, especially in southern cities. The number of European immigrants settling in southern states was small compared to their concentration in the North. In fact, in 1850 only 5 percent of the free population of the South was foreign-born, while in the North as many as one in seven people was born outside the United States.[98] However, a close examination of antebellum demographics reveals that most southern cities attracted a significant number of immigrants.[99] For example, in 1850, immigrants comprised more than one-fifth of the residents of Charleston, South Carolina; over one-quarter of the population of Savannah, Georgia; and nearly one-third in Mobile, Alabama. In most southern cities, immigrants made up an even larger portion of the male workforce than they did of the population as a whole.[100]

In a few urban areas immigrants outnumbered native-born workers. On the eve of the Civil War at least half of the adult white population of Savannah was foreign-born. Indeed, it seems that Lower South cities, and especially port cities, attracted the highest concentration of immigrants. In Baton Rouge, 47 percent of white working men were foreign-born; in Nashville the figure was about 41 percent. In Georgia, about one-third of the immigrants were unskilled laborers, and just under one-third were skilled artisans, most of whom worked in construction trades and on the railroad. Smaller cities, or those in the up-country, tended to attract less immigrants, including Macon and Athens, where foreign-born men headed only about 20 percent of households in 1860.[101]

Similar patterns hold true for cities in the Upper South, especially Richmond, where during the 1850s the growth of the foreign-born population outpaced any other category, increasing 166 percent. During the same period, the population of northern-born white workers in Richmond increased 97 per-

---

98. Ira Berlin and Herbert G. Gutman, "Native and Immigrants, Free Men and Slaves: Urban Workingmen in the Antebellum American South," *American Historical Review* 88 (December 1983): 1176.

99. Earlier studies of the urban South make little reference to the importance of immigrants in southern cities. See, for example, the brief treatment of immigrants in urban Virginia in David R. Goldfield's *Urban Growth in the Age of Sectionalism: Virginia, 1847–1861* (Baton Rouge: Louisiana State University Press, 1977), 124–125.

100. Berlin and Gutman, "Natives and Immigrants," 1177–1178.

101. Ibid., 1180–1181; and Gillespie, *Free Labor in an Unfree World*, 167–168.

cent.[102] By 1860 foreign-born white workers made up 39 percent of Richmond's population, and about 36 percent of the skilled white workers in that city. In Baltimore as much as 28 percent of the population was foreign-born in 1850, and by 1860 the Upper South port city of Baltimore was home to two-thirds of Maryland's immigrant population.[103]

Petersburg fits with the larger pattern of foreign-born residence in the antebellum South, but only to a certain degree. Immigrants made up an important segment of the working class; however, the actual number of immigrant workers was lower than other southern cities. (See table 7.) The important role that free blacks played in filling both skilled and unskilled occupations helps to explain why fewer immigrants chose to locate in Petersburg. In 1860, free blacks comprised 30 percent of the male workforce and claimed 64 percent of unskilled jobs. (See table 8, A–B.) The proportion of black workers in Petersburg was higher than in any other southern city. Even in the industrial giant of Richmond free blacks filled just 30 percent of unskilled jobs.[104] Immigrants reaching Virginia, especially unskilled Irish workers, must have found the competition of free blacks for jobs on the railroad and internal improvement projects intense in Petersburg. Many no doubt moved on to other southern cities where competition for jobs was less pronounced.[105]

Those immigrants who did work for a time in Petersburg found a mixed response from the local community. Some locals lauded unskilled Irish laborers for their industrious nature and good work habits in the construction of the Petersburg Water Works in 1856. A. D. Banks, editor of the local Democratic paper, recognized the competition between Irish immigrants and free black workers, and found the Irish to be the superior workmen. He remarked that "it quite astonishes our lazy colored population to see the way these men of strong muscle make the sods fly; and what is more in their favor, notwithstanding the

102. Kimball, "Place and Perception," 61–62.

103. Berlin and Gutman, "Natives and Immigrants," 1181, 1183; and Christopher Phillips, *Freedom's Port: The African American Community of Baltimore, 1790–1860* (Urbana: University of Illinois Press, 1997), 195–196.

104. Berlin and Gutman, "Natives and Immigrants," 1183; and Bureau of the Census, Population Schedules, Petersburg, Va., 1860.

105. For an examination of Irish immigrants in the South, see David T. Gleeson, *The Irish in the South, 1815–1877* (Chapel Hill: University of North Carolina Press, 2001), esp. chapter 8.

quarrelsome disposition attributed to laborers generally on public works, we have not had one of the above number, since their arrival in this city, before the Mayor for disorder of any kind."[106] Before long, however, negative accounts of immigrant behavior surfaced. Less than a year after praising the upstanding behavior of Irish workers, Banks derisively reported finding three Irish tailors drunk and lying in a doorway.[107] Reports of immigrant drunkenness and misbehavior became a regular feature in the local reports section of Petersburg newspapers. In 1858 the gossip column reported the arrest of laborer Davy McCracken for public drunkenness, noting the Irishman was found in "a very obstreperous humor" and "immortalized himself by ripping some of the shirt buttons" off the arresting policeman. The court released McCracken after he agreed to leave town. Another Irish immigrant, David Strawn, was put on a train for Richmond, although the charge against him was unclear.[108] That same year the Democratic paper reported that German butcher Maurice Van Rice, "a man of intemperate habits," died in the city jail after an arrest for being drunk in public.[109]

Whether welcome or not, immigrant workers filled a small but important place in the Petersburg workforce. By 1860, 11 percent of free men in Petersburg reporting an occupation were born outside the United States. Immigrant members of the PBMA reflected the same trend, with 11 percent of the elite group reporting emigrating to the United States from England, Ireland, Scotland, France, and Germany.[110] The number of northern workers locating in Petersburg was also small in comparison to other southern cities; white northern-born men made up only 4 percent of adult free males in 1860.[111] The relatively small number of immigrants meant that Petersburg did not develop the ethnic neighborhoods and enclaves that formed in some cities. In Richmond, where Germans made up about one-quarter of the white population, immigrants were central to the politics and economy of the city. There, Germans formed cohesive communities, easily recognizable by virtue of their retail shops, beer

106. "The Water Works Laborers," *Daily Southside Democrat*, 6 May 1856.

107. "A Portion of a Man Found on the Side-Walk," *Daily Southside Democrat*, 4 March 1857.

108. "Police Matters," *Daily Express*, 24 August 1858.

109. "Death from Intemperance," *Daily Southside Democrat*, 1 February 1858.

110. Membership list, PBMA Papers, ViU.

111. Bureau of the Census, Population Schedules, Petersburg, Va., 1860.

halls, and saloons. They also formed a German militia unit, established a German-language newspaper in the early 1850s, and became active members of the Democratic Party.[112] In Petersburg, the smaller immigrant population was more integrated into the mainstream of white society and although a few ethnic organizations formed, including the Irish Hibernian society, immigrants made less of an impact on local politics and the economy as distinct interest groups.

Most of Petersburg's immigrant workers were born in the British Isles of Scotland, Ireland, and England, but a significant proportion were natives of the German states. A handful hailed from such diverse locations as Italy, France, Holland, Poland, Switzerland, and Portugal. Most European immigrants appeared to blend into the white society of Petersburg with little evidence of discord. Many sought to become citizens of Virginia and of the United States. Between 1820 and 1860 at least 385 appeared before the Petersburg Hustings Court to take a citizenship oath or to declare their intent to become a citizen. Once a person declared his or her intent to become a citizen and denounced any alliance to "any foreign State or Potentate," he or she could complete the process by taking an oath of citizenship after a two-year wait. Like some northern states, Virginia was interested in attracting skilled workers born in other countries and offered incentives to those who located in the Commonwealth. State law exempted "artizans, mechanics, and handicraft tradesmen," migrating into Virginia from "all taxes except the land tax," for five years providing they practice their trade during their time of residence.[113]

A number of skilled immigrants found considerable success in Petersburg. Charles Miller, a confectioner originally from Hanover, Germany, first appeared on city tax rolls in 1836. He operated a baking house and confectionery at 113 Sycamore Street in partnership with native Virginian George Peace. In the 1830s and 1840s, Miller's tax records suggest that the business was moderately successful. During that period he owned at least two slaves, one of whom

112. Werner Steger, "'United to Support, But Not Combined to Injure': Free Workers and Immigrants in Richmond, Virginia during the Era of Sectionalism, 1847–1865" (Ph.D. diss., George Washington University, 1999), 159–162, 167. For a brief account of immigrant involvement in politics that fits with Steger's findings, see Fred Siegel, "Artisans and Immigrants in the Politics of Late Antebellum Georgia," *Civil War History* 27 (1984): 221–230.

113. Joseph Tate, *A Digest of the Laws of Virginia* (Richmond: Shepherd and Pollard, 1823), 55–58. Figures on citizenship compiled from Hustings Court Minute Books, 1820–1860.

likely was a deliveryman for his business. Miller demonstrated his commitment to his new country when he took the oath as a U.S. citizen 16 April 1840. On the eve of the Civil War, the confectionery of Miller and Peace employed five men and annually produced candies and pastries worth at least $35,000.[114] Scottish shoemaker Robert Penman experienced similar success in Petersburg. Arriving sometime before 1843, before the end of the 1840s he established a shop and decided to remain in Petersburg. In 1847, Penman became a citizen of the United States. His boot and shoemaking shop at 3 Bank Street employed at least six journeymen and four apprentices by 1860, producing $6,000 worth of shoe stock that year.[115]

Other immigrants were equally successful in Petersburg. Stone mason Robert Wright, who emigrated from England before 1842, operated a marble works on Tabb Street in partnership with Scottish immigrant James Bowie. In 1860, these two recent citizens employed ten journeymen stone workers. Bowie managed to accumulate real property valued at $8,000, but Wright held even more in 1860, with property valued at $10,000.[116] Scottish baker Richard Adams was slightly less successful, holding property worth $7,500 in 1850. He chose to follow the path of many itinerant artisans and moved his baking operations to Richmond in the 1850s. It was apparently a wise move. In 1860, Adams owned real estate worth $30,000 in the Richmond area.[117]

Even though Petersburg attracted fewer immigrants than other southern cities, the 1850s witnessed a dramatic growth in the number of foreign-born workers, increasing more than 60 percent. In his study of Irish immigrants in the South, David T. Gleeson argues that the South was particularly attractive to immigrants in the 1850s because many workers believed wages to be higher in

114. Ferslew, comp., *Second Annual Petersburg Directory*, 143; Personal Property Tax Lists, 1836, 1838, 1843, 1847; Hustings Court Minute Book 1838–1840, 242; and Bureau of the Census, 1860 Census, Schedule 5.

115. Ferslew, comp., *Second Annual Petersburg Directory*, 153; Hustings Court Minute Book 1846–1847, 147; Bureau of the Census, Population Schedules, Petersburg, Va., 1860; and Bureau of the Census, 1860 Census, Schedule 5.

116. Ferslew, comp., *Second Annual Petersburg Directory*, 150; Hustings Court Minute Book 1841–1842, 184; Hustings Court Minute Book 1846–1847, 21; Bureau of the Census, Population Schedules, Petersburg, Va., 1860; and Bureau of the Census, 1860 Census, Schedule 5.

117. Bureau of the Census, Population Schedules, Petersburg, Va., 1850; and Bureau of the Census, Population Schedules, Richmond, Va., 1860.

that region than in the North or the West.[118] Many foreign-born workers came first to the cities of the old Northeast, worked for several years, then traveled south seeking opportunities in cities such as Petersburg. Of the foreign-born men reporting an occupation to census enumerators in 1850, more than half were skilled workers and just over 45 percent were merchants or professionals. In sharp contrast with other southern urban areas, less than 2 percent of immigrants were unskilled workers. By 1860 the number of unskilled foreign-born workers jumped to 19 percent of all immigrant workers, due mostly to the number of Irish and German men who located in Petersburg to work on the railroad or internal improvement projects. Immigrant commitment to their new homeland increased in the 1850s as well. Just over 41 percent of all foreign-born residents seeking to become citizens declared their intent or took the citizenship oath in that decade. The number of northern-born workers rose in this period as well, but with different implications. Whereas the immigrant population witnessed an increase in the number of unskilled laborers, most northern-born migrants continued to be skilled artisans. In the 1850 and 1860 census enumerations, more than 60 percent of the white northern-born men living in Petersburg reported skilled artisan occupations. Few unskilled whites came to Petersburg from the North. In 1850 there were only two, and that increased to a mere four in 1860.[119]

In the 1850s, anti-immigrant sentiment grew along with an increase in the number of foreign-born workers in the United States. With over two million immigrants arriving in the 1850s, many skilled workers found themselves in a rapidly changing society and in a work environment growing in ethnic diversity. Many skilled artisans shared a distaste for foreigners and were attracted to the Know-Nothing nativist movement and American Party in the 1850s. In the South, the Know-Nothing movement attracted a variety of supporters, particularly once the national Whig Party fell into collapse. Southern Know-Nothingism tied closely to support for the Union and was condemned by Democratic opponents as an abolition party. In fact, in many areas of the South, Know-Nothings only half-heartedly supported nativism.[120] Instead, in cities such as Baltimore, St. Louis, New Orleans, and others, urban workers supported the

118. Gleeson, *The Irish in the South*, 24, 27; and Wells, *Origins of the Southern Middle Class*, 164–65.

119. Bureau of the Census, Population Schedules, Petersburg, Va., 1850 and 1860.

120. Gleeson, *The Irish in the South*, 107–113; and Philip Morrison Rice, "The Know-

Know-Nothings in hopes that their dominance would bring needed jobs on public works projects. In large cities where Know-Nothings gained control of city politics, they managed to disrupt the "patron-client relationships that employers had used to keep wages low and labor docile."[121] Nevertheless, some southern cities sprouted nativist brotherhood societies, such as the Order of United American Mechanics and the Benevolent Order of Bereans. In the mid-1850s a few southern cities, including Louisville and New Orleans, witnessed election riots when nativists tried to prevent immigrants from voting.[122]

In Petersburg, nativist sentiment never erupted in such violent and dramatic fashion; however, the Know-Nothings formed an element in city politics in 1854 and 1855. A. D. Banks, editor of the *Daily Southside Democrat*, expressed concern over the formation of a Know-Nothing "secret enclave" in June 1854. Although not a Catholic and claiming to be of "pure American blood," the editor expressed concern over the outspoken anti-Catholic and anti-foreign elements of the movement and denounced them as "conspirators against the liberties of the land, as traitors to the Constitution."[123]

The *Daily Southside Democrat's* announcement of the movement's decline two months later was a bit premature. The editor gleefully noted that the "spavined, wind galled hacks, to whom the organization is indebted for its existence, are in a desperate frame of mind."[124] Yet the Know-Nothings persisted in Petersburg through 1855, fostered by April rumors of an uprising of local foreigners allegedly planning to attack the city and kill the native inhabitants. Apparently part of an April Fool's hoax, the report of the impending violent attack put fear in many Petersburg residents. Some were so convinced of the immigrant threat that an appeal was sent to the mayor of Richmond and the governor of Virginia for armed reinforcements.[125]

Nothing Party in Virginia, 1854–1856," *Virginia Magazine of History and Biography* 55 (1947): 61–75.

121. Towers, *Urban South*, 24.

122. Laurie, *Artisans into Workers*, 103–106. For a history of the national impact of the Know-Nothing movement, see Eric Foner, *Free Soil, Free Labor, Free Men: The Ideology of the Republican Party Before the Civil War* (1970; reprint, New York: Oxford University Press, 1995), 226–260.

123. "Know-Nothingism in Petersburg," *Daily Southside Democrat*, 28 June 1854.

124. "In a Decline," *Daily Southside Democrat*, 29 August 1854.

125. "T-h-u-n-d-e-r-a-t-i-o-n," *Daily Southside Democrat*, 2 April 1855.

Later the same month the organization announced a slate of Know-Nothing candidates for local office, revealing the participation of local artisans in the movement. Six of the eight nominees were members of the Petersburg artisan community. The nativist movement in Petersburg attracted men across class lines, but none of the leaders were members of the PBMA. The party nominated local physician Thomas Withers for the House of Delegates, and tobacconists Samuel Williams and Gilbert V. Rambaut for mayor and tax collector, respectively. Withers was a prominent physician in partnership with John B. Strachan. He must have had other important investments because his personal estate was valued at $60,000 in 1860. Williams and Rambaut were also men of mark who rose above the ranks of middling mechanics. Curiously, Rambaut joined the PBMA in 1835, but withdrew in 1846. Hatter John R. Eckles received the Know-Nothing nomination for chamberlain, brickmaker Charles T. Scott for street commissioner, and journeyman cabinetmaker Alexander Moody for keeper of the powder magazine.[126] Eckles manufactured and sold hats and caps for the country trade, and at one time owned at least three slaves. Scott and Moody, however, were more representative of the working men of Petersburg. Scott managed to own one slave for a period in the 1840s, but could make no other claims to wealth. Moody remained a journeyman, employed by cabinet-maker John Morrison; in 1860 his entire personal estate was worth only $50.[127] The Know-Nothings secured only a single office, Rambaut won as tax collector, and in the fall of 1855 A. D. Banks's prediction of a decline in the movement finally materialized.[128] In the last few years before the Civil War economic panic and depression served to unite Petersburg white artisans of all ethnic backgrounds. Artisan concerns turned to focus on competition from another segment of southern society. In the period surrounding the Panic of 1857 the attention of white artisans in Petersburg concentrated on politics across the color line and competition from free blacks.

The political participation of middling white artisans in Virginia is difficult to trace. In his examination of Baltimore, St. Louis, and New Orleans, Frank Towers demonstrates that artisan workers made significant contributions to

126. "The K. N. Nominations," *Daily Southside Democrat*, 23 April 1855.

127. Bureau of the Census, Population Schedules, Petersburg, Va., 1860; member list, PBMA Records, ViU; Petersburg, Va., Personal Property Tax List, 1847; and advertisement, *Daily Southside Democrat*, 13 October 1853.

128. "The Election," *Daily Southside Democrat*, 9 May 1855.

city politics and that their large numbers pushed their issues forward on the political agenda. Much like the northern cities of New York and Philadelphia, southern cities with a population of more than 150,000 had to reckon with artisans.[129] Such was not the case in antebellum Petersburg. Although mechanics in other places were politically active in the early republic, the freehold requirement that denied the vote to those without property kept many middling Virginia artisans out of the formal political circle until the 1851 constitutional revision, when male suffrage became universal. According to Virginia law, voters were required to own twenty-five acres of land or a town lot with a dwelling. Those who boarded or leased property were ineligible to vote.[130] In most northern states universal male suffrage allowed artisans to become a factor in urban politics. In New York skilled workers established ties to formal political parties that expressed the interests of mechanics, and artisan votes were often crucial in New York City mayoral and council elections. Philadelphia mechanics similarly organized to form the all-important General Trades' Union to protect the workingman's place in industrializing Pennsylvania.[131] In northern cities the major political parties, and even local party organizations, paid some attention to the mechanic voting block because artisan political interests often fit with larger party goals. As a numerically significant segment of the population, the mechanic vote could help win an election. With the exception of the largest cities, such was not always the case in the antebellum South.

In most of the South, where politics were largely locally based and tied to an agricultural economy, the political interests of mechanics did not fit well with the ideology of any single political party. Even in southern states that granted white manhood suffrage from an early date, artisans were unable to match the political influence of their northern counterparts. For example, in Georgia a political division emerged between masters and journeymen about the time that the Second Party system was evolving in the 1830s. Instead of empowering skilled workmen, universal suffrage created a new dilemma. There, the Whigs became the party of upwardly mobile master mechanics, while the journey-

129. Towers, *Urban South*, 1–3.

130. Tate, *Digest of Laws*, 183–184; and Charles S. Sydnor, *Gentlemen Freeholders: Political Practices in Washington's Virginia* (Chapel Hill: University of North Carolina Press, 1952), 29–31.

131. Wilentz, *Chants Democratic*, 63–64, 71–72; Bruce Laurie, *Working People of Philadelphia, 1800–1850* (Philadelphia: Temple University Press, 1980), 85–104.

men who faced a bleak economic future, found little representation in state or local politics. Although Georgia journeymen possessed the right to vote in favor of legislation that privileged white labor over slave, they were often afraid to exercise that power. As opportunities for independence withered, mechanics were hesitant to vote in opposition to the masters who were, in many cases, now their employers.[132]

In Virginia, middling mechanics faced an even more dismal political situation. Until 1851 those without substantial holdings in real property could not vote at all. Worse yet, most political power was concentrated at the local level, in either the county or Hustings Court, which became self-perpetuating bodies under local elite control.[133] That body held the power of appointment for most local offices, ensuring that personal connections were the most important qualification for officeholding.[134] Petersburg and other Virginia cities found local power vested in the Hustings Court, which met monthly to perform the tasks of city government and to deal with legal matters such as will probates, arrest hearings, small civil suits, and all criminal cases involving slaves or free blacks. Although most Virginia cities, including Petersburg, were Whig strongholds, party affiliation was of little consequence at the local level. The master mechanics of the PBMA and city lawyers were frequent holders of local office and beneficiaries of the patronage of the Hustings Court, but few of the middling mechanics of Petersburg ever found their way into positions of power. More significantly, because many middling mechanics had no political voice and no influence on the perpetuation of the local court system, city officials had little reason to consider the needs and interests of Petersburg's laboring classes.

Yet despite their lack of political influence, on several occasions in the antebellum era middling mechanics combined to make a political statement. In all three documented cases, middling Petersburg artisans felt the pinch of economic distress and chose to lash out at competition from black labor. There

132. Gillespie, *Free Labor in an Unfree World*, 141–142.

133. William G. Shade, *Democratizing the Old Dominion: Virginia and the Second Party System, 1824–1861* (Charlottesville: University Press of Virginia, 1996), 50; and Richard P. McCormick, *The Second American Party System: Party Formation in the Jacksonian Era* (Chapel Hill: University of North Carolina Press, 1966), 179–180.

134. Charles S. Sydnor, *The Development of Southern Sectionalism, 1819–1848* (1948; reprint, Baton Rouge: Louisiana State University Press, 1968), 39–42.

can be little doubt that the employment of slaves or free blacks in skilled trades placed potential stress on the livelihood of white artisans. Slave artisans worked for a lower wage, and free blacks were often willing to work for less in order to undercut white labor and obtain employment.[135] In communicating their anger at being forced into contest with blacks, Petersburg middling mechanics used their whiteness to express indignation at the injustice of bourgeois masters and factory owners seeking to save on labor costs by employing slaves or free blacks. As was common in other southern cities, Petersburg artisans stressed the importance of white workers to maintaining the racial superiority of southern society.[136]

The first movement of Petersburg white artisans to end competition from blacks materialized in a legislative petition to ban slaves from mechanic occupations. Submitted to the General Assembly in 1831, the mechanics' memorial came at an opportune time, when all of Virginia was wrestling with the slavery question in the aftermath of the Southampton County rebellion of Nat Turner. In the climate of anti-black hysteria following that uprising, Petersburg artisans had little fear that their political statement would result in retaliation from upwardly mobile masters. Theirs was only one of many legislative petitions demanding governmental action to deal with the perceived problem of slaves and free blacks in Virginia. In addition to numerous petitions, post-insurrection Virginia saw an increase in support for colonization, a legislative debate over the future of slavery in the Commonwealth, and a general disdain for both free blacks and slaves.[137]

For Petersburg mechanics, this was the perfect time to express their opposition to the use of slave mechanics, and especially the competition they faced from skilled slaves hired out to individuals or factories. The artisans used the traditional language of republicanism to express their concerns. The petitioners based their claims on the importance of white mechanics, who formed the

135. Luther Porter Jackson, *Free Negro Labor and Property Holding in Virginia, 1830–1860* (New York: D. Appleton-Century, 1942), 67–68; Richard D. Wade, *Slavery in the Cities: The South 1820–1860* (London: Oxford University Press, 1964), 33–38; Ira Berlin, *Slaves Without Masters: The Free Negro in the Antebellum South* (New York: Vintage, 1974), 234; and Starobin, *Industrial Slavery,* 158–159.

136. Roediger, *Wages of Whiteness,* 52.

137. Alison Goodyear Freehling, *Drift Toward Dissolution: The Virginia Slavery Debate of 1831–1832* (Baton Rouge: Louisiana State University Press, 1982), 170–175.

"bone and sinew" of the community, and argued that removing competition from slaves would benefit "society in general." They claimed that prohibiting the employment of slave artisans meant that white mechanics would no longer be "driven from a community" in which they are "patriotic" citizens.[138] But most middling mechanics were not "citizens" of Virginia in the fullest sense because a substantial number could not vote. They lacked the power and connections necessary to challenge the slaveholders who held political control in the state. This petition would be denied, and it would be more than a decade before Petersburg artisans made another public case to end competition from black labor.

The 1840s witnessed a heightening of competition between white and black mechanics in Virginia. In Richmond, the Tredegar Iron Works began using slave labor as early as 1842, with the intention of cutting costs and "controlling white labor." In that facility, the management forced skilled white workers to sign a five-year contract, agreeing to limit their mobility and to train slaves to work along side them in the mill.[139] In 1845, "A Citizen" wrote to the *Richmond Daily Whig* to express the position of many middling white artisans on the increase in competition between white and slave mechanics. Borrowing language from the 1831 Petersburg mechanics' petition, he argued for the abolition of slavery in Virginia because "as long as we cultivate our lands with slaves, and bring them up to trades (which ought to be confined exclusively to white citizens,) thus compelling our people to leave the State, and seek employment elsewhere, or remain here and endure the alternative, so mortifying and repugnant to the feelings of freemen, of being compelled to labor side by side, with the slave, and to have their services estimated by those of slaves." He continued: "Thousands of our young mechanics, Carpenters, Blacksmith[s], Bricklayers, &c, 'the bone and sinew' of the land, from this *cause alone,* annually leave Virginia and go to some of the free States of the West."[140] Two years later in 1847, workers at the Tredegar works walked off the job, refusing to return unless slaves were removed from skilled positions on squeezers and puddle rolls. The

138. Legislative Petition, Petersburg City, 1831, quoted in Freehling, *Drift Toward Dissolution,* 175. Note: this petition cannot be located at the Library of Virginia.

139. Charles B. Dew, *Ironmaker to the Confederacy: Joseph R. Anderson and the Tredegar Iron Works* (New Haven: Yale University Press, 1966), 23–24; and Kimball, *American City, Southern Place,* 169–174.

140. Letter to the editor by "A Citizen," *Richmond Daily Whig,* 11 December 1845.

attempt to rid the works of slaves failed when Tredegar's superintendent fired the striking workers, replacing many of them with more slaves.[141]

Petersburg workers felt similar pressures during the 1840s, leading to the second collective action against black competition. At the end of the decade, Petersburg white journeymen formed an organization to protest the use of slaves in skilled trades. In January 1849, the journeymen developed a preamble and resolutions outlining their position. Petersburg mechanics were not abolitionists who opposed the institution of slavery. In fact, many artisans aspired to own slaves and identified with the values of the slave society. What they objected to was being forced into direct competition with slave laborers and seeing their occupational status "degraded" by enslaved mechanics. Although they respected the rights of property and "the privilege of the owner to employ his slave in honest labor," they regarded "the teaching of any Negro any branch of the mechanic arts as prejudicial to the interests, and injurious to the morals of the laboring White man." They also resolved not to work for any master mechanic who employed a "Negro" for the "purpose of teaching said Negro any branch of mechanic arts."[142] It is unlikely that the journeymen of Petersburg changed the hiring habits of local masters. No evidence points to a sustained journeymen's organization persisting in the city at that time. As in Richmond, Petersburg journeymen lacked the political clout to challenge the established order that put planters, merchants, and successful master mechanics in positions of leadership where they could sustain their own labor needs in slavery. However, this attempt at mobilization demonstrates that Petersburg middling artisans felt competitive pressures from black workers and from the evolving market economy as well.

In the late 1850s, Petersburg mechanics finally formed and maintained an organization aimed at protecting their position in industrializing society. Like earlier collective measures, the Petersburg Mechanic Association (PMA) organized around the issue of black competition. Following the 1851 Virginia constitutional convention, all white men gained the right of suffrage. The 1851 political reforms created a *Herrenvolk* democracy in Virginia, finally affirming the superiority of all white men and granting them the full rights as citizens

141. Dew, *Ironmaker to the Confederacy*, 24–26; and Kathleen Bruce, *Virginia Iron Manufacture in the Slave Era* (New York: Century, 1930), 225–227.

142. "Meeting of Mechanics," *Republican*, 24 January 1849.

regardless of their property holdings.[143] When Petersburg artisans chose to organize in the face of economic distress, they used the republican language of citizenship to lash out at free blacks only.

Just before the Panic of 1857 hit the nation in full force, groups of Petersburg artisans began to meet to discuss "business of the utmost importance" and in the "interest of every Mechanic." The movement originated with the mechanics of the city's south ward, but soon spread to a city-wide organization.[144] The *Daily Express* reported that at least five hundred mechanics showed up for a meeting at the south ward Engine House in July 1857; the room was so filled to overflowing that the group adjourned and reassembled at the Center Market House in downtown Petersburg.[145] At a series of early August meetings, the group committed a set of resolutions and a constitution to paper. Those appointed to draft the resolutions were genuinely middling mechanics, struggling to survive in the late antebellum economy. Most were involved in construction and manufacturing trades. Although the number of positions available in these trades suggest they were flourishing, Petersburg carpenters, wheelwrights, and machinists found fewer opportunities to achieve independence. Among the committee members were wheelwright John W. Leath, painter William Jarvis, machinist James E. Tyson, coach trimmer George Johnson, carpenter Ferdinand Pucci, and shoemaker Robert Penman. The movement gained wide support among middling artisans, but also hoped to capture the attention of successful master mechanics. The large show of solidarity among middling men impressed the editor of the *Daily Express,* but he noted that the movement "only lacks the active co-operation of *leading men.*"[146]

Calling themselves the Petersburg Mechanic Association, this new organization had two purposes. Its first aim was to elevate and protect the mental and social condition of artisan workers. To accomplish this, the group planned a Mechanics' Lyceum and a library accessible to masters, journeymen, and apprentices alike. The purpose of the educational activities was "improving those who are already workmen, and dignifying mechanism so that instead of its being considered degrading to labor, it will be looked upon as the highest honor

143. Shade, *Democratizing the Old Dominion,* 278–281.
144. "Attention Mechanics," *Daily Express,* 24 July 1857.
145. "Mechanics Meeting," *Daily Express,* 27 July 1857.
146. "The Mechanic's Movement," *Daily Express,* 10 August 1857.

to be known as a skillful mechanic."[147] But the main goal, and the reason they believed that some considered manual labor degrading, was the employment of free African Americans in many skilled occupations. These men believed that before an artisan should trouble himself with education, he must first secure his position in the economic world. Their biggest concern was that "a large portion of the mechanical branches of business is monopolized by a class of persons, wholly irresponsible as citizens, known as free negroes, much to the detriment of poor tradesmen of this city." They blamed free black mechanics for the "present depressed conditions of mechanical business" in Petersburg, and considered them "as a curse on our working interest."[148]

The PMA managed to attract the "active cooperation" of a few members of the PBMA, with at least two members of the elite artisan group holding dual membership in both organizations. Master carpenter James Minetree was one of those chosen to draft a constitution for the PMA, and bricklayer Alfred Archer was first vice president of the new organization.[149] The PBMA makes no mention of the new group in their official record, however, the PMA were allowed to assemble in the PBMA-owned Mechanics' Hall, and an honorary PBMA member gave one of the first lectures the PMA sponsored. D'Arcy W. Paul used the opportunity to advocate the values of the emerging middle class. He lectured the assembled mechanics on industry and economy, "the two prime elements of success in life," and temperance, "a great essential to a pure and honorable life." It seems that the PBMA saw little threat in the new group, which the local newspaper dubbed the "Mechanics' Association Junior."[150]

Whatever their interests in self-improvement through lectures and education, PMA members were first concerned with removing threats to their economic position in the community. The mechanics wanted free blacks banned from skilled occupations, believing that "inasmuch as free negroes are not allowed to be Doctors, Lawyers, Merchants or Tradesmen," so they should have "no more right to compete with our employment by undertaking mechanical arts." At the basis of their claim was the reason they believed that whites should

147. "The Mechanics Meeting of Saturday Night," *Daily Express*, 18 August 1857.

148. Ibid.

149. "The Mechanic's Movement," *Daily Express*, 10 August 1857; and "Mechanics Association," ibid., 7 September 1857.

150. "Lecture Before the Mechanics' Association Junior," *Daily Express*, 14 November 1857.

be given preference over blacks: "because the white man is a citizen and must perform all duties which may be required him as such—the free negro is not a citizen, is totally irresponsible and performs no duty for the sustainment of the laws of our State or City."[151] Despite the PMA's protests, the movement had little influence on the employment of African Americans in either skilled or unskilled occupations. By the late 1850s, free blacks accounted for 30 percent of the total workforce and 14 percent of skilled occupations. Their value to a local economy that was increasingly profit-oriented, and ruled by elite planters, merchants, and master mechanics, ensured that middling white artisans would not be able to change the well-established system.

Most artisan political expression was fundamentally conservative and did not actually seek to challenge the established order of slaveholding Virginia society.[152] Middling artisans used the language of republicanism and of citizenship to express their political desires through petitions and journeymen's and mechanics' associations, but did not directly challenge the conventions of southern society. With the exception of the strike of a few journeymen printers in one shop, no major labor conflicts occurred in Petersburg before the Civil War. Those who chose to remain worked within the existing social and economic structures and aspired to slave ownership and the bourgeois values of successful masters. Those who could not find a place in the new order often moved on. Similar to workers in nearby Richmond, Petersburg middling artisans still strove to become a part of the *Herrenvolk* democracy of late antebellum Virginia.

For middling white artisans, life in antebellum Petersburg meant adapting to a changing economy. Between 1820 and 1860, Petersburg became the second largest center for tobacco manufacture in Virginia and gained a reputation for its cotton textile mills and iron forging industry. For many skilled workers who were willing and able to adapt to industrial work, the era offered new ways of gaining a competence. For a few determined masters, it meant prosperity and advancement to elite status as a merchant or factory owner. The period was one of significant change for all, whether upwardly mobile or not. Work cultures altered as journeymen became wage laborers, and the apprentice system an

151. "The Mechanics Meeting of Saturday Night," *Daily Southside Democrat*, 18 August 1857.

152. Steger, "'United to Support, But Not Combined to Injure,'" 100; Wells, *Origin of the Southern Middle Class*, 179–180.

avenue to obtain inexpensive labor or provide poor relief. By 1860, larger firms and manufactories were rapidly replacing independent artisan shops. Excluding those laboring in tobacco factories, the average workplace in Petersburg employed fifteen men. When the industry across the Appomattox River in Chesterfield County is included, the workplace average rises to twenty-three. (See table 9.) The composition of the workforce changed as well, as immigrants and northern mechanics found opportunities in industrializing Petersburg. The uncertainty of the changing economy also meant an instability in the workforce, leading many natives and immigrants to move on when prospects did not materialize in Petersburg. Many of those who stayed adapted to the slaveholding culture of the South and aspired to own or lease slaves for their home or business. Middling artisans also subscribed to the conservative political views of the slaveholding elite, and even after gaining universal suffrage, failed to make any real attempts to challenge the existing social and political order.

Most white artisans found their position in southern society somewhere in the middle between the elite masters of the PBMA and the general laboring classes of Petersburg. For many, like carpenter Monroe Birchett, the new industrial reality meant that life was a constant struggle. Near the end of the antebellum era, his station in life had not advanced. He owned no real property and only a few goods worth a meager $25. Birchett also had little influence with local politicians, even though by that time he had the right to vote. On the other hand, he fared better than the African American population of Petersburg, who formed a permanent underclass, whether enslaved or free.[153]

153. Personal Property Tax Lists, 1856; and Bureau of the Census, Population Schedules, Petersburg, Va., 1860.

Late antebellum/Civil War–era Petersburg   Virginia Historical Society, Richmond

Watercolor by William Simpson showing an antebellum view of Mechanics' Hall, constructed by the Petersburg Benevolent Mechanic Association.

City of Petersburg, *Harper's Weekly,* December 1862

Petersburg courthouse and retail shops, ca. 1865

Library of Congress, Prints and Photographs Division [cwpb 02883]

Johnson's Mill on the Appomattox River is indicative of local industrial development, ca. 1865.
Library of Congress, Prints and Photographs Division [cwpb 03864]

Petersburg industrial milling complex, ca. 1865
Library of Congress, Prints and Photographs Division [cwpb 03714]

Civil War images such as this one point to considerable economic growth in local manufacturing.   Library of Congress, Prints and Photographs Division [cwpb 00613]

Blandford Church and churchyard, where the Petersburg Benevolent Mechanic Association met in 1826 to pledge money for the apprehension of blacksmith Sceva Thayer's murderer, ca. 1865. Library of Congress, Prints and Photographs Division [cwpb 00544]

Civil War–era Petersburg   Library of Congress, Prints and Photographs Division [cwpb 00609]

The five railroad lines crossing in Petersburg significantly contributed to the city's economic growth, ca. 1865.   Library of Congress, Prints and Photographs Division [cwpb 01854]

The Appomattox River flowed into the James River at City Point, making water transport another important market outlet, ca. 1865.

African American workers at City Point, ca. 1865. The carrying trade employed many in Petersburg's free African American community.

During the siege of Petersburg, Federal troops found City Point landings convenient, ca. 1865.   Library of Congress, Prints and Photographs Division [cwpb 04346]

Physician Richard Eppes employed many Petersburg artisans at his Appomattox Manor plantation. During the siege, General Ulysses S. Grant used a building on its grounds as his headquarters.   Photo by the author

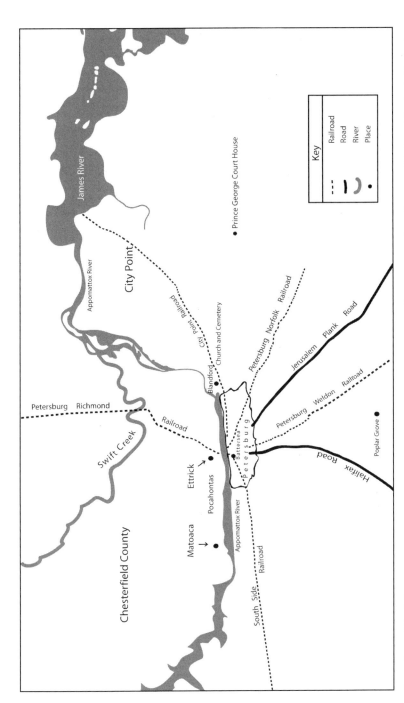

Petersburg, Virginia

Map by Youngstown State University, Media and Academic Computing

Key

Railroad
Road
River
Place

James River

Appomattox River

City Point

Prince George Court House

City Point Railroad

Blandford
Church and Cemetery

Petersburg Norfolk Railroad

Jerusalem Plank Road

Petersburg Weldon Railroad

Petersburg Richmond

Railroad

Swift Creek

Chesterfield County

Matoaca

Ettrick

Pochontas

Appomattox River

South Side Railroad

Battersea

Petersburg

Halifax Road

Poplar Grove

Petersburg on the Appomattox

KEY

1. Dunlop Tobacco Factory
2. Southside Railroad Depot
3. Appomattox Iron Works
4. Farmer's Bank
5. Trapezium House
6. St. Paul's Episcopal Church
7. Tabb Street Presbyterian Church
8. Mechanic's Hall
9. Courthouse
10. Centre Hill
11. Washington Street Methodist Church
12. Harrison Street Baptist Church
13. Blandford Church & Cemetery

4

The Paradox of Freedom

BLACK ARTISANS IN PETERSBURG

Because of his "uncommonly devoted attention to, and care of his late master during a most dangerous illness," black boatman John Brander became a free man in April 1822. Brander's benefactor was his former owner and Petersburg tobacco manufacturer James Dunlop. Dunlop fell ill while at Lynchburg and apparently Brander provided care "by which probably his life was preserved." In return, Dunlop rewarded Brander by granting him a deed of emancipation and entering it into the record of the Petersburg Hustings Court on 18 April 1822.[1] Brander's experience was not unique. Emancipation through deeds and wills was common in antebellum Petersburg and was one of three factors that contributed to the city's large free black population. In addition to local emancipations, the city attracted many newly freed African Americans from the surrounding counties of Dinwiddie, Chesterfield, and Prince George. In 1810, Petersburg could count more than 1,000 free blacks among its citizens, and by 1830, that number doubled to 2,032.[2] With the largest free black population in Virginia, natural increase became a third important factor in the population's growth rate. A significant portion of Petersburg's free black population came to the town because the growing industrial economy offered many employment opportunities. As many as 292 of these African Americans were men who practiced skilled artisan trades with varying degrees of success.

African Americans made up a significant number of the free workers in antebellum Petersburg. Their labor in tobacco factories, on infrastructure projects, and in skilled and semiskilled artisan occupations was an important contribution in the industrial development of the town. Free blacks were most

---

1. Petersburg, Va., Hustings Court Minute Book 1820–1823, 303, Library of Virginia, Richmond, Va. (hereafter cited as Vi).

2. Suzanne Lebsock, *The Free Women of Petersburg: Status and Culture in a Southern Town, 1784–1860* (New York: W. W. Norton, 1984), 91; and James G. Scott and Edward A. Wyatt, *Petersburg's Story: A History* (Petersburg, Va.: Titmus Optical, 1960), 65.

welcome in unskilled occupations, where they consistently accounted for more than half of the city's male laborers. In 1850, 70 percent of the unskilled male workers were free blacks, with the figure dipping to 64 percent in 1860. Although free blacks found racial prejudice and legal restrictions limited their ability to prosper in skilled and semiskilled occupations, the opportunities available to them in southern cities such as Petersburg proved to be more lucrative and less restricting than those of skilled blacks in northern cities. In 1850, free blacks accounted for 13 percent of skilled occupations in Petersburg. Despite an influx of immigrant and northern workers in the 1850s, the number of skilled blacks held steady and even increased slightly to 14 percent in 1860.[3] Relations between black and white artisans in Petersburg were also generally more cordial than in northern cities. There is little evidence of racial strife and discord, except in times of economic distress. When financial downturns affected the economy, and especially when financial panic swept the country in 1857, skilled black workers became the scapegoats of white labor and were subjected to a campaign to rid the city of free black artisans. But white complaints had little effect on the position of free black workers, who already formed the backbone of the unskilled workforce and were making headway into the skilled sector. The importance of free blacks to the economy of Petersburg makes it worthwhile to more closely examine the role of skilled African American workers in the years 1820 to 1860.

The skilled free blacks of Petersburg shared many experiences with their urban counterparts in other southern cities, but there are a number of distinctions that made their lives unique. As was true for other Upper South cities, there was no defined "brown elite" of lighter-skinned individuals who gained higher social and economic status.[4] Among the male workers, blacks outnumbered mulattoes in all trades almost three to one. But unlike their counterparts

3. Statistics on free black workers were tabulated from the 1850 and 1860 manuscript census population schedules. Occupation is not designated before 1850, making earlier calculations impossible.

4. For an examination of class distinctions based on color among the free African American community, see Bernard E. Powers, *Black Charlestonians: A Social History, 1822–1885* (Fayetteville: University of Arkansas Press, 1994), 36–51, 56–61; and Whittington B. Johnson, *Black Savannah, 1788–1864* (Fayetteville: University of Arkansas Press, 1996), 4, 55–58, 77–78. A similar argument can be found in John Blassingame, *Black New Orleans, 1860–1880* (Chicago: University of Chicago Press, 1973), 1–22.

in other cities in the region, Petersburg's African Americans were able to gain positions in an assortment of skilled occupations.[5] Most of those occupations clustered in the service, transportation, and building trades, which matches the experiences of free blacks in the Lower South cities such as Charleston and Savannah.[6] Similarly, in Baltimore free African Americans gained a stronghold in semiskilled shipbuilding positions, including that of caulker.[7] To more closely examine the lives of free African American workers in Petersburg, and to understand what made them unique, it is important to look at the way that they fit into the demographics and economy of antebellum Petersburg.

Petersburg was attractive to free African Americans because of the unique opportunities offered by growing industries. The tobacco factories, transportation improvements, and manufacturing focus extended possibilities for free blacks to gain employment, offered potential for economic success, and created an appealing community life. This city that in so many ways resembled industrializing cities in the North, was radically different demographically. Petersburg gained the largest free black population in Virginia by 1850, claiming even more than Richmond, the urban industrial giant of the South.

The free black population of Petersburg rapidly increased following the enactment of the Virginia manumission law of 1782, which empowered owners to set free any slave under the age of forty-five. According to historian Luther P. Jackson, at least 120 slaves were set free in Petersburg between 1784 and 1806 through deeds of emancipation.[8] Slaves manumitted from the plantation communities surrounding Petersburg also found the growing town an attractive place to settle. Women formed the majority of the Petersburg free black population, totaling 55 percent in 1850. The town attracted many free African American women because employment as domestic servants or as laborers in the tobacco factories was readily available. The free black population also be-

5. For Baltimore, see Christopher Phillips, *Freedom's Port: The African American Community of Baltimore, 1790–1860* (Urbana: University of Illinois Press, 1997), 74–77, 109–111. For Richmond, see James Sidbury, *Ploughshares into Swords: Race, Rebellion, and Identity in Gabriel's Virginia, 1730–1810* (Cambridge: Cambridge University Press, 1997), 204–208, 216–219.

6. See Johnson, *Black Savannah*; and Powers, *Black Charlestonians*.

7. Charles G. Steffen, *The Mechanics of Baltimore: Workers in the Age of Revolution, 1763–1812* (Urbana: University of Illinois Press, 1984), 41.

8. Luther P. Jackson, "Manumission in Certain Virginia Cities," *Journal of Negro History* 15 (1930): 281.

came a source of its own increase. When opportunity and financial situation permitted, Petersburg blacks purchased the freedom of friends and relatives. In fact, after 1806 one-third of the slaves emancipated in Petersburg were set free by blacks.[9]

The rapid increase in manumissions following the passage of the 1782 law led to alarm among the whites of Virginia and to a movement to restrict the abilities of an owner to emancipate his or her slaves. White Petersburg residents petitioned the Virginia General Assembly in 1805 for help in halting the growth of the free black population. Responding to similar pleas across the state, in 1806 the legislature passed a law requiring that newly emancipated slaves leave the Commonwealth within twelve months. Those failing to leave could be "apprehended and sold by the overseers of the poor of any county or corporation, in which he or she shall be found, for the benefit of the literary fund."[10] Applying to anyone manumitted after 1 May 1806, the law temporarily slowed the tide of freedom in the state and in Petersburg. Between 1807 and 1810 city deed books recorded no manumissions at all.[11]

But free blacks were an important element in the workforce of the South, and as Frank Towers shows, especially critical to the economy of growing towns and cities.[12] Their labor was necessary in homes and tobacco factories, on internal improvement projects, and in the carrying trade of Petersburg. Many of the occupations they filled were race-typed jobs that working-class whites found distasteful. In 1850, whites made up less than half of the unskilled general laborers in Petersburg. As Ira Berlin has shown, free blacks were willing to work for less than whites and often on the same terms as slaves, making their labor the least expensive alternative for many employers.[13] For this reason and others, the 1806 law was generally not strictly enforced. In 1816 the legislature relaxed the law by allowing newly emancipated slaves to petition any

9. Joseph Tate, *A Digest of the Laws of Virginia* . . . (Richmond: Shepherd and Pollard, 1823), 500; Bureau of the Census, *Seventh Census*, 258; and Lebsock, *Free Women of Petersburg*, 96.

10. Tate, *A Digest of the Laws*, 502.

11. Jackson, "Manumission in Certain Virginia Cities," 289.

12. Frank Towers, *The Urban South and the Coming of the Civil War* (Charlottesville: University of Virginia Press, 2004), 46–47.

13. Bureau of the Census, Population Schedules, Petersburg, Va., 1850; and Ira Berlin, *Slaves Without Masters: The Free Negro in the Antebellum South* (New York: Vintage, 1974), 228–229.

city or county court for permission to remain in that locality. Applicants had to provide evidence of their "general good character and conduct," and to have a notice posted on the courthouse door for five weeks to allow anyone to come forward with evidence to the contrary. This law remained in effect throughout the antebellum era, but in Petersburg, it was only on rare occasions that the city Hustings Court denied permission to a free person requesting to remain in the city.[14]

The largest growth in the free African American population came between 1810 and 1830, but numbers moved steadily upwards throughout the antebellum era. Once legal restrictions eased, the African American population increased from 2,032 in 1830 to 2,616 in 1850. At that time Petersburg's free blacks made up slightly more than 18 percent of the city's total population of 14,010 and more than one-quarter of its free population. These figures mean that Petersburg had the highest proportion of free blacks of any southern city. (See table 10.) In 1850, Richmond counted 2,369 free blacks, who made up just 8.5 percent of its total population of 27,570. Other southern cities also lagged behind Petersburg in the ratio of free blacks to the total population. Even in Baltimore, which counted over 25,000 free blacks in 1850, free African Americans made up just 15 percent of the total population, and 15.3 percent of the total number of free people, white and black.[15]

The population of free blacks in Petersburg peaked in the 1850s. They numbered 3,244, in 1860, but their proportion of the total population dipped to just under 18 percent and slightly over one-quarter of the total free population.[16] Although the proportion of free African Americans dipped slightly, Petersburg attracted more free blacks than other areas of the South. The strong concentration of African Americans who made the city their home in the period between 1810 and 1830 allowed free blacks to gain a solid hold on many unskilled occupations. The foothold established early in the century made Petersburg a destination for many recently emancipated African Americans who came in

14. Jackson, "Manumission in Certain Virginia Cities," 290; and Tate, *A Digest of the Laws,* 502–503.

15. Bureau of the Census, *Statistical View of the United States: Compendium of the Seventh Census* (Washington, D.C.: Beverley Tucker, Senate Printer, 1854), 397–398.

16. Bureau of the Census, *The Seventh Census of the United States 1850* (Washington, D.C.: Robert Armstrong, 1853), 258; and Bureau of the Census, *Population of the United States in 1860: The Eighth Census* (Washington, D.C.: GPO, 1864), 519.

search of employment or because family already resided there. The continued growth of the free black population explains why Petersburg attracted fewer European immigrants. Mostly seeking out unskilled work opportunities, immigrants found much competition from Petersburg's long-established African American population.

In fact, when the fluid community of free blacks and slaves is considered in the demographic mix, Petersburg was a city where blacks outnumbered whites until 1860.[17] Of this free black population 292 individuals have been identified as holding skilled occupations.[18] The most common occupations were barber, blacksmith, boatman, bricklayer, carpenter, cooper, and shoemaker, but a significant number of African Americans also worked as butchers, stonemasons, cartmen, and gardeners. These skilled men were set apart from the majority of free blacks who worked at unskilled jobs. Of 453 free black men reporting occupations to census enumerators in 1850, more than half claimed to be employed as laborers, and many of these worked in the growing number of tobacco factories.[19]

Whether skilled or unskilled, most free blacks lived in the Pocahontas section of Petersburg, on the north side of the Appomattox River. In this area, black-owned businesses and houses clustered to create a sub-community. The bridge across the Appomattox connecting Pocahontas with the rest of Petersburg was the earliest local work of internal improvement, completed in 1752.[20] Free black businessmen located their operations in and near Pocahontas to serve the needs of other African Americans. H. C. Howlett's coal and wood yard offered fuel for their fires and stoves, but faced competition from a similar yard owned by James Lynch. Business partners Albert and George A. Farley, along with W. S. Harrison, operated a grocery store just across the Pocahontas Bridge on Second Street, a convenient location for workers returning home after a hard day's work in the tobacco factories in the center of town. In the 1840s, the terminal for the Richmond and Petersburg Railroad located in Poca-

17. Population figures for 1850 revealed a total of 7,345 blacks and 6,665 whites. In 1860 the tables were turned slightly when the census counted 8,924 blacks and 9,342 whites in Petersburg.

18. Skilled black artisans have been identified from the 1850 and 1860 census schedules, city directory, and newspaper advertisements.

19. Bureau of the Census, Population Schedules, Petersburg, Va., 1850.

20. Scott and Wyatt, *Petersburg's Story*, 19.

BLACK ARTISANS IN PETERSBURG

hontas and offered nearby opportunities for blacks employed in the carrying trade. This terminus was about three-fourths of a mile from that of the Petersburg Railroad. Since there were no tracks between stations and no railroad bridge spanned the river, all goods continuing south had to be unloaded and hauled by cart or wagon to the other station. Living in Pocahontas was convenient for cartmen, wagoners, and others like E. T. Bledsoe, who worked as an assistant ticket agent for the Richmond and Petersburg Railroad.[21]

African Americans also lived in other areas, including Blandford on the southern edge of the city and Gillfield in the central business district. This neighborhood became the site for the black Gillfield Baptist Church, which moved from Pocahontas to a permanent structure there in 1818.[22] The church was a central institution in the lives of many Petersburg blacks. As in other southern cities, it formed the most visible and influential black organization in the community. As Ira Berlin and others have shown, Gillfield Baptist brought together the Petersburg African American community, free and enslaved, in membership and in church leadership. Congregational records demonstrate that free blacks and slaves served together in leadership positions. Officers and committee memberships were divided to ensure that both enslaved members and free African Americans received representation, and provides evidence of the existence of a fluid urban community.[23]

In addition to Gillfield, which was the largest church, blacks formed the Third Baptist Church and Harrison Street Baptist Church, where slaves made up the majority of worshipers. African American ministers served these churches, but beginning in 1831, following the Nat Turner rebellion, a white supervisor attended all services. These churches filled more than the spiritual needs of Petersburg blacks; they also offered moral guidance and, on occasion, financial assistance to the needy. Gillfield Baptist routinely disciplined members for committing such offenses as fighting, living in sin, destroying property, and swearing. Blacks could also look toward the church in times of dire straits.

21. William D. Henderson, *Petersburg in the Civil War: War at the Door* (Lynchburg, Va.: H. E. Howard, 1998), 17, 25.

22. Scott and Wyatt, *Petersburg's Story*, 286.

23. Ira Berlin, *Generations of Captivity: A History of American-American Slaves* (Cambridge, Mass.: The Belknap Press of Harvard University Press, 2003), 227–230; and Record Book, vol. 2, 1834–1849, Gillfield Baptist Church Records, Special Collections, University of Virginia, Charlottesville, Va.

Gillfield Baptist administered an insurance fund and a "poor saint treasury" that offered a small measure of aid to impecunious parishioners.[24]

The churches formed the backbone of social activities for members and the community through sponsoring picnics, holiday concerts, and fundraising fairs. Near the end of the antebellum era, Gillfield Baptist claimed over 1,200 members and aimed to build a new church at a cost of more than $7,000. The construction brought a rare show of biracial cooperation in Petersburg. At the August 1859 cornerstone ceremony, prominent whites from the Blandford and Petersburg Masonic lodges deposited a list of the church members and officers, coins, city newspapers, and list of local Masonic officers, in a box placed inside the cornerstone. In great ceremony Freemasons laid the stone while a brass band played, and Reverend Thomas G. Keen, of the white First Baptist Church, offered an "address for the occasion." Although whites dominated the cornerstone ceremony, the construction of the new church employed some free blacks. Christopher Stevens, a prominent African American carpenter and deacon of the Gillfield Baptist Church, acted as contractor to oversee the completion of the interior of the new facility, which could comfortably accommodate 1,400 in its auditorium.[25]

Economic opportunities, such as the one Stevens enjoyed as a contractor for this large building project, were one of the main reasons free blacks chose to locate in Petersburg between 1820 and 1860. In 1860, Stevens owned property worth $300 and employed two black apprentices in his carpentry business.[26] The ability to succeed in skilled trades such as carpentry, blacksmithing, shoemaking, coopering, barbering, and the carrying trade allowed a number of African Americans to experience economic prosperity and property ownership that made them important and powerful members of the black community. Barber Henry Elebeck, whose father came to Petersburg from Pennsylvania, owned property worth $1,000 in 1850, including several houses and lots in

24. Lawrence Leroy Hartzell, "Black Life in Petersburg, 1870–1902" (M.A. thesis, University of Virginia, 1985), 9–10; and Johnson, Black Savannah, 7.

25. "Amusement at Gillfield Church," Daily Express, 23 December 1857; "New Church," ibid., 14 May 1858; "Gillfield Church Fair," ibid., 14 June 1859; "Laying a Corner Stone," ibid., 11 August 1859; "Gillfield Baptist Church," ibid., 17 August 1859; and Luther Porter Jackson, Free Negro Labor and Property Holding in Virginia, 1830–1860 (New York: D. Appleton-Century, 1942), 96n.

26. Bureau of the Census, Population Schedules, Petersburg, Va., 1860.

town.[27] When Shadrack Brander, a prominent cooper, died in 1834, his estate was valued at more than $1,000, and an inventory of his work-yard in Blandford included 1,300 barrel staves, one lot of cooper's tools, a wagon, two cows, and three horses.[28] Boatman Joseph Jenkins Roberts operated a successful line of flatboats on the Appomattox River in the 1820s, but chose to emigrate to Liberia in 1829. There he partnered with William N. Colson, a Petersburg barber, to form a merchant shipping company to trade in fancy goods. Colson died soon after arrival in Africa, but Roberts prospered financially, and eventually became the first president of an independent Liberia in 1848.[29]

The Elebeck, Roberts, and Colson families were among the most financially successful and prominent African American families in Petersburg, so it is not surprising that their members experienced prosperity in their life endeavors. But the same success that made the black community proud also angered white mechanics, who resented the competition these free black workers represented. In times of economic distress, black mechanics and businessmen came under attack from middling white artisan workers who believed that their economic situation could be improved through eliminating such competition. Life for skilled black workers was a precarious existence where the possibility of success was often limited by the color line.

In the antebellum South, whites often viewed free African Americans with suspicion and disdain. Many towns passed ordinances restricting the movement of free blacks, codifying segregation, and limiting their employment to certain occupations. Yet in growing cities such as Petersburg, their labor was integral to the local economy. This paradox constantly concerned many in the city that grew up at the falls of the Appomattox River. In addition to making up more than half of the male unskilled labor in Petersburg, free blacks held a significant number of skilled occupations. Determined free blacks in traditional

27. Ibid.; Luther P. Jackson, "Free Negroes of Petersburg," *Journal of Negro History* 12 (1927): 371–372; and Jackson, *Free Negro Labor,* 157.

28. Petersburg, Va., Hustings Court Will Book 3: 82; and Luther P. Jackson, "Business Enterprise Among Free Negroes in the Early History of Petersburg," *Progress-Index,* 9 January 1939.

29. Jackson, *Free Negro Labor,* 147; Luther P. Jackson, "Negro Labor and Property-Holding in Petersburg Before Emancipation," *Progress-Index,* 11 October 1931; and James W. Smith, "The Role of Blacks in Petersburg's Carrying Trade and Service-Oriented Industry, 1800–1865," *Virginia Geographer* 16 (1984): 16.

African American occupations such as barbering and the carrying trade, and even a few in white-dominated occupations, were capable of considerable economic success despite the limitations placed on African Americans by southern whites.

Just under half of all skilled blacks worked in construction and building trades. (See table 11.) Carpenters and bricklayers were the most common occupations with 57 and 32, respectively, but blacks held positions as brickmakers, painters, whitewashers, plasterers, coopers, sawyers, and caulkers as well. Blacks also found a stronghold in transportation and personal service positions. There can be little surprise that barbering, in the process of becoming a predominately African American profession, led this category with 25 employed. Other significant service-related occupations included cartman, drayman, wagoner, and gardener. A third important category fell to those employed in forging trades, where blacksmiths outnumbered all others with 36 employed. Forging-related trades such as machinist, and tinner included free blacks as well. Clothing and shoes employed 26 free blacks, but 25 shoe and boot makers dominated the category. Petersburg could claim only one tailor in the city's free black community, and a smaller number of skilled blacks worked in food and tobacco trades. Five of these were butchers, and another 5 listed their occupation as miller. Two listed their trade as tobacconist, and other occupations included baker, candy maker, and fisherman. Fourteen worked in the container crafts as coopers, and the single free black skilled in furniture making was an upholsterer.

Studies of Upper South cities find that little distinction was made between mulattoes and free blacks of darker complexion with regard to occupational designation or special privilege. In Baltimore most free blacks were dark-skinned, and in general, the society did not place much emphasis on the skin color of the black population.[30] The same holds true for skilled workers in Petersburg. Most of the free blacks enumerated in the 1850 census, the first to designate color difference, were listed as "black," and the skilled workforce also reflects a trend toward a darker populace. Of 292 skilled workers identified in the census and city directories, 215 were listed as "black" and only 77 as "mulatto."[31]

Blacks outnumbered mulattoes in every occupation except barbering. Of

30. Phillips, *Freedom's Port*, 62–63, 105–106.

31. Although color designation was subject to the judgment of the census enumerator, it is the only available indication of distinction within the free African American community.

the twenty-five African American barbers identified, fourteen were designated as mulatto on the census. This occupation was traditionally held by blacks throughout the South, and because of the wide patronage barbers received from whites, one historian has called barbers a sort of African American aristocracy.[32] The only white barbers in antebellum Petersburg were Charles Ellmer, an immigrant from Switzerland, and William Morris, who brought his skills in fancy hair design from New York. Elite barbers, often mulattoes, operated "white shops" and did not serve the black community. Usually dressed in clean white jackets and aprons, they were known for providing attentive personal service. Mulatto barber John K. Shore operated a shop in the Powell Hotel in the 1840s and 1850s, where he rented space for $5 per month. Shore furnished his shop with a maple working chair crafted by white cabinetmaker Samuel Coldwell and a dressing glass mirror purchased from merchants Donnan and Dunn. He also dressed well. In 1849 Shore's personal receipts included one for the purchase of a merino vest and cravat at the cost of $4.75, and a $2 bill from Petersburg tailor William R. Wilkins. It was not uncommon for barbers to own real estate in antebellum Virginia. Shore's business was successful enough to allow him to purchase a house and lot in Petersburg, for which he paid $200.60 in 1855. In 1860, Shore moved his shop out of the Powell Hotel to a building at the corner of Franklin and Sycamore streets. This rented space cost him $25 each quarter, and featured a barber pole painted by local painter John Brewer.[33]

Other mulatto barbers gained prominent economic status in the community. William N. Colson, who later partnered with Joseph Jenkins Roberts in a Liberian merchant venture, was highly successful in his four-chair barbering operation on Sycamore Street. Colson also owned a half interest in another barber shop on Bollingbrook Street, which he operated with Henry Elebeck. When Colson died in 1836, the partnership was owed $134.22 on outstanding accounts. His personal estate included a five-room house on Lombard Street, filled with mahogany furniture, china, silver plate, and an extensive collection of books on history, theology, and biographies.[34] Colson's partner, Henry

32. Jackson, *Free Negro Labor,* 97–98.

33. Ibid., 157, 246; and John K. Shore Papers, Receipts and Bills, 1844–1845, box 19, Colson-Hill Family Papers, 1834–1984, Special Collections, Virginia State University, Petersburg, Va.

34. "Negro Labor and Property-Holding in Petersburg Before Emancipation," *Progress-*

Elebeck, owned several houses and lots valued at $1,000 in 1850. Because he was the son of a prominent black man who came to Petersburg from Pennsylvania in 1802, Elebeck was able to succeed in his chosen profession. The elder Elebeck was so popular in Petersburg that in December 1810 many residents of the town, including the mayor, petitioned the General Assembly to allow Major Elebeck to remain in Petersburg despite a 1793 law that forbade free black residents of other states from settling in Virginia.[35] Another mulatto barber, John Berry, owned a house and lot in Petersburg by the time he was thirty, and could count property worth a total of $800 in 1860. Likewise, Munroe Auter owned $350 worth of property in 1850; and James Ford owned a house and lot worth $175 in 1857.[36]

Although mulattoes dominated barbering in Petersburg, blacks in the trade experienced some financial success. Edward L. Locketh owned real estate worth $800 and had a personal estate valued at $100 in 1860. Albert Stewart's estate, inventoried after his death in 1852, revealed a small amount of household goods and furniture, including twenty books, and a gold watch, hardly the possessions of a poor man. Barber E. Whitehead also had a modest estate, valued at $100 in 1860.[37] Whether mulatto or black, free African American barbers experienced success because they occupied a segment of the service economy that whites largely eschewed. Their ability to succeed financially was not restricted by legal proscription or customary exclusion. Free blacks in other occupations were forced to find a different way to fit into the local economy. Despite the considerable economic success of a number of free African Americans, their presence was not welcomed by all in Petersburg.

In 1855 the editor of the *Daily Southside Democrat* complained that "Petersburg is cursed with free negroes particularly and slaves in general."[38] The sentiment A. D. Banks expressed in his editorial column accurately reflected the

---

Index, 11 October 1931; and "Business Enterprise Among Free Negroes in the Early History of Petersburg," ibid., 9 January 1939.

35. Tate, *A Digest of the Laws*, 492; Bureau of the Census, Population Schedules, Petersburg, Va., 1860; and Legislative Petition, Petersburg City, 15 December 1810, Vi.

36. Bureau of the Census, Population Schedules, Petersburg, Va., 1860; and Jackson, *Free Negro Labor*, 244.

37. Hustings Court Will Book 4: 134–135; and Bureau of the Census, Population Schedules, Petersburg, Va., 1860.

38. "A Nuisance in Fact," *Daily Southside Democrat*, 25 September 1855.

feeling of many white residents. Although African Americans were vital to the industrial economy of Petersburg, their presence in white-dominated southern society was a constant reminder of the complications of antebellum race relations. In a region where dark skin designated servitude and bondage, free African Americans challenged the expectations of white society and formed a class of people in the middle between freedom and slavery. Although often classed with slaves, free blacks enjoyed some of the same rights and privileges as whites, including property ownership. But the list of rights and privileges denied them left no doubt of their secondary status in Virginia. Free blacks could not vote, sit on juries, or testify against whites. After 1832, they were even denied the right to a jury trial, but faced stronger penalties than whites for the same crime. Blacks also shouldered the burden of proving their free status, and at all times carried papers registering their residence and documenting their condition.[39]

Fear that free African Americans would negatively influence otherwise obedient and docile slaves was strong throughout the South and evident in Petersburg. A local newspaper editor expressed the ultimate fear of southern whites in 1858: "Free negro influence is but the stepping stone from our servants quarters to the underground railroad."[40] White Petersburg residents articulated similar sentiment in an 1838 attempt to dramatically reduce the free black population of the city. On that occasion thirty-five residents petitioned the Virginia legislature for aid in curtailing the growing number of blacks who chose to locate in Dinwiddie County. The petitioners asked that the state renew and increase appropriations for African colonization, which they believed would help to lessen this "growing evil."[41] Some argued that "the free negro and the slave should not exist in the same community." Many believed that free blacks aided slaves in the selling of stolen goods and obtaining liquor. The most extreme opposition to free blacks manifested in a movement to rid the Commonwealth of all free blacks and to enslave any free black who chose to remain in Virginia. Advocates of this dramatic solution supported a bill before the state legislature to provide all free blacks who chose to stay in the state with "a suitable master."[42] Fortunately for the African American residents of Virginia, the bill failed, but the

39. Jackson, *Free Negro Labor*, 3–4.
40. "Stampede of Free Negroes," *Daily Express*, 14 September 1858.
41. Legislative Petition, Dinwiddie County, 9 January 1838, Vi.
42. "Free Negroes," *Daily Southside Democrat*, 19 June 1857.

efforts to remove free blacks emphasize the precarious nature of their existence in southern cities.

Free black workers were dependent on a white-controlled society for their livelihood, and the proscriptions and limitations whites dictated hampered their ability to advance. The open and accepted racial prejudice of whites provided a daily reminder of blacks' subservient position in the community. Whites used legal acts to limit and control the actions of free African Americans in Petersburg, as is evident from a series of ordinances the town's Common Hall passed in 1824. Beginning in that year any free African American individual or family choosing to locate in Petersburg was required to report to the master of police, who recorded their occupation and gathered personal information about all free members of the household. Bringing the town into compliance with a statewide black registration law, those who failed to register and those "found to have no honest employment" would be "treated as vagrants and committed to the work house."[43] Anyone employing unregistered African Americans faced a $5 fine. An ordinance that ordered town constables to break up "disorderly and unlawful meetings of slaves, free negroes and mulattoes" grouped free blacks with slaves.[44] They were also included in later city ordinances denying slaves the right to smoke in public and to own or keep a dog, although free blacks could keep a dog with the mayor's written license. Punishment for both offenses was a whipping of at least twenty but not more than thirty-nine stripes.[45]

Legal and social proscriptions affected the ability of free black artisans to practice their trade as they saw fit. Laws and ordinances requiring them to maintain and update their registration certificates restricted them from leaving the town or county of residence. This law limited the earning potential of artisans in the building trades, who often made their living working on projects in the plantation hinterland and other cities in the region. In order to circumvent the restrictions of the registration law, Petersburg bricklayer Henry Mason petitioned the General Assembly for freedom of movement throughout

43. Virginia, *Acts of the General Assembly of Virginia Relative to the Jurisdiction and Powers of the Town of Petersburg: To Which are Added, the Ordinances, Bye-laws, and Regulations of the Corporation* (Petersburg: Edward Pescud, 1824), 43–44.

44. Ibid., 45.

45. "Ordinance Concerning Dogs," *Daily Express,* 15 July 1857; and "Smoking in the Streets," ibid., 20 October 1857.

Virginia. Mason was born a slave in Sussex County, apprenticed and trained as a bricklayer, and even while still enslaved, apparently gained a reputation for fine work. Following his emancipation in January 1844, Mason worked on building projects in Petersburg and occasionally Richmond, but sought more freedom because he found it "difficult at all times to get profitable employment in the town of Petersburg at such wages as his skill as a workman justly and fairly entitle him to."[46] Despite his popularity as a workman, the law required Mason to leave Richmond and return to his trade in Petersburg.[47]

Despite the legal and social restrictions free black workers faced in Petersburg, evidence suggests that they found more opportunities to participate in skilled occupations than did blacks living in northern cities before the Civil War. Figures calculated for 1850 found that artisan occupations accounted for less than 10 percent of black occupations in the northern cities of Brooklyn, Philadelphia, and Cincinnati, and less than 5 percent in Buffalo, Pittsburgh, and St. Louis.[48] In New York City, African Americans comprised a small artisan community, less than 6 percent of all employed blacks, but were largely relegated to the lowest trades, and at best their contribution to the economy was marginal. In early nineteenth-century New York, a number of trades regularly excluded African Americans. City officials routinely denied black applicants for a cartman's license because they feared the riotous behavior of white cartmen seeking to protect their occupation from black competition.[49] In the late 1850s, in Philadelphia, less than one-third of skilled blacks worked in their trade. The concept of a racially mixed workshop was also anathema to northern artisans, making it difficult for parents to find apprenticeship opportunities for their sons. In 1830, the president of the Mechanical Association of Cincinnati was tried before that group for accepting a black apprentice into his shop.[50]

In comparison, southern skilled blacks faced less exclusion and overall oc-

46. Legislative Petition, Richmond City, 22 December 1847, Vi.

47. Jackson, *Free Negro Labor*, 5.

48. Leonard P. Curry, *The Free Black in Urban America 1800–1850* (Chicago: University of Chicago Press, 1981), 260.

49. Sean Wilentz, *Chants Democratic: New York City and the Rise of the American Working Class, 1788–1850* (New York: Oxford University Press, 1984), 48n; and Howard B. Rock, *Artisans of the New Republic: The Tradesmen of New York City in the Age of Jefferson* (New York: New York University Press, 1984), 224–225.

50. Curry, *The Free Black in Urban America*, 18–19.

cupational restriction. The important port cities of New Orleans and Charleston found artisan occupations for more than 60 percent of their free blacks in 1850, while 18 percent of Baltimore's free blacks held artisan occupations.[51] Leonard P. Curry explains this contrast in terms of the comfort level southern city dwellers felt in the presence of African American artisans in general. Slave artisans were a part of southern life before large free black communities formed in places such as Petersburg, and encounters with autonomous African American workers were not unusual. The location of black artisans in southern cities also provided more opportunities for apprenticeships, thus increasing the number of free blacks practicing skilled trades.[52] A racially mixed work environment was also common in southern cities. In Baltimore whites and blacks worked alongside one another in that city's shipyards, although not always in the same occupations.[53] Free blacks in Richmond's construction trades worked together with white workers on numerous construction and internal improvement projects, mingling white and black workers of a variety of skills with gangs of unskilled slaves on a regular basis.[54]

The work experiences of Petersburg free blacks also reflects a more open society characterized by fluid work environments. Although most African American artisans worked at trades traditionally racially designated in the South, blacks could also be found in all but a few elite trades and in more than a few white-operated shops. Some of the most distinguished white artisans in Petersburg opened their shops to black apprentices. A glimpse into the workshop of Daniel Lyon, a prominent bricklayer and building contractor, offers evidence of the mixture of races at work in Petersburg. White artisans, slaves, and free blacks toiled side by side on building projects directed by Lyon. In 1836, he paid taxes on four adult male slaves he employed in his bricklaying business. At about the same time, his workforce included two indentured apprentices, one white and one black. James Read, a white orphan, was bound to Lyon in September 1835 to learn the trade of brick making. Less than two years later, Robert Ricks, a twelve-year-old African American boy was apprenticed to Lyon to learn the trade of a bricklayer. By 1843, Lyon's workshop and household included three white males over age sixteen and six adult male slaves, not counting any wage-

51. Ibid., 260; and Towers, *Urban South*, 46.
52. Towers, *Urban South*, 35.
53. Phillips, *Freedom's Port*, 78–79.
54. Sidbury, *Ploughshares into Swords*, 204–207.

earning journeymen who worked but did not live in the household.[55] In stark contrast to the Cincinnati artisan sanctioned by the mechanics' association for employing a black apprentice, Lyon was one of the most respected and influential men in Petersburg. A founding member of the Petersburg Benevolent Mechanic Association (PBMA), he also served the community as a captain in the local militia, and held office as commissioner of the revenue for several terms in the 1830s.[56]

Bricklayer Benjamin F. Cox also employed a racially mixed workforce. In 1849 the Petersburg Overseers of the Poor bound William Parham, a fourteen-year-old African American boy, to Cox to learn the trade of a bricklayer. Parham entered and worked in a household that already included four adult male slaves. Before Parham's apprenticeship ended, Cox's workforce grew again in 1855 when he leased two young slaves, William and James, at the annual rate of $45 each.[57] Petersburg baker John Patterson opened his shop to train four apprentices between 1820 and 1846, including free blacks William Valentine and Robert Coleman whom he contracted to train as bakers.[58]

Although quite a few of the white-owned workshops in Petersburg were racially mixed, a number of black artisans operated independent businesses that employed only African Americans. Several managed to gain considerable respect and reputation among both whites and blacks in the community and found their services in high demand. Carpenter Henry Claiborn operated a shop on Oak Street at the corner of Sycamore, where he employed at least four other African American men by 1847. A fire in that location in April 1857 cost Claiborn between $300 and $500 in lost stock, but he must have been able to rebuild despite a lack of insurance. When his will was probated in 1867, Claiborn's estate included three town lots and a house, and stipulated that his aged

55. Virginia, Dept. of Taxation, Personal Property Tax List, City of Petersburg, 1836 and 1843, Vi; Petersburg, Va., Hustings Court Minute Book 1832–1835, 17 September 1835, 473; and Hustings Court Minute Book 1836–1837, 20 January 1837, 174.

56. Hustings Court Minute Book 1827–1832, 21 March 1828 (n.p.), 17 February 1831 (n.p.); and 16 February 1832, 75.

57. Personal Property Tax List, 1847; Hustings Court Minute Book 1848–1851, 20 December 1849, 200; and Branch & Company Auction Ledger, 1854–1857, Virginia Historical Society, Richmond, Va. (hereafter cited as ViHi).

58. Hustings Court Minute Book 1820–1823, 20 July 1820, 74, 392; Hustings Court Minute Book 1823–1827, 15 June 1826 (n.p.); and Hustings Court Minute Book 1846–1847, 21.

mother be paid $70 annually from his holdings.[59] Thomas Scott, who owned property valued at $3,100, also employed several free blacks at his carpentry shop in Gillfield, near the Gillfield Baptist Church. When the wooden building housing his shop caught fire in 1859, he suffered a $600 loss but was partially insured. Several of his journeymen were not as fortunate, and sustained "separate losses of from $20 to $30 each" on their tools left in the shop that Saturday.[60]

Even though some white workshops accepted black apprentices, the number of independent African American artisans provided significant opportunities for the perpetuation of skilled black workers in Petersburg. Carpenter and contractor Christopher Stevens trained black apprentices in his business, including Nelson Dugger and Robert Underdeer, who resided in his household in 1860.[61] The barbering partnership of John K. Shore and James Ford took on fourteen-year-old Levy Jones in 1837, with his mother's consent, and agreed to teach him the secrets of the trade.[62] Petersburg Overseers of the Poor placed William Crocker, a twelve-year-old orphan, with William Adkins to learn the shoemaking trade.[63] Even prominent bricklayer Henry Mason took time to train African Americans in his field. Mason's bricklaying apprentice Thomas Garnes remained in Petersburg and gained a reputation as notable as that of his master. Garnes in turn trained subsequent generations of bricklayers whose legacy can be traced to those working in late twentieth-century Petersburg. Garnes became a prominent building contractor and a deacon of the Gillfield Baptist Church, and was reportedly buried in the white Blandford Cemetery when he died.[64]

African American skilled workers found an outlet for their services and skills in places other than city workshops. The city of Petersburg at times used the services of free black artisans for a variety of building and maintenance

59. Personal Property Tax Lists, 1847; Hustings Court Will Book 5: 439; and "Incendiary Fire," *Daily Southside Democrat*, 6 April 1857.

60. "Fire," *Daily Express*, 4 April 1859; and "Negro Labor and Property-Holding in Petersburg Before Emancipation," *Progress-Index*, 8 November 1931.

61. Bureau of the Census, Population Schedules, Petersburg, Va., 1860.

62. Hustings Court Minute Book 1836–1837, 267.

63. Hustings Court Minute Book 1846–1847, 59.

64. "Negro Labor and Property-Holding in Petersburg Before Emancipation," *Progress-Index*, 15 November 1931; and Jackson, "Free Negroes of Petersburg," 380.

needs related to municipal buildings and services. Town authorities hired African American whitewasher Jesse Green and paid him $13 for whitewashing the town jail, and cooper William King received $7.50 for making privy buckets.[65] Each quarter of the year, artisans who performed services or provided goods to the municipality presented the Hustings Court with a bill and received prompt payment.

Those black artisans with special skills found that their reputations allowed them to seek employment outside Petersburg on more than twenty plantations in three surrounding counties. Bricklayer Henry Mason's 1847 legislative petition for freedom of movement aimed to provide him with more mobility so that he could meet the demands of potential customers throughout the state as well as in the local region. Other black artisans also found the countryside a lucrative place to practice their trade. The records and diaries of Richard Eppes, who owned three plantations and at least eighty-eight slaves near Petersburg, shows how outstanding African American artisans found employment in the hinterland. In 1852, Eppes hired black bricklayer Godfrey Mabry to repair a chimney at his Bermuda Hundreds estate. Eppes met with Mabry himself on 13 March to explain "what I wanted done to the chimney."[66] Carpenter Henry Claiborn was in the middle of a large building project for Eppes when his Petersburg carpenter's shop burned in April 1857. Eppes hired Claiborn to construct a new kitchen at his City Point estate, some eight miles outside Petersburg. Including advances of $200 for materials, Claiborn was paid a total of $420.73 for the job, which must have helped to defray some of the losses he sustained in the fire.[67] The contract to build a new kitchen was a well-paying large job for Claiborn, but most of the jobs and services African American artisans provided on area plantations were of a smaller scale. More typical was bricklayer Charles Tinsley's opportunity to earn $5 for fusing the backs of four fireplaces at Eppes's City Point plantation.[68] The early growth of the Petersburg free black population allowed many skilled workers to gain a significant foothold in the local economy. A number of skilled African American workers advanced to middling or almost middle-class status. However, race remained a factor that tempered

65. Hustings Court Minute Book 1853–1856, 100.

66. Richard Eppes Account Book, 1851–1861, 16, ViHi; and 13 March 1852, Richard Eppes Diary 12 March–30 September 1852, ViHi.

67. Richard Eppes Account Book 1851–1861, 74–75.

68. Ibid., 78.

their success. Often classified with slaves, and denied the basic rights guaranteed to rising white artisans, free black mechanics nevertheless sought similar ways to display their economic success. A considerable number of free African American artisans in Petersburg chose to own or lease slaves.

The ownership of slaves by free African Americans is a complex chapter in the history of the antebellum South. It was not unusual for urban southern blacks to own slaves, although Lower South cities, such as Charleston and New Orleans, had a larger percentage of black slaveholders than cities in the Upper South, such as Baltimore or Washington.[69] In the early part of the nineteenth century the practice of free black slaveholding was largely benevolent, and women made up a large number of slave owners. To dodge the Virginia law requiring newly emancipated slaves to leave the state, it was common for free African Americans to "own" relatives and friends. Many of these situations ended with deeds of manumission being granted as soon as feasible. Others retained legal ownership, but most slaves held under such circumstances led a virtually free existence.[70] In 1830, Petersburg counted fifty free black slave owners, most of whom owned only one or two slaves.[71] Between 1832 and 1860, African American slave owners granted one-fifth of the manumissions in Petersburg. Examples from that period bear witness to the benevolent nature of black slaveholding in the early antebellum period. In an 1835 deed of manumission, Joe Jackson freed his son Robin Jackson because of his "natural love and affection" for his offspring. Carpenter Thomas Walden freed his wife, Nancy Mumford, and their two children Elizabeth and Catherine, in 1832. He had purchased his wife and eldest daughter five years before, and the second child was born later. Benevolent manumissions were sometimes made without the bonds of actual kinship. In 1838 Daniel Jackson, a minister in the African Baptist Church, freed Isham Cox five years after purchasing him from tobacco warehouse owner Robert Bolling.[72]

As slavery became more profitable in the 1840s and 1850s, the number of slaves owned by African Americans in the South fell. In one estimate, the num-

69. Curry, *The Free Black in Urban America*, 46–47; and Phillips, *Freedom's Port*, 94–95.

70. John Hope Franklin, *The Free Negro in North Carolina, 1790–1860* (1943, reprint; New York: W. W. Norton, 1971), 159–161.

71. Carter G. Woodson, *Free Negro Owners of Slaves in the United States in 1830* (New York: Negro Universities Press, 1924), 34–35.

72. Jackson, "Manumission in Certain Virginia Cities," 296–297.

bers of black slave owners may have decreased by as much as three-fourths.[73] The motives of some African American slaveholders shifted as well. Although some blacks continued to hold title to friends and relatives who enjoyed a free existence, others bought or leased slaves for their labor. The desire to accumulate property—real, personal, and slaves—was not uncommon among blacks in antebellum cities. Ira Berlin even suggests that relatively well-to-do free African Americans were as disdainful of slaves and poor free blacks as were their white counterparts. He suggests that these free blacks "became imbued with the very racial attitudes that prevented them from fully enjoying the benefits of their elevated class position" through their attempts to identify with the white upper class.[74] These attitudes included owning slaves for profit. Although free blacks owned less property and slaves than did their white counterparts, it was not always because they had a different value system, but sometimes because their economic opportunities were more limited. As Leonard P. Curry demonstrates, in those urban areas where free blacks found favorable patterns of employment, they acquired relatively large amounts of property, including slaves held for profit.[75] A number of the skilled free black workers in Petersburg fit this pattern of slave and property ownership.

At least twenty-two skilled African Americans in Petersburg, about 8 percent, owned or leased slaves in 1830. Blacksmiths, artisans in building trades, and those involved in the carrying trade were most likely to employ slave labor in their business. One of the earliest to do so commercially was blacksmith John Booker. Trained as a blacksmith while himself enslaved, he managed to save enough money to purchase his freedom in 1808 for $700.[76] The fact that Booker held or leased three to five slaves in the 1820s and four in 1830 is curious, considering his own experience with bondage. But perhaps in Petersburg slave owning or leasing seemed the most viable option for Booker's labor needs. In the early nineteenth century the iron-welding component of a blacksmith's trade required the labor of an assistant, called a striker. It was in this capacity that a blacksmith's slaves operated, and explains the high incidence of slave owning of that trade. In 1860, about one-fifth of all African American blacksmiths in Virginia owned or leased slaves. That Booker had four slaves was

73. Curry, *The Free Black in Urban America*, 46–47.
74. Berlin, *Slaves Without Masters*, 275–276.
75. Curry, *The Free Black in Urban America*, 47–48.
76. Jackson, "Manumission in Certain Virginia Cities," 293.

unusual; most blacksmiths owned only one slave and rarely more than three.[77]

Other Petersburg blacksmiths used slaves in their business. Armistead Wilson, who spent most of his working life as a slave, owned or employed a slave assistant after gaining his freedom in 1856. Emancipated after paying his owner John F. May the sum of $800, Wilson experienced considerable financial success. In 1860 he also owned real property worth $1,600.[78] Ned Stokes, who was emancipated sometime before May 1838, also fit the pattern of blacksmiths. He held or leased one slave for at least five years. Property records indicate that he paid tax on a male slave in 1838 and in 1843 he still held one slave. Stokes's blacksmith business must have been successful because he was able to own real property worth more than $1,000.[79] Finally, although his situation is more sketchy, blacksmith Shadrack Joiner owned or leased slaves for his business. Records indicate that he paid tax on three adult male slaves in 1847.[80]

Artisans in the building and carrying trades found uses for slave labor in their businesses as well. Carpenters and contractors, including Thomas Scott and Christopher Stevens, reportedly leased slaves as a part of their workforce. The addition of slave carpenters or laborers contributed to a complex mixture of free and slave workers on projects such as that Stevens secured for construction of the interior of the new Gillfield Baptist Church. This large project must have employed Stevens's leased slaves as well as his regular free workers and his two apprentices. Tax records suggest that boatmen John McCreay and John Sampson and cartmen Arthur Parham and Addison Crawford used slaves commercially. Coopers Shadrack Brander and M. Joiner may also have owned or leased slaves for their labor.[81]

Financially successful African American artisans were those most likely to own or lease slaves for their labor, but prosperous blacks were also liable to be in an economic position to practice benevolent slave owning and to grant deeds

77. Woodson, *Free Negro Owners of Slaves*, 35; and Jackson, *Free Negro Labor*, 206–207, 217–218.

78. Hustings Court Minute Book 1853–1856, 518; Jackson, *Free Negro Labor*, 157, 197, 218; and Bureau of the Census, Population Schedules, Petersburg, Va., 1860.

79. Personal Property Tax Lists 1838, 1843; Hustings Court Minute Book 1838–1840, 44; and "Negro Labor and Property-Holding In Petersburg Before Emancipation," *Progress-Index*, 8 November 1931.

80. Personal Property Tax Lists, 1847.

81. Jackson, *Free Negro Labor*, 225–226; Jackson, "Manumission in Certain Virginia Cities," 293; and Personal Property Tax Lists, 1836, 1838, and 1847.

of manumission. A case in point is that of boatman John Updike, who came to Petersburg from Rhode Island sometime around 1824. Somehow Updike managed to skirt the law forbidding out-of-state blacks from settling in Virginia, and began the successful operation of a small fleet of boats between 1824 and 1862. His operations used both free laborers and slaves, whom he leased on an annual basis.[82] But Updike also bought at least two slaves with the intent to free them. In 1831, he purchased a slave named Rheuben Rhenalds from black cooper Shadrack Brander, then issued a deed of emancipation to Rhenalds on 18 November of the same year. In the mid-1850s, Updike performed a similar act of humanity for a woman named Jane Green, whom he purchased from a white owner, then manumitted through a deed issued 18 January 1855.[83] Updike could well afford to be generous. His carrying business included two sloops and a fifty-two-ton schooner named the *William & Mary*, and he owned more than $1,000 worth of property including his home on East Alley near the Pocahontas bridge.[84] Other successful African American artisans held nominal ownership of family members or friends, and eventually granted them freedom. In 1850, whitewasher Jesse Green purchased his wife and four children for $665, then manumitted them by deed a month later. In 1855, barber Thomas Sturdivant manumitted Robert and Thomas Sturdivant, who were most likely his sons. The following year bricklayer Henry Mason granted a deed of emancipation to his wife Susan.[85]

Black slaveholding was a complex dimension of life in a slave economy. Some owned slaves to guarantee that friends or relatives could remain in the Commonwealth. However, evidence indicates that some free African American artisans shared the motives of their white counterparts. In the greatest paradox of freedom, these African Americans, some once enslaved themselves, chose to own the labor of others. Perhaps some black slaveholders believed that membership in the master class would foster relations across the color line with

82. James W. Smith, "Role of Blacks in the Petersburg Carrying Trade," 16; and Jackson, *Free Negro Labor*, 212n.

83. Hustings Court Minute Book 1827–1832, n.p. (17 November 1831); Hustings Court Minute Book 1853–1856, 193; and Jackson, *Free Negro Labor*, 193.

84. Jackson, *Free Negro Labor*, 240; "Business Enterprise Among Free Negroes in the Early History of Petersburg," *Progress-Index*, 9 January 1939; and W. Eugene Ferslew, comp., *Second Annual Directory for the City of Petersburg* (Petersburg, Va.: George E. Ford, 1860), 128.

85. Jackson, *Free Negro Labor*, 196; Hustings Court Minute Book 1853–1856, 361, 477.

the white artisans they encountered in their daily work routines.

The work environment in antebellum Petersburg necessarily placed whites and blacks together in many workshops. It was not unusual for white and black journeymen to work alongside each other and in the company of enslaved artisans. These men, who spent most of their waking lives at work, developed complex webs of association and conflict. At times competition from African American artisans led to hostility and white attempts to banish them from the town. But, as James Sidbury found in Richmond, the proximity of white and black workers may also have helped to break down some racial barriers.[86] As Petersburg became more industrialized and a few upwardly mobile white master mechanics responded to the pull of new markets by expanding their shops into merchant firms, advancement opportunities withered for many free black and middling white artisans. In some cases these men must have discovered common grievances.

It is also likely that whites and blacks did more than work together. In Richmond, white and black workers patronized the same grocery stores, drank liquor in the same grog shops, and formed common alliances as they gathered at the end of the workday to drink, gamble, and relax.[87] Among the working people of Petersburg similar alliances were forged across the color line. In 1856, white carpenter Monroe Birchett, whom we met in the previous chapter, was again arrested and required to post bond for allowing a slave named Edmund to stay with his family in their home on Donough's alley. Complaints by witnesses suggest an untoward relationship existed between the slave Edmund and Birchett's seventeen-year-old daughter. A newspaper account of the incident claimed that "evidence of gross impropriety" abounded and condemned "the intercourse between slaves and the white people who harbored them."[88] Birchett's position in life was certainly made more difficult when the mayor ordered him to "give security for good behavior in the sum of $100" and sent his wife, Martha Childs, to the poorhouse. Whatever the true circumstances of the case, it is possible that this poor white carpenter found more in common

86. Sidbury, *Ploughshares into Swords*, 201–204.
87. Ibid., 208–209.
88. "The Slave Edmund and the Monroe Birchett Family," *Daily Southside Democrat*, 25 September 1856.

with a slave than he did with the white elite who controlled the economy and the courts in Petersburg.[89]

Most evidence of association between blacks and whites is found in records of criminal arrests and sanctions placed on those who crossed legal and social boundaries dividing the races. Since interaction between whites and blacks outside work was socially and legally discouraged, the public record does not reflect positive examples of those relationships. Records exist only for those negative incidents that were reported (and for those who got caught), but it is likely that biracial cooperation was not uncommon in Petersburg. That such racial mixing was believed to be habitual can be seen in a newspaper report of a burglary at a local jeweler's store. Although a white youth perpetrated the crime, the newspaper editor claimed that "evil associations" with free blacks were to blame. He warned parents that "we daily meet white boys hand in glove in company with free negroes of the lowest grade."[90] In fact, it was rather common for whites, free blacks, and slaves to be involved together in criminal activity. White artisan Nelson Coleman and a slave named John were arrested for stealing four bridles and a saddle from the shop of William French. Although whites and blacks were often arrested together, they faced very different punishments. In the case of Coleman and the slave John, the white man was bound to superior court for trial, but the slave was immediately sentenced to ten lashes and to be burnt in the hand.[91]

Concern about associations between poor blacks and whites usually led to legal sanction. In 1835, whites William Mowberry and Isaac Albright were arrested for being in the company of slaves and for creating "a suspicion that they will do some injury to the good citizens of this town." When the impecunious men could not secure a $500 bond to ensure their good behavior, they were remanded to the town jail.[92] Relationships between the sexes also occurred across the color line. In 1856, black barber Richard Newsome and a slave named Washington were found in Newsome's Short Street shop in the company of two white women, possibly prostitutes. The scandal was reported fully in the *Daily*

89. Hustings Court Minute Book 1848–1851, 17–18, 27–28; and Bureau of the Census, Population Schedules, Petersburg, Va., 1860.

90. "Mayor's Court," *Daily Southside Democrat*, 8 July 1857.

91. Hustings Court Minute Book 1820–1823, 270.

92. Hustings Court Minute Book 1832–1835, 373.

Southside Democrat, revealing that the captain of the night watch found the couples "harmonizing in the full spirit of Liberty, Equality, and Fraternity!" The meetings between Newsome, Washington, and the two women had been going on for some time; witnesses confirmed that the women were seen entering the barber shop after hours on previous occasions. The police arrested all four. The women, unable to post $150 bond each, were jailed. Barber Newsome received a punishment of twenty-five lashes, and the slave Washington endured ten.[93]

The evidence gleaned from court and arrest records suggests that attempts to divide the Petersburg working class along racial lines were not completely successful. As in other urban areas of the Upper South, the working class faced intense economic struggle, whether white or black. In this climate it was not uncommon for free blacks, the enslaved, and poor whites to find common interests and enjoy the same pastimes.[94] However, as late antebellum economic conditions made gaining a competence even more difficult, lines between the races were more firmly drawn. Despite the common experiences of black and white workers in Petersburg, conflict, not cooperation, was the more frequent result, especially in the last two decades of the antebellum era.

Friction between white and black workers tended to coincide with times of economic difficulty and never resulted in the racial confrontations and riots that occurred in northern cities. Most of the contention was one-sided because African American artisans had few legal rights and faced both legal and social proscriptions on their behavior at work and beyond. Although blacks and whites generally worked together without dissension, black artisans became the scapegoats of white workers when times of economic distress reached Petersburg. In 1849 and again in 1857, white artisans organized to protest competition from black mechanics. Watching their opportunities for independence diminish led many white journeymen to lash out at skilled black workers in early 1849. The journeymen met and moved to form a society to protect their own interests in an ever-changing economy. Fearful that their occupations were being degraded, they demanded to be considered "a distinct society, and

93. "Black and White Amalgamation Case," *Daily Southside Democrat*, 9 August 1856.

94. Sidbury, *Ploughshares into Swords*, 231–232; and Midori Takagi, *"Rearing Wolves to Our Own Destruction": Slavery in Richmond, Virginia, 1782–1865* (Charlottesville: University Press of Virginia, 1999), 66–67.

not associates of the Negro." White artisans offered three resolutions to clarify their position on the use of free blacks and slaves in skilled occupations. First, they considered teaching trades to blacks as "prejudicial to the interests, and injurious to the morals of the laboring White man." Next, those journeymen who signed the resolutions insisted that they would "not work for any employer who shall take a Negro in his employ, for the purpose of teaching said Negro any branch of the mechanic arts." Finally, the journeymen tempered their opposition to blacks in the workshop by resolving that "each member is at liberty to engage with any employer using his own slave at the business."[95]

The 1849 journeymen's organization was a short-lived attempt to curb black competition, quickly forgotten in the prosperity of the early 1850s. When serious economic trouble reached Petersburg during the Panic of 1857, journeymen again moved to organize, and in the company of a significant number of master mechanics, they formed the Petersburg Mechanic Association (PMA). Through this fraternal organization they lashed out at African American artisans. Little is known about the response of black artisans to this campaign to remove them from the skilled workforce. During the depression that followed the Panic, black workers, skilled and unskilled, were hit especially hard.

To protect themselves against the changes and fluctuations of an advancing market economy, urban Americans often joined fraternal or benevolent societies. Fraternal organizations, including the Freemasons and Odd Fellows, were social resources for their members and have historically united men from a wide spectrum of social, economic, and even religious positions. Some, especially the Masons, had dual goals of celebrating the importance of manual labor and recognizing the precarious position of craft workers in the new economy through the guarantee of mutual aid. Most fraternal and benevolent groups provided members with a small measure of relief if injured or disabled, similar payment to widows and children of deceased members, and often a burial benefit. But if one foundation of the fraternal organization is its ability to unite many from diverse backgrounds, another important and empowering principle of many such groups is that of exclusion.[96] In the United States, race

95. "Meeting of Mechanics," *Republican*, 24 January 1849.

96. Mary Ann Clawson, *Constructing Brotherhood: Class, Gender, and Fraternalism* (Princeton, N.J.: Princeton University Press, 1989), 11–14.

is the primary basis for exclusion from many white-dominated fraternal and benevolent orders or lodges. In Petersburg, prominent master artisans formed the PBMA to protect their business interests, provide fraternity, and support the mechanic arts for white workers. In the 1850s, the middling white artisans formed the PMA, on similar principles, but also with the express purpose of ending competition from African American mechanics.

Fraternal organizations that excluded African Americans became one more bastion of prejudice in a world where nonwhites found themselves regarded as secondary citizens or worse. In many communities, however, African Americans formed their own fraternal and benevolent organizations that became an important source of strength for the black community. These fraternal and mutual aid societies provided urban blacks with benefits similar to those of white organizations. With its large free black population, Baltimore could count a significant number of benevolent groups. Some were black-sponsored mutual aid societies that guaranteed members support during times of illness and death in exchange for regular payment of dues. Others aimed to promote the intellectual, cultural, and moral development of black Baltimoreans. These included mental improvement societies, lyceums, and bible study groups. Black chapters of the Odd Fellows and the Prince Hall Masons, a black Masonic organization begun in the Revolutionary era, were also prominent in antebellum Baltimore.[97]

The black community of Petersburg likewise found fraternity and benevolent organization to be a source of relief in times of financial stress. As in other southern black communities, one source of aid for needy artisans and their families was the church. All three of the major black churches in Petersburg offered small amounts of financial assistance to members. Gillfield Baptist Church, being the wealthiest black institution in Petersburg, was a significant resource for free African American workers in need of food or medicine. About 1815 successful black artisans and businessmen formed the Beneficial Society of Free Men of Color of the City of Petersburg and State of Virginia. Lasting until the Civil War, this organization recognized the precarious position of free African Americans in the South and aimed to promote temperance and moral behavior and to offer financial relief to members.[98] The Beneficial Soci-

97. Phillips, *Freedom's Port*, 170–175; and Clawson, *Constructing Brotherhood*, 132–133.
98. Jackson, *Free Negro Labor*, 162–163; and Constitution, Rules and Regulations of the

ety aimed to protect the interests of African Americans in the community in a manner similar to the white fraternal organizations in Petersburg, including the PBMA and the PMA.

Those subscribing to the Beneficial Society recognized that the prosperity of free African Americans in Petersburg rested with the "infusion of virtuous qualities," and strove for "the suppression of vice and immorality among our own class of people, and for the inculcation of every honest and correct principle that can render many good, respectable and happy." The members hoped for alleviation of racial prejudice, that "consumate [sic] ignorance that has too long prevaded [sic] the lives of many of us," and "concluded to associate together for the ostensible purpose of administering support to each other, when in sickness or necessity."[99] The Beneficial Society was as much an organization of elite free blacks as the PBMA was of prominent white businessmen. Although there is no extant list of members, the initiation fee of $10 suggests that the roster included the more prominent members of Petersburg's African American community. It is likely that prominent artisans and contractors, such as Henry Mason, Christopher Stevens, and Shadrack Brander, belonged to this group. Successful barbers, such as Henry Elebeck and John K. Shore, may also have held membership.

The Beneficial Society operated as a male-only fraternal group. As such it functioned much like other antebellum organizations. It met once a month, on the first Monday, and fined members for missing a meeting. Immoral and intemperate behavior was also subject to sanction. Any member could be fined for attending a meeting while intoxicated, and for swearing, drinking, or smoking. Members arrested and found guilty of a felony, cock-fighting, gambling, or other "disgraceful behavior" faced expulsion. To be considered for membership, one had to be nominated by a current member and receive the support of two-thirds of the membership. Then there was the matter of paying a $10 initiation fee and twenty-five-cent monthly dues.[100] Membership in the organization offered African Americans the opportunity to associate with other artisans and businessmen and to form bonds of contact that could help to advance their

Beneficial Society of Free Men of Color, Petersburg, Va. (as revised 2 August 1852), Colson/ Hill Papers, Virginia State University, Petersburg, Va.

99. Constitution, Beneficial Society, Colson/Hill Papers.

100. Ibid.

business opportunities and provided moral support for these black men who daily faced the racial prejudice and proscription of the dominant white community.

The benefits of membership went beyond the fraternal association at monthly meetings. Each member was entitled to a square in the cemetery the Society owned and maintained. This was an especially important benefit, because most Petersburg cemeteries excluded African Americans. The Beneficial Society made an initial purchase of land for a burial ground in 1818, and in 1840, bought additional property for the same purpose.[101] The burial benefit extended to the members' parents, if free, their unmarried children, and any brothers under age twenty-one. If a member fell ill, or was disabled, he was entitled to $1.50 per week, providing that the Society's treasury held at least $50. When a member died, his family received a one-time payment of $15, and a widow also was entitled to $1 per week for as "long as she remain[ed] a prudent widow." Funerals were also a serious matter. For the Beneficial Society, as for many fraternal groups, the funeral of a fellow member was an important ritual that signified the kin-like relations that bound members together as "brothers."[102] Members of the Beneficial Society who failed to turn out for the funeral of a fellow member faced a $1 fine.[103]

African American members of the Beneficial Society represented the elite of Petersburg's free black community. The ability of free African American artisans and businessmen to acquire property and to succeed in the antebellum South was affected by many of the same factors facing their white counterparts. The modernization of the Petersburg economy expanded workshops and created a social and economic divide among skilled free blacks, but did not materialize in the creation of a "brown elite" as occurred in some Lower South cities.[104] Those free blacks who advanced under the new conditions viewed themselves as a distinct group and expressed aspirations and concerns that closely mirrored those of the white members of the PBMA. Despite the considerable success of many, racial prejudice was an ever-present factor in the lives of free African Americans. The opportunities available in some occupations

101. Jackson, *Free Negro Labor*, 162–163.
102. Clawson, *Constructing Brotherhood*, 42–43.
103. Constitution, Beneficial Society, Colson/Hill Papers.
104. Powers, *Black Charlestonians*, 47–48; Johnson, *Black Savannah*, 111–112.

allowed them to excel in personal service and carrying trades. But many blacks competed with whites in building and forging trades. For most of the antebellum era, black and white artisans worked side by side in the same workshops and on the same projects without significant conflict. In fact, the presence of high numbers of African American artisans, slave and free, in southern cities reduced the conflict between the races at work. But relations were not always smooth. In times of economic distress, and especially during the Panic of 1857, white artisans lashed out at skilled blacks, blaming them for their reduced economic position.

In times of need, black workers could look to their community for some small measures of assistance. Some even formed a benevolent society modeled after similar organizations in other cities.[105] As Bernard E. Powers Jr. and Whittington B. Johnson have shown for Charleston and Savannah, free African Americans formed institutions that fostered the perpetuation of the black community.[106] In Petersburg, the Beneficial Society and churches, such as Gillfield Baptist, were symbols of the determination of free blacks to maintain a viable existence within a city dominated by powerful whites. The lives of Petersburg's free blacks were also significantly enhanced by the size of their community, which was the largest among Virginia cities. Because the free blacks arrived early in the nineteenth century, they were able to gain a significant stronghold in unskilled occupations. Because the racial climate in Petersburg was not as restrictive as in some northern cities, African Americans also made significant inroads in the skilled trades.

The significance of free blacks in the economy and community of Petersburg requires that their story be told. The industrial growth of Petersburg before the Civil War made it possible for black artisans, such as barber John K. Shore, and carpenter Christopher Stevens, to experience freedom and to prosper in ways not possible for their northern counterparts. Yet in the market economy and industrial city of Petersburg, freedom was not enough to ensure success. Unlike Shore and Stevens, boatman John Brander found little success following the freedom James Dunlop granted him in 1822. Near the end of the antebellum era, Brander owned no property nor any taxable goods or assets. In fact, in the

---

105. Curry, *The Free Black in Urban America,* 196–200.
106. See Powers, *Black Charlestonians;* and Johnson, *Black Savannah.*

1840s, the Overseers of the Poor bound out his teenage daughter as an indentured apprentice because Brander could no longer afford to support her.[107] The gap between successful blacks such as Shore and Stevens and those who failed such as Brander point to the paradox of freedom in the industrializing Upper South.

107. Petersburg City Personal Property Tax, 1838, 1843; Hustings Court Minute Book 1841–1842, 185; and Bureau of the Census, Population Schedules, Petersburg, Va., 1850.

5

Tobacco and Iron

THE FOUNDATIONS OF INDUSTRIAL SLAVERY

Beginning in 1852, Tom Bragg worked for Petersburg brick layer and contractor Daniel Lyon. Bragg was likely a suitable skilled worker, for Lyon continued to employ his services through 1858. Unfortunately, Bragg did not receive wages as a reward for his hard work because he was a slave owned by local tobacconist Charles F. Osborne. Lyon leased Bragg, paying an annual hire fee that increased from $87.50 in 1852 to $130 by 1858.[1] Enslaved men and women, including Tom Bragg, formed an important component of the working class in Petersburg. Tobacco factories and the growing iron foundries and railroad car shops employed large numbers of Petersburg's enslaved workers, but as in other southern cities, slaves worked in many industrial capacities, ranging from highly skilled craft workers to basic manual laborers. This chapter considers the implications of the growing industrial economy and its need for slave labor. As demand for labor grew, the rising costs of purchasing or leasing enslaved workers had important ramifications for industrialists and independent artisans of both races. However, unlike the case in most southern cities, the large free black population of Petersburg offered an alternative source of labor for industrial employers. When other southern cities turned increasingly toward immigrant workers, or paid the increasing cost of enslaved labor, Petersburg industrialists and artisans hired free blacks, who dominated the city's unskilled labor pool. Nevertheless, industrial slaves made an important contribution to Petersburg's antebellum industrial growth and prosperity, and slavery was intimately tied to the lives and livelihoods of the city's skilled artisans.

Across the South, approximately 5 percent of slaves worked in industrial occupations. They labored in tobacco factories, iron foundries, and coal mines, and worked as blacksmiths, carpenters, and joiners. Rural areas and plantations, as the locus for much of southern industry, also employed the majority of

1. Auction Sales Record Book, 1847–1854 and 1854–1867, Branch & Company Records, 1837–1976, Virginia Historical Society, Richmond, Va. (hereafter ViHi).

industrial slave labor. Only about 15 to 20 percent of urban slaves toiled in industry; in cities employment in domestic service was more common. Most industrial slaves were men, but some businesses and factories employed the labor of enslaved women and children.[2] Enslaved men, women, and children made up nearly one-third of the population in Petersburg. In 1850 the slave population was 4,729 and split nearly evenly along gender lines.[3] It is impossible to accurately calculate the number of slaves employed in Petersburg's industrial operations and artisans' shops, but it is clear that they worked in all segments of the economy and were especially critical to tobacco manufacture and iron founding.

Tobacco manufacturing relied heavily on enslaved labor, with slaves owned and slaves hired making up most of the factories' workforces. Late in the antebellum period, many tobacconists also employed a significant number of free African Americans. In 1850, across Virginia as a whole, tobacco factories hired about 40 percent of their slave workers under an annual contract, with the figure jumping to nearly 50 percent by 1860. In some areas, such as Richmond, tobacconists relied almost exclusively on enslaved labor. Examination of census manuscripts suggests that about one-third of Richmond's adult male slaves worked in tobacco factories or iron foundries. The rising cost of slave labor made hiring more popular among industrialists. In 1860, 87 percent of the slaves working for manufacturers in the capital city's first ward belonged to other slave owners, mostly from plantations in the surrounding region.[4]

In 1835, 6 tobacco factories operated in Petersburg with predominantly slave labor. Over the next two and a half decades, the pace of expansion in tobacco manufacture led to a concomitant increase in the number of slaves employed. By 1850, 13 tobacco factories owned 467 slaves, amounting to almost one-tenth of the slave population of Petersburg. Each of the firms or individuals held at

2. Robert S. Starobin, *Industrial Slavery in the Old South* (London: Oxford University Press, 1970), 9–12.

3. Bureau of the Census, *Seventh Census of the United States in 1850* (Washington, D.C.: Robert Armstrong, printer, 1853), 258. The census enumerated 2,376 male and 2,353 female slaves.

4. Claudia Goldin, *Urban Slavery in the American South, 1820–1860: A Quantitative History* (Chicago: University of Chicago Press, 1976), 25–27; Midori Takagi, *"Rearing Wolves to Our Own Destruction": Slavery in Richmond, Virginia, 1782–1865* (Charlottesville: University Press of Virginia, 1999), 24–29; and Ronald L. Lewis, *Coal, Iron, and Slaves: Industrial Slavery in Maryland and Virginia, 1715–1865* (Westport, Conn.: Greenwood, 1979), 4–5.

least a dozen slaves, with Jones and Hudson owning 94. (See table 12.) This pattern continued until the mid-1850s, when rising slave prices led area tobacconists to employ large numbers of free African American men and women. By 1860, the industry dominated the local economy, with 20 establishments employing over 2,500 men and women.[5] Many of the tobacconists belonged to the Petersburg Benevolent Mechanic Association (PBMA), and represented those artisans who were eschewing manual labor for the manager's chair.

Tobacco factories were typically constructed of brick, which reduced the risk of destruction in the all-too-common fires of the antebellum era, and of two to four stories in height. Former slave Henry Box Brown recalled that the Richmond tobacco factory where he worked was similarly constructed. "The building I worked in was about 300 feet in length, and three stories high, and afforded room for 200 people to work in, but only 150 persons were employed, 120 of whom were slaves, and the remainder free colored people."[6]

Petersburg tobacco factory construction offered lucrative contracts to city artisans, including bricklayer and PBMA member Daniel Lyon, and the carpentry and contracting firm of Marks and Murphy. The factory these men built in 1859 for the firm of Biddle and McIlwaine was typical of Petersburg factories. Measuring 45 by 125 feet, the three-story structure consisted of a wood frame faced with brick. Tobacconist John A. Hair's factory of nearly identical dimensions went under construction just a few months later in August 1859.[7] The square construction fit into the existing space available on the city's remaining urban building lots, where these plain buildings with utilitarian architectural style could squeeze between existing businesses. Because the factories located operations on busy city streets, loading and unloading activities took place in the alley behind the building. The most functional factories had flat roofs that doubled as drying space for newly cured and flavored tobacco plugs and twists. A rare exception to the plainness of style was the brownstone stucco factory

5. Joseph Martin, *A New and Comprehensive Gazetteer of Virginia and the District of Columbia* (Charlottesville: Joseph Martin, 1836), 162; Bureau of the Census, 1860 Census, Schedule 5, Products of Industry during the Year Ending June 1, 1860, microfilm; and Stephen E. Bradley, comp., *The 1850 Federal Census Dinwiddie County, Virginia and the City of Petersburg* (Keysville, Va.: Author, 1991), 129–142.

6. Henry Box Brown, *Narrative of Henry Box Brown* (Boston: Brown & Stearns, 1849), 41.

7. "Extensive New Tobacco Manufactory," *Daily Express*, 18 March 1859; and "New Tobacco Manufactory," ibid., 27 August 1859.

constructed in 1857 for PBMA member Robert Leslie. Although square and functional like the other factories in the city, Leslie's new Washington Street building boasted arched windows in a style that blended with the First Baptist Church, which stood adjacent to the factory.[8]

The interior of tobacco factories was designed so that the most hands could be supervised by a minimum number of overseers, and most work took place in large, open rooms. Overseers sat in elevated chairs to better observe the workers. The temperament and character of the overseer dictated factory operations and could sometimes create an unpleasant work environment. In the late antebellum era, most tobacconists relied on overseers to maintain both order and the expected level of production and quality control.[9] Henry Box Brown remembered his overseer as "a very wicked brother, whose soul I commend to Almighty God, hoping that his sovereign grace may find its way, if it is a possible thing, to his sin-hardened soul."[10] Brown reported that the overseer forced them to work fourteen hours in summer and sixteen hours in winter. H. C. Bruce recalled a different experience of his time spent as a tobacco factory slave. Bruce was hired out to various employers during his twenty-nine years as a slave, and had a variety of experiences upon which to draw. He remembered his employment as a tobacco factory worker in Brunswick, Virginia, as a pleasant time. "I enjoyed myself very much. We had good wholesome food and plenty of it, and when the factory closed at sunset we were free to go where we pleased until sunrise the next day."[11] Indeed, although the workday was long, tobacco factories often offered cash payments for overtime work and extra production and allowed slaves to make their own boarding arrangements.[12]

Despite the privileges some tobacco factory slaves enjoyed, all worked hard.

8. Joseph Clarke Robert, *The Tobacco Kingdom: Plantation, Market, and Factory in Virginia and North Carolina, 1800–1860* (1938; reprint, Gloucester, Mass.: Peter Smith, 1965), 209; Edward A. Wyatt, "Rise of Industry in Ante-Bellum Petersburg," *William and Mary Quarterly* 17 (2nd ser. January 1937): 13; and W. Eugene Ferslew, comp., *Second Annual Directory for the City of Petersburg* (Petersburg: George E. Ford, 1860), 159.

9. Takagi, "Rearing Wolves," 89.

10. Brown, *Narrative*, 41.

11. H. C. Bruce, *The New Man: Twenty-Nine Years a Slave, Twenty-Nine Years a Free Man* (York, Pa.: F. Amstadt & Sons, 1895), 71.

12. Richard C. Wade, *Slavery in the Cities: The South 1820–1860* (London: Oxford University Press, 1964), 34–35.

Stemming the tobacco was the first task, and was usually performed by women or children. Laborers moistened the leaves, then the stemmers removed the leaves from their center rib stems. The best leaves were saved for wrapping the finished plugs, with the remainder gathered to dry in bunches or "hands." The most strenuous activity took place in the twisting room, which was typically lined with rows of benches and often described as resembling a schoolroom. Here factory operatives sat as they rolled and twisted the prepared tobacco leaves into long rolls, which were then cut and trimmed to length. Workers created the plugs by prizing the twisted tobacco in a hand-operated screw and lever press. Pressing was the most strenuous activity in the tobacco factory and an almost exclusively male occupation. In the late antebellum era, some factories began to use a hydraulic-powered press, invented and patented by Petersburg tobacconist William Cameron. Pressing remained a manual operation in most factories, however. By 1860 only thirteen factories in Virginia reported the use of hydraulics.[13] After pressing, the plugs were sent for finishing.

Crucial to the production of plug and twist tobacco, the main product of Petersburg factories, were a sweat house and a kitchen. In the sweat house and kitchen workers mixed flavoring extracts over open fires so a trademark taste could be "sweated" into the finished tobacco plugs after removal from the press. Demand from tobacco factories kept local druggists and apothecaries busy mixing the flavoring oils and extracts. Popular seasonings included licorice, rum, sweet oil, bergamot, cloves, mace, and nutmeg.[14] The job of tending the fire in the sweat house often fell to young boys. Although not a difficult task, keeping the fire burning was important to the flavoring process. On occasion a lack of direct supervision led enslaved workers into trouble. When a young slave named Peter strayed from his appointed duties in maintaining the sweat house fire to play a game of marbles, a Lexington factory owner beat him severely and tried to tie him to a tobacco press. Peter escaped and hid within the factory, only to be discovered and suffer a second beating.[15]

Leaving the sweat house fire untended could have dire consequences beyond a beating. In the sweat house, the constant heat from an open fire infused

13. Robert, *Tobacco Kingdom*, 210–212.

14. Ibid., 209–215; and Suzanne Lebsock, *The Free Women of Petersburg: Status and Culture in a Southern Town, 1784–1860* (New York: W. W. Norton, 1984), 182–183.

15. Kate E. R. Pickard, *The Kidnapped and the Ransomed* (1856; reprint, n.p.: Negro Publication Society of America, 1941), 37–40.

oils and flavor into the tobacco plugs, making fires a common occurrence in antebellum factories. When Thomas N. Lee's factory caught fire in late December 1846, the destruction consumed the interior of the establishment, including a small amount of raw and finished tobacco. Lee's $7,000 insurance coverage failed to cover the total amount of the loss, and likely put many out of work, at least temporarily.[16] Brick construction could prevent a building's collapse, but did not protect the important factory interior.

Enslaved workers in Petersburg tobacco factories worked long days in less than ideal conditions. The humid summer months made conditions almost unbearable in factory buildings designed and built to make maximum use of small urban spaces. Employers gave little forethought to ventilation and the undesirable conditions within the factory. But because they lived apart from the factory in most cases, tobacco factory workers could establish a life of their own in the broader urban community of antebellum Petersburg. Their counterparts in area iron foundries found a slightly different experience.

Virginia's iron forging and founding industry made use of slave labor beginning in the early eighteenth century. Many colonial- and early national-era iron furnaces operated in rural areas, with the Shenandoah Valley emerging as the prime region of iron production before 1840.[17] In the late antebellum era, Richmond eclipsed the Valley to become the state's leading iron producer. Local foundries and forges in the capital city satisfied demand for finished iron products, including storefronts, steam machines, metal tools, and even railroad cars and engines. Tredegar Iron Works, the largest and most famous of Richmond's iron producers, included a rolling mill with nine puddling furnaces producing pig iron that was then rolled into bar iron. Nearby stood the Armory Works, only slightly smaller in size and production. These mills employed enslaved workers in general labor and semiskilled occupations beginning in the late 1830s, especially in the rolling mill and blacksmith shops. The Armory Works stopped employing slaves after 1858, but Tredegar continued to rely on them. In 1860, Tredegar counted 80 slaves among its workforce of approximately 780.

16. "Fire," *Republican*, 1 January 1847.

17. Lewis, *Coal, Iron, and Slaves*, 20–23, 30–31; and Kathleen Bruce, *Virginia Iron Manufacture in the Slave Era* (1930; reprint, New York: Augustus M. Kelley, 1968), 231. For an important study of rural iron making, see Charles B. Dew, *Bond of Iron: Master and Slave at Buffalo Forge* (New York: W. W. Norton, 1994).

The tight labor market of the Civil War led the iron works to increase its slave labor pool to 135 by 1862.[18]

Although always operating on a smaller scale than Richmond, in the 1840s and 1850s iron founding formed an important segment of Petersburg's economy as well. The city did not have rolling mills, but concentrated on forging iron tools, implements, and machines to meet local demand. Manufacturers imported raw iron from Richmond and mills in the surrounding countryside to forge tools and machines. The manufacture of tobacco was a race-typed industry, with only a few exceptions the exclusive domain of enslaved and free African Americans, but iron forging required skilled metal workers. Petersburg iron forging began in small blacksmiths' and machine shops and expanded relative to the region's demand for tools, implements, and machines. White artisans governed most metal work, although it was not unusual for African Americans or the enslaved to practice the trade.[19] Robert E. Redwood's 1834 advertisement was typical of an enterprising antebellum blacksmith of either race, noting that his machine shop manufactured wheat machines, horse powers, fan mills, and a "Virginia Negro Wheat Machine" entirely suitable for "negroes and mules."[20]

Metal working required more of an initial investment than other trades, so only the wealthiest blacksmiths tended to use slaves. Before a metalworking artisan could expand his workforce by purchasing or leasing slaves, he had to raise enough cash or credit to purchase a bellows, anvils, and other expensive tools for handling and shaping iron.[21] Even though Petersburg could count some very ambitious blacksmiths, none ever employed slave labor on the scale of the tobacco factories. The partnership of PBMA members Sceva Thayer and William M. Peterson was an enterprising firm that exemplifies the move to incorporate slave labor in metal working. Located on Old Street near the Appomattox River, their blacksmith shop was founded in the early years of the

18. Charles B. Dew, *Ironmaker to the Confederacy: Joseph R. Anderson and the Tredegar Iron Works* (New Haven: Yale University Press, 1966), 18–19, 27; and Lewis, *Coal, Iron, and Slaves*, 34.

19. Approximately 30 percent of the 123 blacksmiths traced through the 1850 and 1860 manuscript census were free African Americans.

20. Advertisement, *American Constellation*, 14 June 1834, 21 June 1834.

21. T. Stephen Whitman, *The Price of Freedom: Slavery and Manumission in Baltimore and Early National Maryland* (Lexington: University Press of Kentucky, 1997), 21–22.

nineteenth century. By 1820, Thayer paid taxes on seven slaves, including three adult men who likely worked in the blacksmith shops. Thayer owned more than the average number of slaves for a skilled artisan, but his holdings were not large enough to allow him to remove himself from the manual labor of metal crafting, and in all likelihood he worked alongside his enslaved workers. Thayer and Peterson's blacksmith shop did not persist long enough to take advantage of the growing demand for machines that followed the coming of the railroad in the 1830s. Following Thayer's murder in late 1826, the partnership dissolved and the number of slaves in the household dropped to three and included only one adult man.[22]

On the eve of the Civil War, demand led to larger metalworking and forging establishments and to the increased use of slave labor in the trade. In 1860 Petersburg had three substantial iron foundries and a car shop operated by the Southside Railroad. Most of Petersburg's foundries emerged from expanded blacksmiths' shops, such as that of Thayer and Peterson, and tended to employ slaves as part of the workforce. The Petersburg Iron, Bell, and Brass Foundry grew from the blacksmith shop of Pennsylvania native Uriah Wells to employ as many as two hundred in the manufacture of iron goods, including steam locomotives and railroad cars. In 1850, Uriah Wells also owned nine male slaves between the ages of twenty and forty. Although there are no extant employment records for the company, these men no doubt worked in some capacity at the Petersburg Foundry.[23]

The Southern Foundry owned by William H. Tappey and George L. Lumsden also grew from a blacksmith's shop into a producer of machines, tools, and steam engines. Among the seventy hands employed in 1860 were several slaves. Tappey and Lumsden each owned slaves personally and leased slave labor for the foundry. In 1853 on behalf of the foundry, the partnership hired a man named Scott for $85 and Edwin for $100. In the same transaction, Tappey paid $35 to hire a woman or girl named Frances for his household.[24]

Whether in tobacco manufacturing or iron forging, slavery clearly became central to the major industrial segments of Petersburg's economy. Slaves most obviously dominated the race-typed occupations in tobacco factories. After

22. Petersburg, Va., Personal Property Tax List, 1820, 1823, 1838, Library of Virginia, Richmond, Va. (hereafter cited as Vi).

23. Bradley, *1850 Federal Census*, 141.

24. Auction Sales Record Book, 1847–1854, Branch & Company Records, ViHi.

slave labor costs increased in the 1850s, slaves and free African Americans toiled side by side in tobacco factories. Although their presence was less significant in the white-dominated forging trades, enslaved workers were often employed and generally tolerated in semiskilled and unskilled positions in the iron industry. In these and other industrial capacities, slave labor proved to be a flexible labor source that continued to form an important component of the antebellum workforce.

In the urban environment, industrial slavery offered advantages to the employers of slave labor and to the enslaved, who experienced more freedom of movement than their counterparts on surrounding plantations. Petersburg industrial employers and artisans who could afford slaves found that options for obtaining slave labor included direct purchase or entering into a lease agreement, usually on an annual basis, to hire needed workers from owners who had a surplus of enslaved labor. Capital investment in slave labor made up a substantial portion of industrialists' business investments, just as it did for plantation owners. Allen Archer, a prominent bricklayer, employed a number of slaves in his contracting firm, and like many Petersburg artisans, his workforce included a combination of slaves owned and hired. In 1850, he owned a dozen slaves, but in previous years he leased at least one slave from the estate of Thomas Y. Wynn.[25] Rising slave costs in the 1850s increased the operating costs for many industrial employers. When metal worker and tinner George W. Adams died in July 1858, his eight slaves were valued at $4,050, accounting for 72 percent of the worth of his entire estate.[26]

Independent artisan employers often operated with a flexible mix of white, slave, and free black labor, but owners of larger industrial complexes and factories often tried to avoid free labor. Especially true in the manufacture of tobacco, southern factory owners believed that slave labor was more efficient than free labor. Looking to proslavery ideologues such as George Fitzhugh and J. D. B. DeBow for business advice, they pointed to the power of white labor and its increasing militancy in the northern workplace as a model to be avoided.[27] Indeed, white workers in the South's largest cities were already mak-

25. Bradley, *1850 Federal Census*, 133; and Petersburg, Va., Hustings Court Minute Book 1841–1842, 102, Vi.

26. Petersburg, Va., Hustings Court Will Book 4: 482, Vi.

27. See, for example, George Fitzhugh, *Sociology for the South or the Failure of Free Society* (Richmond: A. Morris, 1854), esp. chapter 2.

ing demands and creating work stoppages. Strikes in Baltimore's iron industry in the 1850s demonstrated the dangerous nature of white labor. In that city, at the conclusion of the unrest workers formed a General Mechanics Union to push the political demands of free labor.[28] Fear of labor militancy kept many southern businessmen from switching to white labor, even when the cost of slave labor rose significantly in the 1850s. While Richmond tobacco factory proprietors continued to own nearly 60 percent of their workforce as late as 1860, Petersburg tobacconists took advantage of the city's large free black labor pool. This was expedient because occupations in tobacco manufacturing, such as twister and press operator, were already race stereotyped, so much so that few whites could be persuaded to accept employment in a tobacco factory.[29] By 1860, most tobacconists in the city employed a combination of slaves owned, slaves hired, and free African Americans.

A considerable number of antebellum industrial employers who believed that owning their enslaved workforce was the best option found that as slave prices increased in the decade before the Civil War, hiring slave labor on an annual basis allowed them to cut manufacturing costs. Although slave labor was available for short-term hire, by the month or even the day on occasion, most employers of industrial slaves found that contracting for a year provided the most workforce security. Not only did hiring slaves on an annual basis offer more stability than a monthly contract, it was considerably less expensive than purchasing such workers. Upon entering into an annual hire contract, the industrial employer could calculate the cost of labor for the entire year. Most hire contracts were payable in three to four installments, allowing artisans and industrialists to save capital and spread out the cost.[30]

Slave hiring could be negotiated at any time, but business for annual contracts usually occurred in the two weeks following the Christmas holiday. Although city authorities tried to limit hiring transactions to the central market square, potential hirees congregated at busy intersections in downtown Petersburg causing congestion and sometimes making it nearly impossible for traffic

28. Frank Towers, *The Urban South and the Coming of the Civil War* (Charlottesville: University of Virginia Press, 2004), 87.

29. Takagi, *"Rearing Wolves,"* 82–89; and Robert, *The Tobacco Kingdom*, 199–200.

30. Takagi, *"Rearing Wolves,"* 22–23; and Robert, *Tobacco Kingdom*, 200.

to pass.[31] At other hiring sites, commission merchant firms, including Thomas Branch and Company, acted as brokers for regional plantation owners and other slave masters who sought to lease their surplus labor. The iron foundry owned by William H. Tappey and George L. Lumsden often hired slaves through Thomas Branch and Company, as did cordwainer Thomas Byrne. Bricklayer Daniel Lyon hired his helper Tom Bragg from this large firm too.[32]

Diversification of plantations in surrounding Dinwiddie, Chesterfield, and Prince George counties contributed largely to the population available for annual hire in Petersburg. As tobacco depleted valuable nutrients from the soil, many planters switched to less labor-intensive staple crops such as wheat, corn, and peas. This shift in production across the Upper South meant a slave labor surplus existed in the region, and led many slave owners to lease workers to work in industry. In 1860, nearly 13 percent of Petersburg's slaves were hired from owners living outside the city, with almost three-fourths originating from the three surrounding counties. Others belonged to slaveholders hailing from at least thirty Virginia cities and counties, with a handful living as far away as New Orleans or St. Louis. Someone living in New York owned twelve Petersburg slaves.[33]

The widespread use of a combination of enslaved and free black labor and the prominence of self-hire practices shows that Petersburg was a city in transition from slavery to freedom even before the Civil War. Christopher Phillips demonstrates the long-lasting impact of a gradual changeover from slavery to freedom in pre–Civil War Baltimore. There free African Americans came to outnumber slaves, creating a black community characterized by a fluid mix of free and unfree.[34] Petersburg experienced a similar transition in the late antebellum era. Although not completed before civil war erupted, slaves and free

31. "The Last Meeting," *Daily Southside Democrat*, 19 December 1853.

32. Auction Sales Record Book, 1847–1854 and 1854–1867, Branch & Company Records, ViHi.

33. Bureau of the Census, *Population of the United State in 1860: The Eighth Census* (Washington, D.C.: GPO, 1864), 516–519; and Bureau of the Census, Population Schedules of the Eighth Census of the United States, 1860, roll 1389, Virginia, Slave Schedules, vol. 2. Although not a fixed category of schedule two in 1860, the Petersburg enumerator carefully listed the place of residence for each absentee slave owner.

34. Christopher Phillips, *Freedom's Port: The African American Community of Baltimore, 1790–1860* (Urbana: University of Illinois Press, 1997), 2–4.

blacks enjoyed a coexistence that brought them together after work as well as on the factory floor. Hiring and living arrangements in Petersburg often allowed the enslaved to enjoy some personal autonomy.

The nature and flexibility of industrial slavery in an urban environment meant that some slaves were permitted to live at large and negotiate their own employment. Although illegal in Virginia, the practice of self-hire, as it was known, was not uncommon. Self-hire offered industrial slaves much flexibility and control over their lives. In exchange for providing his or her owner with a regular cash payment, the slave could negotiate the terms of his or her employment contract. A rare enforcement of the 1782 law against self-hire occurred in 1826 when Jack, a tobacco factory slave belonging to James and John Dunlop, was arrested and jailed for "being allowed to go at large and hire himself out." The tobacconists were fined $20 for this transgression.[35] More commonly, local authorities turned a blind eye to the practice of self-hire because slaves were crucial to Petersburg's growing industrial economy.

Self-hire was often coupled with "living out," whereby the employer further cut operating costs by permitting the industrial slave to arrange his or her own room and board. The practice of "living out" was generally not sanctioned, and in many cities, slaves living apart from the workplace or their owner were only allowed to do so with written permission.[36] In Petersburg, however, authorities did little to control the practice. In some cases, slave workers were treated more like wage laborers, given a small amount of money monthly to find their own housing. This arrangement allowed workers to maintain a sense of control over their lives, and to mix with the wider urban working class community, black and white. Enslaved workers rented rooms in boarding houses, lived with relatives, or simply disappeared into the night once the workday was complete. The situation of Sharply, a tobacco worker in Benjamin Tucker's tobacco factory, was not unusual. Sharply's owner, William Blow, lived in Sussex County and hired his slave to the Petersburg tobacco manufacturer through an agent identified as Captain Ledbetter. Sharply lived in a boardinghouse maintained by a free African American woman at the corner of Bollingbrook and Sixth streets.[37]

35. Hustings Court Minute Book 1823–1827, n.p. (16 November 1826).

36. Wade, *Slavery in the Cities*, 62–65; and Rodney D. Green, "Industrial Transition in the Land of Chattel Slavery: Richmond, Virginia, 1820–60," *International Journal of Urban and Regional Research* 8 (1984): 244.

37. "Rebellious," *Daily Express*, 15 September 1858.

So long as Sharply arrived at the factory at the appointed hour and put in a full day's work, the rest of his time was his own. In Petersburg, after work many industrial slaves trudged across the Pocahontas Bridge to the city's large African American neighborhood of the same name, or to Blandford where many blacks congregated for social interaction.

In cities across the Upper South, tobacco factory slaves were most likely to benefit from "living-out" arrangements. Unlike industries dependent on water-power, the manual nature of tobacco manufacture required no special power arrangements, so factories often located on small lots in the center of urban areas where boarding possibilities made the construction of worker dormitories less essential. Slaves in other industries experienced less latitude and control over their living situation. At Richmond's Tredegar Iron Works, for example, enslaved workers were housed in tenements within the gates of the industrial complex. They received no cash payments for living expenses, as the company distributed food and clothing, and even maintained a slave hospital to provide medical care.[38] In Petersburg enslaved workers experienced a freedom of movement that was both necessary to the nature of the city's industries and troublesome to local authorities who sought to maintain law and order.

Much like other southern cities where enslaved labor was important, Petersburg was an open city with few restrictions on the movement of industrial slaves. Although authorities regularly expressed concern over the uncontrolled movements of the urban slave community, attempts at enforcing the law were sporadic and largely unsuccessful. Local officials were often at their wits' end because they could offer little incentive for positive behavior and slaves' illicit activities were often hard to detect.[39] Enslaved workers blended into urban working-class neighborhoods, where they mixed easily with the city's large free African American community. In 1860, the African American population of Petersburg was 8,924, including 3,244 free and 5,680 enslaved. When combined, the enslaved and free black population accounted for 49 percent of the total.[40] In Petersburg, enslaved workers patronized black-owned businesses, attended African American churches, mixed with whites in local taverns and

38. Dew, *Ironmaker to the Confederacy*, 26.

39. Takagi, "*Rearing Wolves*," 65–68; and Whittington B. Johnson, *Black Savannah, 1788–1864* (Fayetteville: University of Arkansas Press, 1996), 89–93.

40. Bureau of the Census, *Population of the United States in 1860: The Eighth Census* (Washington, D.C.: GPO, 1864), 516, 519. Total Petersburg population in 1860 was 18,266.

grog shops, and even formed families that sometimes united the free and the enslaved.

It is impossible to accurately trace the movements of Petersburg's industrial slaves, but it is safe to assume that many lived among the city's large African American population in the East Ward. The neighborhoods of Pocahontas and Blandford, separated by the Appomattox River and connected by a bridge, formed the locus for free blacks, who owned considerable amounts of property and operated a number of independent businesses.[41] Industrial slaves who hired their own time and "lived out" sought housing in these neighborhoods often among friends or family. Others boarded with anyone willing to accept their small payment, or simply pocketed their board money and lived on the streets. This ambiguousness often frustrated the efforts of city authorities to keep some sort of control over both the enslaved and free black populations.

The clearest evidence of the activities of the urban slave community comes from the attempts of Petersburg authorities to control their behavior. Concern over the after-work behavior of slaves and their interaction with the free black community led Petersburg and state officials to enact a number of laws and ordinances aimed at restricting their movements. These were tightened following Nat Turner's 1831 rebellion in Southampton County, but enforcement remained a challenge. Laws forbade slaves from gathering together in groups for any type of activity without proper white supervision, from owning dogs, and from smoking in the street, and forbade drinking and gambling. The town's sergeant, or sheriff, rang a nightly bell commencing the evening curfew at 8:00 p.m. in winter and 9:00 p.m. April through September. After curfew, slaves traveling city streets needed a written pass, or faced arrest and a whipping if caught going at large. Petersburg officials formed a night watch to patrol the streets and arrest lawbreakers. It was the duty of the ten-man night watch to "explore the streets of the city during the night, and apprehend all negroes found strolling about more than half an hour after the ringing of the bell, without a pass, and all other persons who may be found violating the laws of the State or the ordinances of the city."[42]

On occasion, upstanding white citizens fell victim to the law. Petersburg

41. Lucious Edwards, "Free Black Property Holders in Petersburg, Virginia: 1865–1874" (M.A. thesis, Virginia State College, 1977), 14.

42. Petersburg Common Council, *The Charter and Laws of the City of Petersburg* (Petersburg: O. Ellyson, 1852), 74–77 (quote p. 77).

miller and longtime city flour inspector Richard F. Hannon was fined $15 for allowing his slaves to have a party at his residence in December 1854. The night watch discovered seventy to eighty people "carrying on at a great rate," about 2:00 a.m. at Hannon's Blandford home.[43] Because Hannon was white he got off with a fine. African Americans caught violating the illegal gathering ordinance received lashes, whether slave or free. The nature and size of the party at the Hannon home prompted the editor of the *Daily Southside Democrat* to remind Petersburgers that gatherings of slaves were illegal under both Virginia law and city ordinance. The editor reprinted sections of state law and local ordinances to remind readers of the power of the night watch to "apprehend all suspicious, riotous, idle, and disorderly persons, white or black, loitering or strolling about such places, or in the streets, at *unseasonable hours.*"[44]

After Turner's rebellion, white Virginians were especially sensitive to rumors of slave rebellion or insurrection. White Petersburg residents were naturally alarmed in 1855 when the local newspaper reported that someone uncovered a plot to kill the whites of the city. Reporting this alarming news in Saturday's edition, the editor warned residents to "be on the watch" and to read Monday's paper for more details. Petersburg officials sent word to the mayor of Richmond and appealed to the governor for armed protection. What a panicked weekend must have passed in Petersburg before discovering that the threatened insurrection was only an April Fool's hoax.[45] The willingness to assume the worst suggests that Petersburg authorities were aware of their tenuous hold over the African American community of the city. Until the abolition of slavery in 1865, the common council and mayor of Petersburg struggled constantly to balance the need for urban order and control with industrialists' demands for slave labor.

Drinking, gambling, and other illicit nighttime activities were not the only social or cultural enjoyments for the urban slave community. On Sundays and special holidays, enslaved Petersburgers found solace in the city's black churches. Although a number of free and enslaved men and women attended white churches, especially the Washington Street Methodist Church, many more attended one of the city's three African American churches. After 1831

43. "Unlawful," *Daily Southside Democrat*, 29 December 1854.

44. "City Jottings," ibid., 4 January 1855.

45. "Startling Disclosure! Awful Discovery!" *Daily Southside Democrat*, 31 March 1855; and "T-h-u-n-d-e-r-a-t-i-o-n," ibid., 2 April 1855.

Virginia law prohibited slave worship services, except under white supervision, but this did not stop African Americans from forming some of the largest churches in the state. Three of Petersburg's Baptist churches were the domain of the area African American community. Enslaved members predominated at the Harrison Street Baptist Church, slaves and free blacks each made up a significant part of the congregation at the Gillfield Baptist Church, while free African Americans held domain at the Third Baptist Church.[46] Gillfield Baptist Church records most clearly show the interaction of slave and free blacks in a mixed congregational setting. For example, in 1846 congregants selected fourteen free and fifteen enslaved members to serve as officers. During the antebellum era, the church regularly designated the status of members and officers, sometimes using the euphemistic term "servant" to indicate the enslaved.[47]

The after-work activities of the African American community were generally tolerated because the labor of enslaved workers such as Tom Bragg was essential to the industrial economy of antebellum Petersburg. The tobacco factories, iron foundries, and artisan shops sought a steady labor force that in many cases mixed slave labor with free. Throughout the antebellum period, the composition of the industrial workforce ebbed and flowed along with the regional economy. Early in the era, industrial employers owned most of their enslaved workforce. This shifted as the regional plantation economy diversified and a surplus of hired slave labor became available. Coinciding with increasing slave prices in the 1850s, slave hiring was widely adopted in the city. Many industrial employers, especially tobacconists, adapted to rising slave prices by hiring from the city's large free black community, and on occasion from the pool of available white labor. The resulting urban mélange created a working-class community where whites and blacks, slave and free, mixed after work in grog shops, alleys, and taverns. Slaves were increasingly allowed to hire their own time and to live apart from their owner or employer.

This relative quasi-freedom allowed men like Tom Bragg to disappear into the night once the workday ended, and gave them more control over their time than their counterparts on plantations or those forced to live in company dormitories. The relative freedom of the urban environment was always tenuous

46. Luther P. Jackson, "Free Negroes of Petersburg, Virginia," *Journal of Negro History* 12 (1927): 384–385.

47. Record Book, vol. 2, 1834–1849, Gillfield Baptist Church Records, Special Collections, University of Virginia, Charlottesville, Va., n.p.

and the bonds of slavery could be tightened at any time, reminding slaves that they were not truly free. This happened for Tom Bragg in 1859, when bricklayer Daniel Lyon opted not to renew his annual hire contract. The commission merchant negotiating his hire leased Bragg to the Southside Railroad at an annual rate of $140.[48] For at least two years, he labored to maintain and construct the railroad operating between Petersburg and Lynchburg. Bragg disappeared from the historical record in 1860, and one can only hope that he lived long enough to get a taste of real freedom.

48. Auction Sales Book, 1854–1867, Branch & Company Records, ViHi.

6

Between Class and Caste

THE CULTURE OF SOUTHERN ANTEBELLUM ARTISANS

As the fiftieth anniversary of the Declaration of Independence approached in 1826, members of the Petersburg Benevolent Mechanic Association (PBMA) busied themselves with special preparations in celebration of the "Jubilee of American Freedom." The master mechanics used the opportunity to "congratulate each other" on the arrival of this patriotic event, and established a special committee to plan the association's participation in the town's July Fourth parade.[1] Like their northern counterparts, white Petersburg mechanics embraced a tradition of republicanism, rooted in the Revolution, which celebrated the role of manual labor and the independence of small producers in America. Despite sharing an attachment to independence and the virtues of republicanism, southern artisans were different from those who lived and worked in the North. The institution of chattel slavery in southern society brought direct and indirect benefits to white workers, and complicated their views of republicanism and their interpretation of free labor. While the arrangement committee of the PBMA made diligent plans to celebrate Independence Day, at least half of all the organization's members owned slaves. Slaveholding offered artisans membership in the South's master class. Owning the labor of others gave them a stake in the perpetuation of the institution and complicated workers' political response to the industrialization of southern society. The common bond of slaveholding, or the aspiration of slaveholding, bound artisans to the southern planter class and formed a caste system more significant than the evolving class divide. Their celebration of a free labor ideology included a dimension that supported unfree labor and often sought it out. This important distinction highlights the difference between workers in the antebellum North and South.[2]

1. Minutes, 16 June 1826, Petersburg Benevolent Mechanic Association Records, 1826–1836, Virginia Historical Society, Richmond (hereafter cited as ViHi).

2. For an examination of southern artisan ideology in the Revolutionary era, see Charles G. Steffen, *The Mechanics of Baltimore: Workers in the Age of Revolution, 1763–1812* (Urbana:

Slavery and race were constant points in question for southern workers. While some white southern mechanics benefited from slavery through direct participation in the institution, all enjoyed the elevated status that their whiteness afforded. Yet slavery had its disadvantages for white southern mechanics. When Petersburg journeymen and middling artisans organized to protest competition from black labor in 1857, their declaration that "we do not aim to conflict with the interests of slave owners" was lauded in the local newspaper. In a column following the mechanics' meeting, the newspaper editor expressed relief that the group was not condemning slavery, warning "that would have been bad and dangerous ground to have trod on."[3] Property in slaves formed the backbone of the southern economy, and mechanics' protests against slave labor often fell on deaf ears. Southerners would always put their right to protect their property in slaves before the rights and demands of the white working class. Through their participation in or acceptance of slavery, southern artisans necessarily lived different lives from northern masters and journeymen.[4] Despite this meaningful distinction, through the formal language of republicanism mechanics in both regions voiced many common concerns. Exploring the contradictions between republicanism and slavery helps to give meaning to their commonalities and differences.

In the years following the American Revolution, artisan workers espoused a republicanism that emphasized their role in upholding the values of virtue, equality, citizenship, and especially, independence. Linking these concepts with a producer ideology, their republicanism celebrated the contribution skilled workers made to the community and the economy. Perhaps most important, artisan republicanism rested on the belief that society was dependent

---

University of Illinois Press, 1984). For the late antebellum artisan experience, see Frank Towers, *The Urban South and the Coming of the Civil War* (Charlottesville: University of Virginia Press, 2004). For the southern free labor ideology, see James L. Huston, *Calculating the Value of the Union: Slavery, Property Rights, and the Economic Origins of the Civil War* (Chapel Hill: University of North Carolina Press, 2003), 40–49.

3. "The Mechanics' Meeting of Saturday Night," *Daily Southside Democrat*, 18 August 1857 (first quotation); and "The Mechanics' Meeting Saturday Night," ibid., 19 August 1857 (second quotation).

4. Michele Gillespie, *Free Labor in an Unfree World: White Artisans in Slaveholding Georgia, 1789–1860* (Athens: University of Georgia Press, 2000), 133; and Towers, *Urban South*, 142–143.

on the labor of small producers. Artisans' confidence in their position in the new republic included an expectation that industrious apprentices and journeymen could achieve the goal of a "competence" or independence as master mechanics.[5]

However, republicanism was a complex ideology that adapted and changed with the advancing industrial economy. Some mechanics, especially small masters and journeymen who found themselves in jeopardy of being displaced in a changing economy, adapted their republicanism to include a critique of capitalism and to emphasize their belief that republican values were rooted in the small shop.[6] Master mechanics who prospered and became manufacturers or merchants incorporated a bourgeois notion of liberal capitalism into their republicanism, but still used the language of the revolution to define and measure their success. The division within the artisan community became manifest in separate organizations and celebrations that served to emphasize the growing division between masters and journeymen.[7]

White southern artisans shared much the same worldview as northern mechanics in the nineteenth century. They experienced change in the organization of work and in their position in society in ways similar to that of their northern counterparts. Frank Towers demonstrates that for large southern cities artisans organized politically and formed an important element in the voting block.[8] It is not surprising, then, that southern mechanics also embraced and adapted the major values of artisan republicanism. Michele Gillespie shows how Georgia mechanics "built self-conscious communities based on the

5. See Howard B. Rock, *Artisans of the New Republic: The Tradesmen of New York City in the Age of Jefferson* (New York: New York University Press, 1979), 142–143; and Sean Wilentz, *Chants Democratic: New York City and the Rise of the American Working Class, 1788–1850* (New York: Oxford University Press, 1984), 62–63. For republicanism in a southern context, see Steffen, *Mechanics of Baltimore*, 281–283. For an important discussion of the development of republicanism in the post-Revolutionary era, see Joyce Appleby, *Capitalism and a New Social Order: The Republican Vision of the 1790s* (New York: New York University Press, 1984).

6. See, for example, Gary J. Kornblith, "Becoming Joseph T. Buckingham: The Struggle for Artisanal Independence in Early-Nineteenth-Century Boston," in *American Artisans: Crafting Social Identity, 1750–1850*, ed. Howard B. Rock, Paul A. Gilje, and Robert Asher (Baltimore: Johns Hopkins University Press, 1995), 123–129; and William S. Pretzer, "From Artisan to Alderman: The Career of William W. Moore, 1803–1886," in ibid., 135–139, 146–147, 151–152.

7. Wilentz, *Chants Democratic*, 93, 95–96, 102–103.

8. Towers, *Urban South*, 1–4.

principles of artisanal republicanism." She notes that artisans in Augusta used republicanism as a tool to conceive of themselves as a political community in the 1790s. Charles G. Steffen demonstrates that Baltimore artisans used their radical republicanism to demand more democracy and less restriction on political participation in the immediate post-Revolution period. However, after 1800 many mechanics traded their well-defined artisan identity for a new one based on the independence granted to white men in a slaveholding society. In fact, southern mechanics did not believe the tenets of republicanism extended to slave and free black artisans. Like their northern brethren, they reserved their expressions of equality, independence, and the duties of citizenship for whites only.[9]

The white artisans of Petersburg made their own expressions of republicanism; however, their ideology was not a static concept, but was adapted and employed in a variety of ways as structural realities changed for mechanics and their ranks split into middle and working classes. Instead of being a defining factor of change, their republicanism should be viewed as one of several changing factors in nineteenth-century Petersburg. The republicanism expressed by the successful members of the PBMA, for example, was different from the ideology more middling mechanics embraced near the end of the antebellum era.

The upwardly mobile members of the PBMA laid claim to the tradition of artisan republicanism and made it an important part of their celebrations and the formal oratory of their organization. Republicanism became the language of these successful masters, who adopted it and shaped it to fit their position in the new economy. Although economic realities changed for many members of this group who no longer participated directly in the labor of their shops and firms, they continued to value manual labor and to respect the virtue of independence. Theirs became a republicanism that accepted the acquisitive nature of the individual whom the market revolution made possible. As they moved out of manual labor into middle-class roles as merchants and contractors, republicanism became the rhetoric that bound them to their heritage as artisans and to their employees who faced a new reality of life-long wage labor. In a southern society dominated politically and socially by elite planters, PBMA members could not hide their roots in manual labor. Celebrating their working-

9. Gillespie, *Free Labor in an Unfree World,* 38–39, 61 (quotation p. 38); and Steffen, *Mechanics of Baltimore,* 281–283.

class roots through the language of republicanism helped establish the credibility of certain types of manual labor, particularly that performed by skilled whites.

Initially, the mechanics of the PBMA used republicanism to justify and celebrate the role of manual labor in southern society. In a region dominated by commercial agriculture, where the largest class of manual laborers was enslaved, it was natural for white mechanics to feel the need to elevate and support their position within southern society. By laying claim to the Revolution and stressing their role as citizens, artisans sought to prove that manual labor was a noble undertaking. At the PBMA's first annual meeting in January 1826, President Francis G. Yancey used the language of republicanism to honor the status of mechanics in society. The bulk of his speech offered evidence that the mechanic arts were not degrading occupations, but ones deserving of prominent recognition. Yancey embraced the republicanism of the classical Greeks, including Aristotle, as the original founders of the mechanical arts, and then offered Benjamin Franklin's contributions as examples of the importance of mechanics to society. He rhetorically asked the assembly, "Will any one be disposed to cast a stigma on the Mechanic Arts, or to speak disrespectfully of the followers of the various branches? Is not this a nation of Republicans, where all are equal?"[10] Board of officers member Luzon Whiting reinforced Yancey's message in his own speech, reminding the group that "there are no branches of productive industry deserving a more elevated standing than Mechanics."[11]

Republicanism remained a useful tool for reinforcing the status of mechanics in an ever-changing economy, but was often employed in moderate ways. As Werner Steger suggests for Richmond, the association the upwardly mobile masters of the PBMA formed was ultimately a conservative organization. Steger found that in Richmond "the rhetoric of the virtuous republican artisan was used to realign the interests of the artisan with those of the middling entrepreneur and the professional classes such as lawyers and physicians."[12] For most members of the PBMA, those interests merged completely as the masters

10. Annual address, 10 January 1826, Minutes, PBMA Records, ViHi.

11. Minutes, 10 January 1826, Petersburg Benevolent Mechanic Association Papers, 1825–1921, University of Virginia Library, Charlottesville (hereafter cited as ViU).

12. Werner Steger, "'United to Support, But Not Combined to Injure': Free Workers and Immigrants in Richmond, Virginia During the Era of Sectionalism, 1847–1865" (Ph.D. diss., George Washington University, 1999), 90, 100 (quotation p. 90).

became entrepreneurs or entered the professional classes themselves. Yet they continued to express themselves in the language of artisanal republicanism and celebrated manual labor long after they removed themselves from the actual production process.[13] Expressions of artisanal republicanism were still an important part of the annual meeting in 1834, when a PBMA member proclaimed "that the time is not remote when the Southern artisan will vie for intelligence and wealth with any in the world."[14]

These masters had significant reasons for embracing republicanism. It helped to underscore their relationship with manual labor and to minimize the developing differences between masters and journeymen in Petersburg. By touting the harmony of the artisan community and celebrating the mechanic arts they focused on a common past and hoped to quell any labor unrest on the part of journeymen-turned-employees. PBMA members also sought to elevate the status of mechanics across the South. In a region, and especially in a city, where manual labor was often identified with slavery and blackness, it was important to make a distinction between white and black and to establish the white mechanic alongside other whites in the business sector. White artisans had to work hard to demonstrate that their lives and livelihoods were set apart from the rhetoric of the proslavery argument that proclaimed that the existence of slavery exempted southern whites from manual labor. The very nature of such an argument implied that manual labor was degrading to whites. Therefore, PBMA members used the language of republicanism to redefine their heritage in the mechanic arts as "virtuous" and necessary.[15] Emphasizing the importance of artisans to society through republican language meant proclaiming the virtue of white manual labor as vital to the community and indeed, the nation.

Whatever their rhetoric, by 1834 a significant number of PBMA members were no longer mere mechanics struggling to uplift manual labor in the South. Most were businessmen with investments to protect and reputations to uphold. That year the association president was carpenter Beverly Drinkard, a pros-

13. Kornblith, "Becoming Joseph T. Buckingham," 128–129; and Wilentz, *Chants Democratic*, 302–306.

14. Minutes, 13 January 1834, PBMA Papers, ViU.

15. For an extended discussion of proslavery republicanism, see Larry E. Tise, *Proslavery: A History of the Defense of Slavery in America, 1701–1840* (Athens: University of Georgia Press, 1987), 347–362.

perous building contractor and entrepreneur who owned between nine and twelve slaves.[16] Vice President Daniel Lyon, a brick contractor of equal wealth, was also a captain in the Petersburg militia and town commissioner of the revenue.[17] PBMA treasurer Robert Ritchie was a prominent muslin manufacturer and treasurer of the Petersburg Hustings Court.[18] These men who were espousing artisanal republicanism and celebrating the importance of manual labor were actually some of the most powerful and wealthy men in Petersburg. Many had not engaged in actual manual labor for years.

As Michele Gillespie argues for Georgia, and others have claimed for northern artisans, republicanism was an important unifying tool that brought mechanics together on political and other issues. In Georgia, mechanics supported political equality for all, and particularly for the artisan community. As political parties formed in the early republic, Georgia artisans became staunch supporters of the Jeffersonian Republicans. Baltimore craftsmen employed republicanism to support a unicameral assembly for Maryland, low property qualifications for office holding, and to some degree even biracial voting. New York mechanics used republicanism to express their positions on important issues such as opposition to a national bank, support for education, and even the seizure and redistribution of land.[19] Although debates were less radical in the more politically homogeneous South, republicanism was a vital component of artisan solidarity. Republicanism may have been the link that led Petersburg master mechanics to form the PBMA in 1825. One account suggests that the group formed following the uncoordinated attempt of local artisans to plan a special welcome for Revolutionary War hero the Marquis de Lafayette, who visited Petersburg during his tour of the United States in the fall of 1824. At a meeting of mechanics and manufacturers in the workshop of cabinetmaker M. D. I'Anson, they planned to construct an arch to honor Lafayette. Unfortunately, the general's travel plans brought him to Petersburg before the arch

16. Petersburg, Va., Personal Property Tax List, 1823, 1836, Library of Virginia, Richmond (microfilm, hereafter cited as Vi).

17. Petersburg, Va., Hustings Court Minute Book 1827–1832, n.p. (21 March 1828) (17 February 1831) (microfilm), Vi.

18. Hustings Court Minute Book 1823–1827, n.p. (15 June 1826); and Hustings Court Minute Book 1832–1835, 299.

19. Gillespie, *Free Labor in an Unfree World*, 45–47; Steffen, *Mechanics of Baltimore*, 281; and Wilentz, *Chants Democratic*, 214–215, 237–239.

could be constructed.[20] The mechanics met again and formed the PBMA in 1825.

Events such as George Washington's birthday, General Lafayette's visit, and especially Independence Day brought Petersburg artisans together in cross-class exhibitions of American nationalism. As David Waldstreicher argues, in the early republic artisans believed they were "full participants in the virtuous, orderly, patriotic public." The participation of masters, journeymen, and apprentices in large numbers minimized the appearance of the social and economic differences that befell the artisan community after 1820.[21] Yet as Susan G. Davis shows for Philadelphia, artisanal symbols, as well as the events themselves, were planned and manipulated by men who called themselves mechanics but no longer worked with their hands.[22] In Petersburg, it was the upwardly mobile members of the PBMA who engineered artisan parades and celebrations.

Soon after its organization, the PBMA used the language of republicanism to bring members together for important events, especially the Fourth of July, which celebrated the traditions of the Revolution and the roots of republican thought. Across the United States, Independence Day was a special holiday that brought artisans together to participate in parades and dinners that usually featured many toasts and orations celebrating the birth of the nation and the place of mechanics in American society.[23] Mary Ann Clawson notes that celebration of a ritual holiday is an important hallmark and bonding tool of fraternal organizations, and for mechanics' societies Independence Day was the highpoint of the year.[24] The PBMA made special plans to celebrate the fiftieth

20. "Lafayette," *Intelligencer and Petersburg Commercial Advertiser*, 15 October 1824; and James G. Scott and Edward A. Wyatt, *Petersburg's Story: A History* (Petersburg, Va.: Titmus Optical, 1960), 69.

21. David Waldstreicher, *In the Midst of Perpetual Fetes: The Making of American Nationalism, 1776–1820* (Chapel Hill: University of North Carolina Press for the Omohundro Institute of Early American History and Culture, 1997), 104–106 (quote p. 105).

22. Susan G. Davis, *Parades and Power: Street Theatre in Nineteenth-Century Philadelphia* (Philadelphia: Temple University Press, 1986), 125–130.

23. Rock, *Artisans of the New Republic*, 139–143; Simon P. Newman, *Parades and the Politics of the Streets: Festive Culture in the Early American Republic* (Philadelphia: University of Pennsylvania Press, 1997), 83–119.

24. Mary Ann Clawson, *Constructing Brotherhood: Class, Gender, and Fraternalism* (Princeton, N.J.: Princeton University Press, 1989), 42–43.

anniversary of the Declaration of Independence, or the "Jubilee of American Freedom," as it called the 1826 event. Three months before the holiday, the group appointed a special committee to organize the association's celebration and another subcommittee to coordinate their activities with those arranged by the town's officials. Committee members were all prominent masters, including bricklayer Allen Archer, watchmaker William Cooke, stone cutter Fielding Bell, cabinetmaker Samuel White, blacksmith Sceva Thayer, and hatter George Henderson, who was ironically an English immigrant. For the parade, PBMA members wanted to assume the appearance of military order, so they arranged to subdivide the group into platoons, each led by a PBMA director. To make a "more respectable display on the occasion," the group appointed a military member to act as adjutant, and the association chose bricklayer Allen Archer as standard bearer. More special meetings in June finalized preparations for the parade. The group designed a membership badge of blue ribbon that the mechanics were urged to wear "on the left side of the coat, passed from the first to the third button hole." Military members who would be marching with their militia units during the parade were asked to wear the badge on their uniforms "as a mark of Respect for the Association." The association resolved to place an ad in the newspaper calling the children and apprentices of members to a meeting "for the purpose of their making arrangements for celebrating with us."[25]

By 16 June, the main committee was certain that participation of the membership would be strong because all were "too well aware of their patriotism, and of the friendly feelings they entertain for each other, to suppose they would let slip an opportunity, such as the day of Jubilee approaching to congratulate each other on its arrival."[26] On 4 July, Petersburg witnessed a lively procession. A small militia detachment of the Petersburg Jefferson Volunteers led the way, followed by the commissioned militia officers of the 39th Regiment, the town committee of arrangement for the event, and the full company of the Petersburg Jefferson Volunteers. The PBMA was sixth in line, after the band providing musical accompaniment for the event. The militia companies of the Petersburg Light Infantry Blues and the Petersburg Independent Volunteers rounded out the parade.[27]

The thriving members of the PBMA did not have exclusive claim to the lan-

25. Minutes, 11 April, 16 June, 30 June 1826, PBMA Records, ViHi.
26. Minutes, 16 June 1826, PBMA Records, ViHi.
27. Ibid.

guage of republicanism in antebellum Petersburg. Journeymen and more middling masters used the rhetoric and precepts of republicanism in their own
quest for organization and political action. Their crusade to uphold the significance of their work and position in southern society differed from the earlier
PBMA campaigns. Time and class divisions shaped the middling mechanics'
rhetoric. Late antebellum Virginia was far removed from the immediate influence of the American Revolution. Similarly, the hand of industrialization
and economic modernization already made wage labor a permanent reality for
many in their group. When faced with economic distress in the wake of the
Panic of 1857, the middling mechanics of Petersburg formed their own association to guard their place in society and promote the education of a future
generation of working men. Although their organizing language lashed out at
free black workers, these white mechanics used the egalitarian language of
artisanal republicanism to justify their actions, but adapted it to fit southern
society. As northern artisans often claimed, the Petersburg mechanics believed
that organizing and supporting skilled workers was in the interest of the common good because mechanics could protect society and the community from
wealthy and corrupt men only concerned with their individual interests and
personal accumulation of wealth.

But as southerners, their claims found the biggest threat from men who
employed African Americans in skilled positions, and their republicanism had
a definite racial component. The artisans argued that excluding blacks from
skilled occupations placed mechanics on equal footing with other professionals, "enabling us to be participants in the promotion of the best interests of our
city, our State or common country, and driving from position the designing
demagogue—allowing men of practical senses to aspire to any eminence his
countrymen may desire him to occupy."[28] Excluding blacks from artisanal occupations thus provided for the elevation of white mechanics who aspired to
higher position in society. The mechanics also appealed to the responsibilities
of white men as virtuous citizens, claiming that "he is a blind man to his own
welfare who does not, in all cases, support the white mechanic in preference
to the negro." They argued that "the white man should have the preference,
because the white man is a citizen and must perform all the duties which may

28. "The Mechanics' Meeting of Saturday Night," *Daily Southside Democrat*, 18 August
1857.

be required of him as such."[29] Most members of the Petersburg Mechanic Association (PMA) were middling artisans who faced a growing reality of lifelong wage labor or permanent journeyman status. When confronted with a new economic reality that made reaching master status unlikely, rather than discard the republican ideals of an earlier generation, they adapted the concepts of independence, virtue, and the common good to fit their new circumstances, and looked to separate themselves from those who were beneath them on the ladder of status and position. In Petersburg, as in other growing southern cities, this meant separating themselves from free African Americans.[30]

The divergent ways that masters and journeymen used the language of republicanism were symptomatic of the growing divisions within the artisan community. A brief look at the iron foundry of Tappey and Lumsden in Petersburg helps to illustrate the changes industrialization and the market revolution brought to this community of workers and their dividing conceptions of republicanism. Blacksmith William H. Tappey, who came to Virginia from Hanover, Germany, operated a well-established blacksmith shop in Petersburg by 1846. Besides general smith work, such as shoeing horses, Tappey specialized in "tobacco factory, mill work, railing, house and farm work, making and laying cast-steel Axes, equal to any."[31] Tappey took advantage of the changes in the local economy to expand his operations by focusing on industrial work, and entered into partnership with Virginia-born pattern-maker George L. Lumsden. Together the partners established the Southern Foundry on Washington Street, near Tappey's original blacksmith shop, just across from the Jarratt Hotel. Although their operations, often known as the Tappey and Lumsden foundry, were nearly destroyed four or five times by fire, the two prospered and increased their undertakings to meet the needs of growing local industry.[32] By 1855, the foundry forged and built mail cars for the railroad and in 1859 built a steam-powered printing press for the Petersburg *Daily Express*.[33]

Growing demand for the iron products of the Southern Foundry led to an

29. Ibid.

30. For examples from Baltimore and St. Louis, see Towers, *Urban South*, 46–49.

31. "Take Notice," *Republican*, 30 December 1846.

32. "Destructive Fire–Burning of Tappey's Southern Foundry," *Daily Express*, 10 April 1858.

33. Editorial, *Daily Southside Democrat*, 22 June 1855; and "The City Water as a Motive Power," *Daily Express*, 2 May 1859.

increase in the scale of operations. Tappey and Lumsden became "bosses" to a growing group of wage earners. The seventy molders, blacksmiths, pattern makers, and engineers employed at the Southern Foundry at the end of the antebellum era were journeymen with little hope of achieving the independence Tappey knew when he opened his first blacksmith shop in Petersburg. The annual production of at least $70,000 worth of iron goods clearly separated the proprietors from their workforce on an economic and a social level.[34] Tappey and Lumsden moved into the ranks of the newly developing middle class, and joined other upwardly mobile master mechanics in the PBMA. George Lumsden became a member of the organization in 1838, and William H. Tappey followed in 1856. Lumsden's personal wealth in 1860 included property holdings valued at $4,000 and a personal estate worth $10,000, exclusive of his holdings in the foundry. Tappey's assets grew from real estate worth $2,500 in 1850 to include property valued at $7,000 and other personal possessions worth $15,000 in 1860. Both owned personal slaves, and in 1860 Tappey employed an Irish girl as a domestic servant.[35]

The journeymen at the Southern Foundry mostly faced a different reality, one based on permanent wage labor. Of thirty-three Tappey and Lumsden employees identified in the 1859 Petersburg city directory, not one owned real property or other personal effects worth more than $100. The average age of foundry employees was twenty-eight, and 68 percent of the workmen reporting an age to census enumerators in 1860 were over the age of twenty-five. In an earlier generation, these skilled workmen might have aspired to master status and become owners of their own workshops, but in the face of the changes in late antebellum Virginia, most rarely achieved traditional artisan independence. While their employers enjoyed a new lifestyle that afforded them the attentions of servants and affiliation in elite organizations, the mechanics at the Southern Foundry adapted to life as wage laborers. Mechanization, and the division of labor, brought new opportunities for some enterprising artisans, but also formed a class divide between masters and journeymen.

At the end of the antebellum era, masters and journeymen still used the

34. Bureau of the Census, 1860 Census, Schedule 5, Products of Industry during the Year Ending June 1, 1860, microfilm.

35. Bureau of the Census, Population Schedules, Petersburg, Va. (Washington, D.C., 1850, microfilm); Bureau of the Census, Population Schedules, Petersburg, Va. (Washington, D.C., 1860, microfilm); and Personal Property Tax Lists, 1843, 1856.

formal language of republicanism to emphasize their important position in the community, but their claims to unity in manual labor were no longer true. Men like William H. Tappey could point to their beginnings as journeymen and small masters and hope to inspire a drive to succeed in their employees. They used republicanism to account for their own economic prosperity, and to justify new arrangements in their workshops and factories. But independence became more a dream than an attainable goal for the journeymen employed in Petersburg's larger shops, foundries, and factories. Their republicanism evolved into a competing interpretation that justified their organization and protests of unfair work practices on the part of their employers.[36] Although successful masters and journeymen celebrated independence, and still stressed the virtues of manual labor and the importance of artisans as citizens, they were in reality divergent groups whose unity was quickly becoming a vestige of the past.

The experiences of Tappey and Lumsden, and of the mechanics who worked for them, closely mirrored the experience of skilled workers in many northern communities and towns. The industrial development and resulting shift in work relations were not unique to Petersburg, but common throughout the developing United States in the antebellum era. Yet even with a growing wage labor force caused by a division of labor and mechanization, Upper South communities were different. The major defining difference between Petersburg and northern industrializing communities was the existence of racial slavery.

By 1820, the legal institution of slavery was largely absent from the northern states of America.[37] Even though the market revolution led to decreasing independence for many skilled workers in both regions, artisans in the North labored under a wage system and competed only against free men and women. Not so in the South, where the bulk of the workforce consisted of men and women whose labor was owned by someone else. Slavery bastardized the con-

36. Wilentz, *Chants Democratic*, 102–103.

37. Slavery was abolished by state constitutions in Vermont (1777), Ohio (1802), Illinois (1818), and Indiana (1816); and through constitutional interpretation in New Hampshire. Massachusetts ended the institution through a judicial decision (1783), and gradual emancipation acts in Pennsylvania (1780), Rhode Island (1784), Connecticut (1784 and 1797), New York (1799 and 1817), and New Jersey (1804) ended slavery in the remaining states. Leon F. Litwack, *North of Slavery: The Negro in the Free States, 1790–1860* (Chicago: University of Chicago Press, 1961), 3n.

cept of a free labor ideology that was so strong and prevalent in artisan communities in the North, perhaps preventing organization of southern workers across racial lines. As Eric Foner has argued, the "definition of free labor depended on juxtaposition with its ideological opposite, slave labor."[38] Under the principle of free labor, northern artisans defended the superiority of their way of life in opposition and contrast to the slaveholding South. In the South, artisans who celebrated the superiority of free labor also often owned, or aspired to own, the labor of others.

Southern free laborites had a radically different view of free labor. They insisted that the key to southern survival, and holding the fealty of poor whites, rested with fostering large-scale industry and the mechanical arts. Some promoted the use of slaves in manual labor occupations in factories, and did not see the contradiction inherent in their philosophy. Concentration on manufacturing with slave labor, they argued, made it possible to unite all segments of white southern society. It gave planters an outlet for their agricultural products, provided new customers for merchants, and elevated the social status of white artisans, raising them out of poverty to claim a bigger share of the wealth. Slaveholding was an integral part of the free labor plan, and not seen as an inconsistency.[39] In fact, according to Bruce Laurie, southern free labor advocates encouraged mechanics to aspire to slaveholding status "for the purpose of alleviating that domestic drudgery which in non-slaveholding states falls so heavily on the wives and daughters of men of limited means."[40]

This difference illustrates a serious contradiction in the rhetoric of artisans North and South, even though both used similar language and supported free labor. Southern mechanics conveniently ignored their relationship to enslaved labor (and presumably even free blacks) when celebrating the place of artisans in society. In his presidential address to the first annual meeting of the PBMA in 1826, Francis G. Yancey applauded the free labor status of mechanics in the South. He proclaimed, "We are a nation of freemen, possessing equal rights."

38. Eric Foner, "Free Labor and Nineteenth-Century Political Ideology," in *The Market Revolution in America: Social, Political, and Religious Expressions, 1800–1880*, ed. Melvyn Stokes and Stephen Conway (Charlottesville: University Press of Virginia, 1996), 100.

39. For an in-depth examination of free labor politics in the South's largest cities, see Towers, *Urban South*, 109–148.

40. Bruce Laurie, *Artisans into Workers: Labor in Nineteenth-Century America* (New York: Noonday, 1989), 55–56.

Rejoicing in the position of artisans in American society he continued: "Perhaps there is no country in the world where plans for the improvement of the condition of man meet so little obstruction as in this." Yet Yancey had only to look as far as his own workshop to find such an obstruction. This master printer and editor of the *Intelligencer and Petersburg Commercial Advertiser* owned at least four adult male slaves who most likely worked in his print shop.[41] Yancey's audience of successful white southern artisans knew that when he spoke of free men with equal rights, he referred to rights allowed to white men only. The location of mechanics in a slaveholding society complicated the comparison between free and unfree labor and meant that their social and political independence often rested on the permanent enslavement of African Americans.[42]

Slavery had a profound impact on the free working class of the antebellum South, and stands out as the most important difference between artisan workers North and South. The existence of slavery and the large African American population of the South buffered the place of white artisans in society, who rose above blacks by the very nature of their whiteness. Artisans, and other southerners, were convinced that the slave system afforded all white men economic opportunity and political equality denied to wage laborers in the North. The identity of northern artisans was more tenuous in the changing society and economy of antebellum America. There, white workers strove to define and embrace their own racial distinctiveness just as their economic status grew more precarious. Artisans North and South defined race as an important part of their identity, but had divergent understandings of whiteness. In the South, society already identified the benefits of belonging to the "master race," and mechanics readily embraced their role as white men in a slaveholding society.[43] Frank Towers shows that in southern cities where white artisans wielded political power, they manipulated the politics of race so that their "campaigns against black labor could fit into either their opposition to slavery or support for it."[44]

Mechanics in northern communities worked hard to cultivate a racial identity that glorified their own whiteness. According to David Roediger, this is

41. Minutes, 10 January 1826, PBMA Records, ViHi; and Personal Property Tax List, 1820, 1823.

42. Gillespie, *Free Labor in an Unfree World*, 171.

43. Ibid., xvii, 39.

44. Towers, *Urban South*, 143.

rooted in the Jacksonian era, when some white workers began to make an uneasy comparison between their position as wage earners and the chattel slaves
of the South. Many comparisons emphasized how new and unfavorable economic circumstances threatened white workers and relegated them to a slave-
like condition. Northern artisans developed a tendency to speak out strongly
against white wage slavery and to support the enslavement of blacks.[45] White
mechanics sought to separate themselves as far as possible both physically and
ideologically from black workers. In the climate of the northern states, where
racial segregation became increasingly codified in the antebellum era, relations
between white and black workers were especially tense.

Only about 5 percent of the nation's black population lived in the North
in the antebellum era, but the antipathy they faced was intense. In northern
states hostility toward black workers stemmed from a fear of competition in
the trades, but whites also worried about a loss of social status resulting from
association with blacks in the workplace.[46] Ronald L. Lewis and Philip S. Foner
provide documentary evidence of the racial prejudice black workers faced in
the North. Some northern states passed laws restricting blacks to certain occupations, and Ohio required African Americans to secure a $500 bond to guar-
antee their good behavior.[47] When northern black workers found skilled jobs in
the North, they were often driven from them by force. There is ample evidence
of the racial strife among northern workers. An 1831 race riot in Providence,
Rhode Island, dissolved into a battle between stone-wielding rioters and the
state militia, resulting in at least two deaths. Philadelphia was the site of race
riots on several occasions, beginning in 1834, when working-class men and
boys attacked blacks in their neighborhoods causing significant property damage. In the 1840s and 1850s, violence erupted in Pennsylvania as Irish workers
lashed out at blacks in the coal mines and on the railroad.[48] Such violent scenes
were repeated in northern cities throughout the antebellum era.

45. David R. Roediger, *The Wages of Whiteness: Race and the Making of the American Work-ing Class* (London: Verso, 1991), 65–69, 75.

46. Litwack, *North of Slavery,* 158.

47. Philip S. Foner and Ronald L. Lewis, *Black Workers: A Documentary History from Colo-nial Times to the Present* (Philadelphia: Temple University Press, 1989), 2–3.

48. Ibid., 115–117; Ronald Takaki, *Iron Cages: Race and Culture in 19th-Century America* (rev. ed., New York: Oxford University Press, 2000), 114–115; Bruce Laurie, *Working People of Phila-delphia, 1800–1850* (Philadelphia: Temple University Press, 1980), 62–63; and Litwack, *North of Slavery,* 159–160.

In northern communities white workers lashed out at blacks who made up a small minority of the working population with little fear of retribution. The racial climate of the North made it unlikely that such actions faced retaliation from authorities or the community. Things were much different in the South, where mechanics faced significant direct competition not only from free blacks but also enslaved artisans on a daily basis. Even had they wanted to, in most areas of the region the conventions of southern society constrained expressions of racial animosity. In Petersburg, blacks made up half or more of the population and played a substantial role in the city's economy. White workers faced competition daily from free African Americans who were willing to work for less, and from enslaved artisans who received no direct wages for their labor. Although most southerners did not own slaves, elite planters and industrialists with a personal stake in the institution of slavery dominated the world of southern mechanics.

In a sense, their status as property may have insulated slave workers from the type of violence blacks in the North routinely faced. Slaveholders jealously guarded their right to do with their chattel property as they saw fit. White workers who challenged that control found little tolerance for their behavior. In a late eighteenth-century legislative petition, a thousand Virginians insisted "that slavery was sanctioned by Scripture and was essential to southern prosperity."[49] Virginians retained strong attachment to the social institution that formed the backbone of their economy with little alteration in the antebellum era. When Petersburg mechanics began to air complaints about black competition in the face of the Panic of 1857, the editor of the Petersburg *Daily Express* warned against lashing out at slavery and slave mechanics: "The right of the master to the labor of his slave is perfect and absolute, and neither his right of ownership or the field in which he may see fit to enter his slave can be made a matter of question or circumscribed a hair's breadth without doing violence to the sovereign right of property and occasioning a social convulsion. It would be overt war on the dominion of the master over his slave, and would be repelled promptly as an outrage."[50] "Any direct physical attack on slave property

49. James Oakes, *The Ruling Race: A History of American Slaveholders* (1982; reprint, New York: W. W. Norton, 1998), 31–32.
50. "The Mechanics' Meeting Saturday Night," *Daily Southside Democrat*, 19 August 1857.

was considered an attack on one of the basic premises of southern society."[51]

This is not to suggest that southern artisans acquiesced to working side by side with enslaved or free black workers. Yet unlike northern mechanics, they rarely lashed out physically against blacks in race riots or other violent attacks.[52] To do so was to go against the grain of the dominant southern ideology. Instead, southern mechanics often responded politically to the threat of competition from black workers. Most of their protests were ineffective and did little to change the social order. They frequently presented petitions to local and state governments demanding the restriction of slave mechanics and free blacks from skilled trades. In Atlanta, two hundred mechanics presented such a petition to the city council complaining that enslaved artisans were underbidding them. Mechanics' organizations in Jackson, Mississippi, and Little Rock, Arkansas, called for legislative action to bar slaves from the skilled trades. The Mechanics' Association of Charleston sent as many as ten petitions demanding an end to slave hiring and competition. On three separate occasions in the antebellum era, economically distressed Petersburg mechanics publicly expressed their displeasure at being forced into competition with blacks. In 1831, they presented a petition to the Virginia General Assembly demanding an end to the employment of slaves and free blacks in skilled trades. In 1849 and again in 1857, white mechanics moved to form a fraternal organization to protect their interests and made similar pleas to limit the employment of blacks in the trades.[53] Like the petitions and protests of other southern mechanics, all of their efforts came to naught because the planter-dominated legislature and slaveholding elites in Petersburg gained little from restricting free black and

51. For discussions of property rights in slaves, see Kenneth M. Stampp, *The Peculiar Institution: Slavery in the Ante-Bellum South* (New York: Vintage, 1956), 201–206; and Robert William Fogel and Stanley L. Engerman, *Time On the Cross: The Economics of American Negro Slavery* (1974; reprint, New York: W. W. Norton, 1989), 232–237.

52. An exception to this convention can be found in the 1858 attack on free African American caulkers in Baltimore. However, this event was closely tied to white artisan resentment of a patronage/client relationship between black caulkers and shipbuilders and became embroiled in a struggle for political power within the city. See Towers, *Urban South*, 139–143.

53. Legislative Petition, Petersburg City, 1831, quoted in Alison Goodyear Freehling, *Drift Toward Dissolution: The Virginia Slavery Debate of 1831–1832* (Baton Rouge: Louisiana State University Press, 1982), 175; "Meeting of Mechanics," *Republican*, 24 January 1849; and "The Mechanics Meeting of Saturday Night," *Daily Southside Democrat*, 18 August 1857.

slave employment. As was true for the South generally, local government in Petersburg, which was controlled by slave owners, viewed any restrictions on the employment of slaves as a threat to the value of personal property.[54]

Because of the importance of slavery to their society, Petersburg mechanics also largely limited their complaints to competition with free African Americans. With few exceptions, slavery was not to be targeted. Only in the wake of the 1831 Nat Turner rebellion in Southampton County did Virginians, including Petersburg mechanics, openly express opposition to and debate the slavery question. A flood of legislative petitions concerning the fate of slavery in the Commonwealth swept over the General Assembly and helped to spark the 1832 debate over whether the institution should be abolished in Virginia.[55] But even then, most petitioners blamed the insurrection on the large free black population in the state.

Throughout the antebellum era, free African Americans shouldered the blame for the ills of society, and since they were not the protected property of slaveholders, it was common for them to be the target of petitions and public complaints. In 1838, residents of Dinwiddie County petitioned the General Assembly to remove all free blacks from Virginia through colonization, which they held to be a "cheap, certain, and humane remedy," to what they believed to be a "growing evil."[56] When the Panic of 1857 struck the economy of Petersburg and middling mechanics moved to organize against black competition, they were careful to limit their complaints to competition from free blacks, although they must have faced rivalry from slave artisans as well. The resolutions of the new PMA carefully avoided treading on "bad and dangerous ground" by asserting that they did "not aim to conflict with the interests of slave owners," but to elevate their own position in society.[57]

There are a number of reasons why black and white violence did not often

54. Ira Berlin, *Slaves Without Masters: The Free Negro in the Antebellum South* (New York: Vintage, 1974), 229–231; and Takaki, *Iron Cages,* 122–124.

55. Merton L. Dillon, *Slavery Attacked: Southern Slaves and their Allies, 1619–1865* (Baton Rouge: Louisiana State University Press, 1990), 158–161; and Stephen B. Oates, *The Fires of Jubilee: Nat Turner's Fierce Rebellion* (New York: New American Library, 1976), 154–158.

56. Legislative Petition, 9 January 1838, Dinwiddie County, Vi.

57. "The Mechanics' Meeting of Saturday Night," *Daily Southside Democrat,* 18 August 1857.

erupt among southern workers. In the South, where blacks formed a permanent underclass, whites did not have to struggle to define their whiteness as important. Southern society already made that distinction. In the South, the place of African Americans was so well defined as inferior by the antebellum era that mechanics counted whiteness as a basic benefit of living in the region.[58] No matter how wide the gap became between Petersburg masters and journeymen, the divide across the color line would always be larger. Through the cultivation of the proslavery argument southern elites encouraged poor and middling whites to distinguish themselves from blacks. John McCardell contends that as class distinctions threatened to create divisions in the South, the proslavery argument shifted away from a defense of slavery as a positive good and instead emphasized the racial differences and the belief that all white men benefited from slavery. Southern literature and the "pseudo science" of such men as Josiah Nott and George R. Gliddon provided evidence of the superiority of whites over blacks.[59]

Many southern artisans did in fact benefit from slavery even if they did not participate directly as slave owners or employers. The plantation economy that rested on luxurious estates producing agricultural products for market meant employment in the hinterland for many white artisans. Mechanics found meaningful employment as itinerants touring through plantation lands. The large scale of agricultural operations and wealth plantations generated led to important relationships between skilled white artisans and planters. Building and forging mechanics including blacksmiths, millwrights, and wheelwrights provided occasional but necessary service to mills, gins, and equipment on plantations.[60] Even some artisans skilled in luxury trades made a decent living off the plantations surrounding Petersburg. In the 1840s and 1850s, the owner of the White Hill plantation in Prince George County regularly hired Petersburg artisans, including saddlers, druggists, wheelwrights, cabinet makers, butchers, and hatters. The account books of City Point planter Richard Eppes show that in 1856 and 1857 he employed fifteen or more white artisans from Petersburg.

58. See Winthrop Jordan, *White Over Black: American Attitudes Toward the Negro, 1550–1812* (Baltimore: Penguin, 1969).

59. John McCardell, *The Idea of a Southern Nation: Southern Nationalists and Southern Nationalism, 1830–1860* (New York: W. W. Norton, 1979), 75–81.

60. Gillespie, *Free Labor in an Unfree World*, 116–121.

Their occupations included founders, druggists, carpenters, painters, bricklayers, cabinetmakers, saddlers, and even a coach maker, and tasks ranged from simple repairs of bed mattresses to construction projects earning the mechanic more than $400. In this way, small amounts of the wealth generated through slave labor on the plantations benefited the white artisans in the community of Petersburg even if they did not own slaves themselves.[61]

But there is another reason why white southern mechanics did not react physically against blacks. The slaveholding aspirations of many southern mechanics further complicated racial relations. James Oakes notes that in 1850, twenty thousand southern artisans owned at least one slave. In the early antebellum era, when slave prices and hire rates were relatively low, many Petersburg mechanics elevated their position in society by becoming slaveholders. For white mechanics, slave ownership was a visible symbol of their success and increasing social and economic status.[62] Of the prosperous members of the PBMA, more than half owned or leased slaves. Quite a few of the more middling mechanics in Petersburg also managed to purchase or lease slaves, although many held slaves only temporarily as their fortunes waxed and waned in the changing economy. In the 1850s, rising slave prices made the purchase or lease of slaves difficult for all but the most successful mechanics.

Yet in the late antebellum era when rising slave costs meant slaveholding was unreachable for most artisans, they still did not respond with violence. At an 1857 Petersburg slave auction, a 40-year-old enslaved blacksmith sold for $1,755, a 10-year-old boy for $1,025, a man of 50, "ruptured slightly" for $605, and a "rather weakly" young man brought $790.[63] The sale notice did not list the purchasers, but it is doubtful that middling white mechanics were among their number. For most Petersburg artisans on the eve of the Civil War, slave ownership was a visible symbol of someone else's success and another structural factor dividing bourgeois businessmen and middling workers. Although the aspiration of slaveholding was realized less and less, white mechanics in Petersburg and other parts of the South continued to reap other benefits from the

61. Account Book, 1839–1869, Charles Friend Papers, ViHi; and Richard Eppes Account Book, 1851–1861; and 1865–1868, 62–77, ViHi.

62. Oakes, *The Ruling Race*, 43, 58–59.

63. "Sale of Negroes," *Daily Express*, 12 December 1857.

slave system.[64] Through economic relationships with slaveholders, and a shared belief in the superiority of white men, Petersburg artisans clung to the notion that they were the social and political equal of elites in southern society.

Artisan workers in antebellum America shared many experiences, whether they lived in the North or the South. Drawing on the traditions of the Revolution they used the language of republicanism to support their claims of the superiority of manual labor and the importance of small producers in the early national era. Upwardly mobile masters in each region adapted republicanism to fit the acquisitive nature of their movement into the middle class and away from manual labor. Journeymen and less successful masters developed a competing interpretation of republicanism and uncovered alternative ways to define independence, emphasizing their responsibilities as citizens and coming to uneasy terms with a life of wage labor.

Despite many similarities in the history of northern and southern artisans, racial slavery stands out as an important distinction. Northern artisans complained that the changing industrial system was relegating them to a slave-like condition. Southern artisans, who often worked in proximity to enslaved workers, knew better. Like their northern counterparts, southern white artisans spurned comparison with, and competition from, African American workers. But with the southern economy resting largely on enslaved labor, southern artisans enjoyed a racial identity that naturally placed them above African Americans. In exchange for the psychological wage of white superiority, southern mechanics understood that they could not openly oppose slavery. When northern workers lashed out physically at blacks, southern mechanics made ineffective protests through conservative channels such as legislative petitions and organized protective organizations. Unlike northern artisans, most southern mechanics believed that they benefited from slavery, even after rising prices made slave ownership a fleeting dream.

At the end of the antebellum era, the busy industrial city of Petersburg bore little resemblance to the little town that had worked so hard to show its patriotism in celebration of the fiftieth anniversary of the Declaration of Independence in 1826. Tobacco factories, cotton mills, and iron foundries replaced many of the small shops where journeymen once believed that putting in a full

64. Gillespie, *Free Labor in an Unfree World*, 171.

day's work would help them earn a competence and open their own workshop. In this respect the experience of the southern artisan was hardly distinct from that of mechanics in antebellum New York City, Philadelphia, or Lynn. In both regions of the country, mechanics continued to espouse the language of republicanism and to celebrate the importance of free labor and independence, but the willingness of southern white artisans to embrace racial slavery forced them to trade their artisanal ideals for the values of the dominant race in a slaveholding society.[65]

65. Ibid., 39.

Epilogue

AND THEN THE WAR CAME

When the Civil War erupted in April 1861, James Coldwell was among the first to volunteer to serve the Confederacy. Enlisting as a private in Company B of the 12th Virginia Infantry, the Petersburg carpenter spent most of the war wielding a hammer instead of a rifle. First he helped build his regiment's winter quarters, then, in 1862, he went to South Carolina, where his job was to keep the telegraph lines in operation. In 1865, he rebuilt the telegraph lines William Tecumseh Sherman's army destroyed during its devastating march to the sea. Although dramatic changes rocked his world in the antebellum era, Coldwell was willing to fight with hammer and hand, or rifle, to preserve his trade and his place as a white man in southern society.[1]

The economic and social changes that transformed Petersburg from a small regional trading center into a bustling industrial city were a part of the gradual shift that affected all of America in the antebellum era. The market revolution created a national economy based on the values of acquisitive capitalism. New technologies in the form of transportation improvements allowed for broader market participation. As better roads, then canals and railroads, crossed the American countryside, domestic manufactures and trade became increasingly important and led to a broader industrialization of the economy.[2] Although the highest concentration of antebellum industry was in the North, southern cities, such as Petersburg, Richmond, and Baltimore, were highly industrialized and articulated developmental goals echoed in any number of growing northern towns and cities.[3]

1. William D. Henderson, *12th Virginia Infantry* (2nd ed., Lynchburg, Va.: H. E. Howard, 1984), 117.

2. Charles Sellers, *The Market Revolution: Jacksonian America, 1815–1846* (New York: Oxford University Press, 1991), 27–28; and George Rogers Taylor, *The Transportation Revolution, 1815–1860* (New York: Harper & Row, 1951), 396–398.

3. Gregg David Kimball, "Place and Perception: Richmond in Late Antebellum America"

In Petersburg, the newly evolving industrial economy brought uneven opportunities for skilled workers. Successful white masters with enough capital and proper personal connections transformed themselves into entrepreneurs, factory owners, and "bosses," and formed the Petersburg Benevolent Mechanic Association (PBMA) to foster their interests. These men constituted the core of an emerging middle class that wielded much power in Petersburg.[4] Along with merchants and lawyers, PBMA members were active in local politics. In a manner consistent with the planter-dominated oligarchies of rural Virginia, members of the emerging middle class controlled the Petersburg Hustings Court, held leadership roles in the state militia, and administered most advisory boards for local educational and poor relief institutions.[5] As was the case in the antebellum North, the masters of the PBMA separated themselves economically, socially, and ideologically from their journeymen employees. They adopted middle-class values, emphasizing temperance and self-improvement through education. Even in the wake of their upward mobility, however, PBMA masters retained ties to their artisanal roots. Although most no longer participated directly in productive labor, PBMA members continued to celebrate manual labor and emphasized the importance of the mechanic arts in the new economy. They adapted the language of artisanal republicanism to fit their new status in the community and to justify their economic success. In line with masters in the antebellum North, these successful southern mechanics-turned-entrepreneurs glorified the artisanal past to promote harmony among their journeymen, who often found fewer opportunities for advancement as the era progressed.

(Ph.D. diss., University of Virginia, 1997); Steven Elliott Tripp, *Yankee Town, Southern City: Race and Class Relations in Civil War Lynchburg* (New York: New York University Press, 1997); Frederick F. Siegel, *The Roots of Southern Distinctiveness: Tobacco and Society in Danville, Virginia, 1780–1865* (Chapel Hill: University of North Carolina Press, 1987); and Frank Towers, *The Urban South and the Coming of the Civil War* (Charlottesville: University of Virginia Press, 2004).

4. Stuart M. Blumin, *The Emergence of the Middle Class: Social Experience in the American City, 1760–1900* (Cambridge: Cambridge University Press, 1989), 134–136; John S. Gilkeson Jr., *Middle-Class Providence, 1820–1940* (Princeton, N.J.: Princeton University Press, 1986), 55–56; and Jonathan Daniel Wells, *The Origins of the Southern Middle Class, 1800–1861* (Chapel Hill: University of North Carolina Press, 2004), 7–11, 179–180.

5. Charles S. Sydnor, *Gentlemen Freeholders: Political Practices in Washington's Virginia* (Chapel Hill: University of North Carolina Press, 1952), 78–81.

White journeymen and less successful masters also had much in common with northern mechanics. Forming the bulk of the skilled workforce were men who entered the antebellum years with a hope of gaining independence and a competence under the traditional artisan system. For most of the middling mechanics in Petersburg, the very definition of independence and the nature of the artisan system altered and work was redefined under the division of labor and new economic realities. Permanent wage labor became a way of life for many, including the journeymen blacksmiths and metal workers who found they could not compete against the large foundries owned by PBMA members William H. Tappey, George L. Lumsden, and Uriah Wells. These artisans also redefined traditional artisanal republicanism to fit their new reality of wage labor. When independence and advancing to master status became a fleeting dream, they looked for other opportunities. Indeed, the increase in industrial establishments and concomitant population growth led some trades to flourish in antebellum Petersburg. A significant number of mechanics adapted to the change by pursuing industrial work at the large foundries, or prospered moderately as wage laborers under carpenters-turned-contractors in the building trades.

Petersburg artisans did not always acquiesce to the realities of the new industrial order. In some cases journeymen vocally protested unfair workshop practices, and apprentices who fell victim to ruthless masters ran away or sought court protection. But unlike mechanics in northern or large southern cities, Petersburg artisans were unlikely to have their political interests defended by either established political party.[6] The dominance of agriculture and slavery in the South ensured that the mechanics' chief complaint, competition from free African American and slave labor, fell on deaf ears. Even after achieving universal white manhood suffrage under the Virginia constitutional revision of 1851, middling white mechanics were often afraid to exercise their right to support legislation promoting the superiority of white labor over black.[7] Also unlike their northern counterparts, Petersburg artisans were not free to lash out

6. Sean Wilentz, *Chants Democratic: New York City and the Rise of the American Working Class, 1788–1850* (New York: Oxford University Press, 1984), 70–73; Howard B. Rock, *Artisans of the New Republic: The Tradesmen of New York City in the Age of Jefferson* (New York: New York University Press, 1979), 71; Towers, *Urban South*, 2–7.

7. Michele Gillespie, *Free Labor in an Unfree World: White Artisans in Slaveholding Georgia, 1789–1860* (Athens: University of Georgia Press, 2000), 141–142.

physically at African American workers. Although African Americans made up 49 percent of the city's population, Petersburg never experienced the race riots and racial violence that plagued northern cities. The political strength of slaveholding planters and industrialists ensured that mechanics channeled their protests through such ineffective means as legislative petitions.

The large concentration of free blacks and slaves in Petersburg also differentiates the experiences of Upper South and northern mechanics. For white artisans, location in the Upper South guaranteed them the psychological wage afforded all members of the dominant race in a slave society. The developing proslavery argument in the antebellum South, with its emphasis on the racial inferiority of African Americans, ensured that the southern working class remained divided across the color line. However difficult their economic position in the new economy, white artisans were always above blacks on the social ladder.[8] Most of the time white and black men worked side by side in Petersburg with few incidences of complaint. In stark contrast to the North, where African American artisans found it difficult to practice their trade, many Petersburg workshops employed a mix of white, black, and enslaved workers. Only in times of economic distress, such as those surrounding the depression following the Panic of 1857, did white artisans mobilize to protest competition from blacks in the skilled trades. Even then, the white artisans who formed the Petersburg Mechanic Association (PMA) avoided criticizing the institution of slavery. Many white mechanics, and a few free blacks, owned or aspired to own slaves. Others benefited indirectly from the institution through their work on the plantations in the hinterland surrounding Petersburg.

Free African American workers in Petersburg also found an experience significantly different from that of their northern counterparts. Although they faced legal and social proscription on a number of levels in Petersburg, African American artisans managed to hold on to 14 percent of the skilled occupations. Free blacks were denied the right to vote and the right to have a jury trial, and had to register and provide proof of their free status. They were sometimes lumped with slaves in city regulations forbidding both groups from smoking in public or keeping a dog. Holding a precarious position in the middle between slavery and absolute freedom, Petersburg African American artisans neverthe-

8. David. R. Roediger, *The Wages of Whiteness: Race and the Making of the American Working Class* (London: Verso, 1991), 52.

less were better off than their northern counterparts. They rarely faced racial violence, and except on a few occasions when white workers felt an economic pinch, worked harmoniously alongside whites and enslaved workers. Although African Americans did not practice elite trades such as silversmithing and coach making, many prospered in flourishing occupations in building and industrial trades. A substantial number became property owners and entrepreneurs, and even formed their own fraternal organization to protect their position in Petersburg society. Like their white counterparts, black artisans adapted to a changing economy and took advantage of opportunities as carpenters, black-smiths, and in traditional African American trades, such as barbering.

In other ways, Upper South artisans were not so different from those in the North in antebellum America. Some managed to advance into an emerging middle class of shopkeepers and factory owners. Others struggled to reach independence in a changing economy and settled for wage labor. As the market economy expanded, Petersburg masters and journeymen each adapted the language of artisanal republicanism to fit their new situation, and both groups continued to celebrate the importance of manual labor to society, although many of the masters removed themselves from productive work. Despite their similarities to northern artisans, Petersburg mechanics lived in a slave society that buffered the intrusion of industrial capitalism for white workers. Artisans in Petersburg, as white men, adapted traditional artisanal beliefs in uniquely southern ways. Their notions of equality, independence, and the superiority of free labor were always qualified as a *Herrenvolk* republicanism, for whites only. By accepting a place in white southern society, they gained a social equality based on race that was not available to northern mechanics. Their social and political identities defined them not just as artisans or workingmen, but as southerners as well.

Beginning in April 1861, with the onset of civil war, those social identities were on the line, and their way of life was irrevocably altered. Before the firing on Fort Sumter on 12 April, Petersburg did not favor secession. The city voted for Constitutional Union candidate John Bell in the presidential election of 1860, and Thomas Branch, the city's delegate to the Convention of 1861, supported remaining with the Union.[9] However, once Virginia became a member

9. James G. Scott and Edward A. Wyatt, *Petersburg's Story: A History* (Petersburg, Va.: Titmus Optical Company, 1960), 169–70; and William D. Henderson, *Petersburg in the Civil War: War at the Door* (Lynchburg, Va.: H. E. Howard, 1998), 18–20.

of the Confederacy, white Petersburgers rallied to the cause and supported the war effort. Petersburg's location just south of Richmond, the new capital of the Confederate States of America, made the city more important than ever. Industrial capacity and rail connections brought Petersburg to the forefront of the Confederate war effort as a strategic center for the transport of materiel and troops, and for the manufacture of armaments. The rush to war altered local priorities, so that tobacco took a back seat to iron forging, textile milling, and other manufacturing concerns directly tied to mobilization for battle. Artisans in those trades now found their skills in high demand as they chose between volunteering to fight for their new country and steady employment in the developing war economy.

Following Governor John Letcher's proclamation calling for troops to support the Confederate war effort, Virginia men rushed to join newly forming volunteer companies and regiments. In Petersburg, men camped on Poplar Lawn, the customary central mustering ground for local militia and now for the city's volunteer troops. Five existing Petersburg militia companies expanded with new recruits beginning on 19 April, and were eventually incorporated into the 12th Virginia Infantry. That regiment's command fell to longtime militia major and Petersburg commission merchant David A. Weisiger, who served as colonel of the 12th Virginia Infantry beginning in June 1861.[10] Among the artisans rushing to support the Confederacy on 19 April was twenty-one-year-old carpenter Henry Blanks, the son of prominent merchant tailor Henry A. Blanks. The younger Blanks joined as a private in Company A, but did not return to Petersburg. He was killed at the Battle of Malvern Hill the following July.[11] New Jersey–born apothecary George W. Emmons enlisted in Company C the same day, but was eventually detailed to Norfolk as a hospital steward. Emmons returned to Petersburg late in the war, then reportedly deserted to the Union in December 1864; apparently having had enough of war, he took a loyalty oath and left for Binghamton, New York.[12]

In May 1861, bricklayer and PBMA member Fletcher H. Archer raised another company, known as the Archer Rifles, also eventually incorporated into the 12th as Company K. Archer resigned as captain of Company K in September

10. Henderson, *12th Virginia Infantry*, 1–3; and Lee A. Wallace, *A Guide to Virginia Military Organizations 1861–1865* (rev. 2nd ed., Lynchburg, Va.: H. E. Howard, 1986), 234–237.

11. Henderson, *12th Virginia Infantry*, 111.

12. Ibid., 123.

1861, and returned to Petersburg, where he served as major and later lieutenant colonel of the 3rd Battalion of the Virginia State Reserves.[13] Machinist John Cooper, a partner in the Cooper and Rodman Foundry and Machine Shop, was among the first to enlist in the Archer Rifles. Cooper's experiences illustrate the importance of skilled artisans to the Confederate war effort. Because he was an accomplished metal worker, Cooper spent most of his enlistment plying his trade. Four months after volunteering, he was working at the Portsmouth shipyard, then in May 1862 he was reassigned to the naval shipyard at Rockett's Landing on the James River near Richmond.[14] Iron molder Alexander Baxter joined the Archer Rifles in late April 1862, but was almost immediately detailed back to Petersburg, where he spent the remainder of the war working in Uriah Wells's foundry.[15]

Petersburg eventually raised seventeen companies to aid the war effort, eleven infantry, three artillery, and three cavalry. Although most Petersburgers enlisted in one of six companies of the 12th, some locals joined companies of the Tidewater-centered 41st Virginia Infantry, which organized slightly later in July 1861.[16] The 12th Virginia Infantry drew most of its recruits from the urban areas of Petersburg, Richmond, and Norfolk. Skilled artisans and clerks, more so than general laborers, filled the ranks of the companies raised in Petersburg. Since many of the companies formed before the war as militia units, most of the men already knew each other and likely had worked alongside one another in Petersburg.[17] This meant that the 12th Virginia was a bit of an anomaly in the rural South, where over 60 percent of the average distribution of soldiers lived or worked on a farm.[18] The 12th and 41st Virginia Infantry regiments were among four units forming a brigade of the Army of Northern Virginia commanded by Brigadier General William Mahone. As a part of these units, Petersburg men saw considerable action at the battles of Seven Pines, Malvern Hill, Second Manassas, Fredericksburg, and Gettysburg.

13. Ibid., 107.

14. Ibid., 118; and W. Eugene Ferslew, comp., *Second Annual Directory for the City of Petersburg* (Petersburg, Va.: George E. Ford, 1860), 150.

15. Henderson, *12th Virginia*, 109.

16. Scott and Wyatt, *Petersburg's Story*, 170; and William D. Henderson, *41st Virginia Infantry* (Lynchburg, Va.: H. E. Howard, 1986), 1–5.

17. Henderson, *12th Virginia Infantry*, 3–4.

18. James M. McPherson, *Battle Cry of Freedom: The Civil War Era* (New York: Ballantine, 1989), 614–15.

Journeymen and middling masters were most likely to enter the army at the rank of private. Of the skilled men identified as joining either the 12th or 41st Virginia Infantry regiments, 85 percent began their service at that rank. Regimental officers, elected by the enlisted men, tended to come from the same rising middle class of merchants and manufacturers dominating the prewar political and economic structure. Either through appointment or officer election, Petersburg merchants and leading artisan-entrepreneurs who joined the 12th Virginia generally entered at a higher rank. Louis L. Marks, partner in the Maney and Marks Lumber Mill, was Company C's first lieutenant. William Beasley, a tobacco factory executive, filled the first lieutenant's post in Company D. Benjamin J. Eggleston, owner of a tobacco box factory, enlisted at the rank of sergeant for Company K in May 1861, but was discharged five months later after he purchased a substitute to fill his place.[19] Thus, the class divide that emerged in the antebellum era was well represented in the 12th Virginia Infantry.

On 19 April, the same day that volunteers rushed to join the Confederate Army, President Abraham Lincoln issued a proclamation instituting a blockade of all Confederate ports. The more than 260 warships blocking Confederate ports by the end of 1861 altered Petersburg's economy in fundamental ways.[20] Although some local businessmen invested in blockade-running ships, the Union blockade greatly curtailed the export of local goods to overseas markets. The tobacco industry, which dominated the prewar Petersburg economy, was especially hard hit. Wealthy tobacconist and PBMA member Robert Leslie learned early in the war that business could not continue as usual. In the spring of 1861, Leslie initiated sending a shipment of tobacco to Great Britain aboard the British *Hiawatha*, but it ran afoul of the Union blockade, was seized in the Hampton Roads area, and was diverted to New York. Between risking seizure and the rising cost of transporting goods across the blockade, Leslie considered continuing tobacco factory operations a losing prospect. He closed his factory and gave the building over to the Confederate war effort for use as a hospital.[21] Most fellow tobacconists followed suit and likewise converted their factories into Confederate hospitals. By September 1861, the countryside felt the crunch as well. The editor of the *Daily Express* urged area planters to prize their to-

19. Henderson, *12th Virginia Infantry*, 109, 123, 140.
20. McPherson, *Battle Cry of Freedom*, 313–314.
21. Henderson, *Petersburg*, 28–29, 32.

bacco and store it at home until "the country becomes more settled," because Petersburg warehouses were already crowded.[22]

Many Petersburg artisans remained in the city, where they helped advance the Confederate war effort in a variety of capacities. Despite the blockade, some industries and occupations found prosperity supporting the war effort. The building firm of Thomas Sheddon and David F. Shields contracted with the government to build 1,900 beds for Confederate hospitals in Petersburg and Richmond.[23] Painter and PBMA member Charles A. Delano painted Confederate and regimental flags to order. Merchant tailor Henry A. Blanks converted his firm to accept contracts for uniforms. Using well-paid female seamstresses, he boasted of the ability to fashion seventy-five to a hundred complete uniforms with ten to fifteen days' notice. Blanks noted, "Encourage a native born citizen or Yankee as you please, but I have the honor of being the only one carrying on the Tailoring business in the city."[24] Petersburg flour and textile mills also benefited from the Virginia's mobilization for war. Area cotton mills converted to war production, turning out sheeting for hospitals, shirting for undergarments, and tent ducking.[25]

Metal foundries reaped the largest gains during the war. Many artisans in metal crafts remained in the city or were detailed back to Petersburg foundries once they joined the Confederate Army. Their skills and special knowledge were vital to the war effort. William Tappey and George Lumsden's Southern Foundry produced an ill-operating revolving cannon, while Uriah Wells's foundry focused on the production of ordnance. The Mount Airy shop of the Petersburg Railroad stepped up production of freight and passenger cars. New industries appeared as well. The Confederate States Navy Powder Mill began gunpowder production near the locks on the Appomattox Canal with nitrate mined in niter beds surrounding Petersburg. The Navy supplied all its cordage needs from a Petersburg rope walk that continued operations until March 1865, employing both white and free black workers. The Army Medical Corps established a laboratory to act as a dispensary for medical supplies.[26]

Quickly creating a connection between Petersburg rail lines, the lack thereof

22. Editorial, *Daily Express*, 7 September 1861.
23. Henderson, *Petersburg*, 32–33.
24. Advertisements, *Daily Express*, 7 September, 28 September 1861.
25. Henderson, *Petersburg*, 35.
26. Ibid., 36, 56–57.

always a curiosity and an advantage to local businessmen in the antebellum era, also occupied skilled workers early in the war effort. The five railroads tying Petersburg to the coast and the interior of Virginia and North Carolina became critical links in the supply line feeding the Confederate Army. They also made the city a central stopping place for the wounded and refugees. Throughout the antebellum era, the carrying trade flourished in Petersburg because the railroads did not directly connect, so freight was unloaded, placed on carts or wagons, and hauled to another terminal to be reloaded onto the cars of another rail line. The offloading of goods kept many Petersburg cart and draymen employed, and ensured that Richmond did not siphon off Petersburg's share of commerce, but complicated the movement of military equipment. Removing the need to load and reload rail cars was especially opposed by African Americans in the carrying trade, many of whom earned a tidy profit during the early months of the war.

Completing a connection and railroad bridge at Petersburg became an early goal of Robert E. Lee, Virginia's commanding general. Writing to the Virginia Convention in June 1861, Lee reported the delay in transporting artillery and troops, and strongly requested that the lines be connected.[27] The Convention approved Lee's request and appointed a committee to determine the best way to connect the Petersburg Railroad, which stretched south to Weldon, North Carolina, and the Richmond and Petersburg Railroad. Concerned about lack of local support for a permanent connection, William T. Joynes, a member of the board appointed by the Petersburg Railroad Company, argued that in order to appease local residents, the connection should be a temporary one, in place only for the duration of the war, and be created at the government's expense. He noted that "it is well known that a great repugnance is felt by the citizens of Petersburg to any connection between the roads in question by means of which produce and merchandise would pass through Petersburg to and from Richmond."[28] On 25 July, workers began laying track and constructing a wooden bridge across the Appomattox River, connecting the two lines by 14 August 1861. Short line extensions from the Southside Railroad and the Norfolk and

---

27. *The War of the Rebellion: A Compilation of the Official Records of the Union and Confederate Armies* (Washington, D.C.: GPO, 1880–1901), series 4, 1: 394 (hereafter cited as OR).

28. *OR*, ser. 4, 1: 485–486.

Petersburg completed the rail junction, allowing the movement of goods and troops directly through the city.[29]

Dray and cartmen likely found their workloads reduced as a result of the rail junction, but the increase in population and bustling nature of the city at war left plenty of opportunity for those in the carrying trade. Over the course of 1861, Petersburg became a magnet for wounded soldiers who filled the hospitals opened in abandoned tobacco factories and for refugees fleeing parts of Virginia under heavy combat. In the spring of 1862, the *Daily Express* editor noted the change, remarking that Petersburg no longer seemed like a little provincial town. The growth of wartime industry and carrying trade coupled with an influx of hundreds of refugees swelled the city's population. The editor proudly supported the importance of Petersburg in the war effort and its recent growth, boasting "no matter how big and important we are, will the Yankees ever take us? No, sir."[30]

Despite the growth in population and industry, Petersburgers began feeling an economic pinch soon after the war started. Common goods grew scarce, so that as early as July 1861, prices for items such as chickens and butter soared. The blockade limited the amount, and raised the price, of imported merchandise available for sale and dry-goods merchants. In August 1861, Davis & Company advertised the availability of home-spun "Cassimore" and southern-made gray satinets for sewing. Noah Walker & Company advertised his stock of "clothing and furniture goods, embracing goods of Southern Manufacture."[31] Finally, it seemed the necessities of war accomplished what years of southern manufacturing conventions could not, and the South moved toward developing a domestic industrial economy. Unfortunately, scarcity of raw materials curtailed expansion. By mid-1863, Uriah Wells closed his metal foundry for long periods because of the short supply of pig iron.[32] Other artisans and factories experienced work stoppages due to a lack of raw materials. The resulting cyclical unemployment only added to Petersburg's economic malaise.

---

29. Henderson, *Petersburg*, 34; and Noah Andre Trudeau, *The Last Citadel: Petersburg, Virginia, June 1864–April 1865* (Boston: Little, Brown, 1991), 6.

30. "A Change," *Daily Express*, 14 May 1862.

31. Advertisements, *Daily Express*, 29 August 1861.

32. Henderson, *Petersburg*, 59.

Petersburg's slave community found their lives disrupted by the war as well. Following the General Assembly's passage of an impressment bill in October 1862, the Commonwealth began demanding that local governments provide slaves to labor on behalf of the Confederate cause. On 5 February 1863, the Petersburg Hustings Court met in response to Governor Letcher's call for 230 male slaves between the ages of 18 and 45 "to labor in fortifications and other works necessary for the public defenses."[33] Both individual and industrial slaveholders complied with the order. Among the 168 pressed into service on the first call were one held by tobacconist James Dunlop, 6 held by Tappey and Lumsden's Southern Foundry, and 11 held by the Petersburg Railroad.[34] As the war progressed, the official call for more slave labor became more frequent. In September 1863, Virginia began requisitioning male slaves up to age 55, requiring Petersburgers to provide an additional 30 that month and another 80 in February 1864. In January 1865, more than 300 of the slaves in Petersburg were in service to the Confederate government and a local census counted a mere 124 male slaves between ages 18 and 55.[35]

By the spring of 1864, the Confederacy's economic hardships led to severe problems in Petersburg. In March, residents held a mass meeting at the First Baptist Church to consider establishing a soup house to aid the poor. Rising food prices reached alarming heights that month when an auction sale brought $15 per pound for loaf sugar and $8 per pound for brown sugar.[36] That spring, devastation characterized the Petersburg economy. Retail trade largely ceased and by June, both major foundries closed. Only the cotton and flour mills under government contract continued operations.[37] Just when it seemed things could get no worse, the Union Army targeted Petersburg in an effort to bring an end to the terrible war.

Beginning 5 May, the Union Army landed at City Point, about nine miles outside Petersburg, and initiated a series of battles aimed at capturing the city. Over the next few weeks, priorities for Petersburgers turned toward the de-

33. Petersburg, Va., Hustings Court Minute Book 1861–1867, Library of Virginia, Richmond (microfilm), 203 (hereafter cited as Vi).

34. Ibid., 204–205.

35. Ibid., 290–291, 350, 435, 445–446.

36. The Mass Meeting Tonight," *Daily Express*, 15 March 1864; and "The Markets," *Daily Express*, 19 March 1864.

37. Henderson, *Petersburg*, 100–101.

fense of their city from the pending Union attack.[38] Some fled the city, but most remained. According to 12th Virginia Infantry surgeon and PBMA member John H. Claiborne, many stayed in Petersburg because "they [didn't] know the danger" or more likely because "they [had] no where to go."[39] The Union advance upon the city came on 9 June, and found an army of "old men and young boys" determined to defend their city.[40] With the aid of some regular Confederate troops, they repulsed the attack, but the cost of driving the Federals off was high. Fifteen residents were killed, eighteen wounded, and forty-five taken prisoner.[41] Among those dead were druggist George Jones and merchant tailor Henry A. Blanks. Instead of falling to the Union Army, Petersburg came under siege for 292 days, and was the last line of defense and the only obstacle keeping the Union Army from taking Richmond.[42]

During the long months of the siege, life in Petersburg became even more difficult. The Union Army continued shelling the city and many homes and businesses suffered physical damage. Pocahontas, the neighborhood where many free African Americans lived, was closest to the Union lines and suffered the most physical damage. Residents from the hardest hit areas formed cities of tents, filling many of Petersburg's vacant lots. The Union cut off access to the Petersburg Railroad, but the Richmond and Petersburg Railroad remained in operation. Business and trade came to a standstill, with the exception of the textile mills, which somehow managed to remain working.[43]

Hunger became a constant concern to Petersburg residents. What small amount of goods that found their way onto the shelves of city stores was priced beyond the reach of most residents. By July 1864, tomatoes sold for $5 a quart, ears of fresh corn $6 per dozen, a dozen eggs cost $10, while bacon and ham brought $9 per pound.[44] Residents, including many soldiers, looked to the Hustings Court for relief. In August, the Hustings Court made plans to provide

38. Trudeau, *The Last Citadel*, 5–9.

39. John Herbert Claiborne to his wife, 7 June 1864, Papers of John Herbert Claiborne, 1861–1905, University of Virginia Library, Charlottesville, Va.

40. See William G. Robertson, *The Battle of Old Men and Young Boys, June 9 1864* (Lynchburg, Va.: H. E. Howard, 1989).

41. Trudeau, *The Last Citadel*, 10–11.

42. Ibid., xiii.

43. Henderson, *Petersburg*, 119–127.

44. "What is to Become of Us?" *Daily Express,* 23 July 1864.

aid and began to gather a list of needy soldiers, and even in greater number, the widows and orphans of soldiers killed in the war. By the time city sergeant John H. Patterson compiled a list of needy soldiers, widows, and children, the Hustings Court deemed it "inexpedient at this time to make any allowance or provisions" for the needy.[45] The record does not offer a clear reason for this change of policy, however, considering the impoverished and besieged Petersburg economy, there may have been no relief to offer.

The siege of Petersburg ended with the withdrawal of the last Confederate troops on 3 April 1865. In the process of evacuation, Robert E. Lee's army destroyed tobacco valued at more than $1 million. The Confederates also set fire to the terminal of the Norfolk and Petersburg Railroad and a bridge spanning the Appomattox River.[46] Nevertheless, the Union forces occupied the city, closing all businesses until the owners agreed to take an oath of allegiance to the United States.[47] The process of restoring order and business began.

Two days later, on 5 April a very short-lived newspaper, *Grant's Petersburg Progress*, appeared. The single surviving issue offers a glimpse of Petersburg in the immediate aftermath of the siege and occupation. The editor noted that the industrial capacity of Petersburg remained viable; he counted five cotton textile mills and seven flour mills. Much of the town remained intact, although almost every church sustained considerable damage. African American residents gladly welcomed the Union troops, according to the editor, and were largely responsible for trying to save the bridge across the Appomattox upon which the Federals entered the city. A New York City reporter traveling with the occupying force described the damage and destruction Union shelling had caused. On Bollingbrook Street, he reported, "chimneys have been raised on every building, windows knocked and splintered to pieces, brick walls crumbled and torn, porches carried away."[48]

The destruction the war caused in Petersburg and across the South provided employment opportunities for returning veterans, including master carpenter James Coldwell. He returned to Petersburg carpentry business and set about rebuilding his city. He eventually served as lieutenant of police and commis-

45. Hustings Court Minute Book 1861–1867, 395–396, 401.

46. "Petersburg," *New York Tribune*, 6 April 1865.

47. Henderson, *Petersburg*, 135–139.

48. Articles, *Grant's Petersburg Progress*, 5 April 1865; and "Petersburg," *New York Tribune*, 7 April 1865.

sioner of the revenue. The war's physical damage could be repaired, but the world of Upper South artisans was irrevocably changed. The war brought an end to the institution of slavery, which had stood as the cornerstone of southern class and race relations. Gone was the bonus wage enjoyed by Petersburg's white mechanics. In the absence of slavery, skilled workers of both races, and southerners of all classes, began a renegotiation of their social world.

Appendix

TABLE 1 Population Figures, Petersburg, Virginia

	1800	1810	1820	1830	1840	1850	1860
A. Population							
Free whites	1,606	2,404	3,097	3,440	5,365	6,665	9,342
Free African Americans	428	1,089	1,165	2,032	2,134	2,616	3,244
Slaves	1,487	2,173	2,428	2,850	3,637	4,729	5,680
Total population	3,521	5,668	6,690	8,322	11,136	14,010	18,266
B. Percent of total population							
Free whites	45.6	42.4	46.2	41.3	48.1	47.5	51.1
Free African Americans	12.1	19.2	17.4	24.4	19.1	18.6	17.8
Slaves	42.2	37.7	36.2	34.2	32.6	33.7	31.0

Sources: Bureau of the Census, *Compendium of the Enumeration of the Inhabitants and Statistics of the United States, as Obtained at the Department of State, From the Returns of the Sixth Census* (Washington, D.C.: Thomas Allen, 1841), 32–34; Henry Howe, *Historical Collections of Virginia* (Charleston, S.C.: W. R. Babcock, 1849), 242; Bureau of the Census, *Statistical View of the United States: Compendium of the Seventh Census* (Washington, D.C.: Beverley Tucker, Senate Printer, 1854), 192–193; Bureau of the Census, *Population of the United States in 1860; The Eighth Census* (Washington, D.C.: GPO, 1864), 516, 519; and Historical Census Browser, University of Virginia, Geospatial and Statistical Data Center: http://fisher.lib.virginia.edu/collections/stats/histcensus/index.html (accessed 10 August 2006).

TABLE 2   Petersburg Benevolent Mechanic Association, 1825–60

	Number	Percent
Construction/woodworking crafts		
Builder	1	.3
Carpenter	41	12.6
Bricklayer	12	3.6
Brickmaker	2	.6
Coach trimmer	1	.3
Coach maker	10	3.0
Glass cutter	1	.3
Marble cutter	1	.3
Millwright	2	.6
Painter	5	1.5
Plasterer	4	1.23
Stone cutter	2	.6
Stone mason	4	1.23
Wheelwright	3	.9
Wood comber	1	.3
Wood sawyer	1	.3
Total	91	28
Clothing crafts		
Clothier	1	.3
Cotton manufacturer	3	.9
Hatter	6	1.8
Shoemaker	8	2.4
Tailor	25	7.6
Weaver	2	.6
Total	45	14
Leather crafts		
Saddler	12	3.6
Tanner and currier	7	2.15
Total	19	6

(Table 2 continued)

	Number	Percent
Food and tobacco		
Apothecary/druggist	4	1.2
Baker	4	1.2
Butcher	6	1.8
Chemist	1	.3
Confectioner	6	1.8
Flour manufacturer	6	1.8
Miller	12	3.6
Tobacconist	23	7.0
Tobacco manufacturer	2	.6
Total	64	20
Furniture		
Cabinetmaker	9	2.7
Upholsterer	1	.3
Total	10	3
Forging/manufacturing crafts		
Blacksmith	11	3.3
Buhrstone manufacturer	1	.3
Founder	2	.6
Gauger	2	.6
Gunsmith	6	1.8
Machinist	10	3.0
Manufacturer	1	.3
Pattern maker	1	.3
Plow maker	1	.3
Rope maker	1	.3
Tinner (coppersmith)	9	2.7
Total	45	14

(Table 2 continued)

	Number	Percent
Printing and paper		
Bookbinder	4	1.2
Printer	22	6.7
Total	26	8
Clocks/jewelry/pianos		
Jeweler	5	1.5
Watchmaker	7	2.1
Total	12	4
Transportation/service		
Engineer	3	.9
Physician/surgeon	6	1.8
Plumber	1	.3
Total	10	3
Boiling crafts/containers		
Potter	1	.3
Soap and candle maker	1	.3
Tallow chandler	1	.3
Total	3	1
Grand total	325*	

Source: Membership list, Petersburg Benevolent Mechanic Association Papers, University of Virginia, Charlottesville, Va.

*Number does not include honorary members.

TABLE 3   Petersburg Benevolent Mechanic Association, Slave Ownership of Members, 1847

Occupation	Number of slaveholders	Number of slaves held	Average holdings
Blacksmith	2	9	4.5
Bookbinder	1	3	3
Bricklayer/maker/stonemason	6	31	5.1
Buhrstone manufacturer	1	1	1
Butcher	3	15	5
Cabinet maker	3	10	3.3
Carpenter	8	13	1.6
Chemist	1	2	2
Coachmaker	3	8	2.6
Confectioner	2	7	3.5
Coppersmith/tinsmith	2	5	2.5
Cordwainer/shoemaker	5	9	1.8
Cotton/muslin manufacturer	2	10	5
Druggist	3	15	5
Engineer	1	1	1
Flour manufacturer	2	9	4.5
Gunsmith	1	1	1
Hatter/hat manufacturer	2	2	1
Honorary member	7	45	6.4
Jeweler/watchmaker	3	5	1.6
Machinist	4	6	1.5
Miller	3	15	5
Painter	1	2	2
Plasterer/slater	2	3	1.5
Printer	3	14	4.6
Saddler	3	14	4.6
Surgeon	3	9	3
Tailor	7	11	1.5
Tanner/currier	2	7	3.5
Tobacconist	9	191	21.2
Weaver	2	3	1.5
Total	97	476	4.9

Source: Petersburg, Va., Personal Property Tax Ledger, 1847, Library of Virginia, Richmond.

TABLE 4   Census Distribution of Skilled Male Workers, Petersburg, Virginia

Skilled workers	1850	1860	% increase
Virginia- or southern-born (white)	698	1,077	54
Northern-born (white)	44	108	145
Foreign-born (white)	77	179	132
Black (free)	76	157	106
Mulatto (free)	47	60	28
Total white	819	1,364	67
Total black	123	217	76

Source: Bureau of the Census, Population Schedules, Petersburg, Va., 1850, 1860 (microfilm).

TABLE 5   Skilled Middling White Workers

Group	Number	Percent
A. Distribution of skilled middling white workers by occupational group		
Construction/woodworking crafts	656	34
Clothing crafts	195	10
Leather crafts	59	3
Food and tobacco	341	18
Furniture	60	3
Forging/manufacturing	349	18
Printing and paper	70	4
Clocks/jewelry/pianos	41	2
Transportation/service	120	6
Boiling crafts/containers	36	2
Total	1,927	

B. Occupational breakdown of skilled middling white workers

Construction/woodworking crafts

Carpenter	333	
Boatbuilder	1	
Bodymaker	2	
Bricklayer	68	
Brickmaker/molder	6	
Carriage/coach trimmer	8	
Coach maker/smith	41	

(*Table 5 continued*)

Group	Number	Percent
Coach painter	2	
Fresco painter	1	
Granite cutter	2	
Joiner	1	
Marble workman	7	
Millwright	10	
Painter	66	
Planing miller	2	
Plasterer	13	
Sawyer	5	
Ship carpenter	2	
Ship chandler	1	
Slater	5	
Stone cutter	26	
Stone mason	23	
Tobacco mill maker	2	
Wheelwright	27	
Whitewasher	2	
Total	656	
Clothing crafts		
Hatter	3	
Merchant tailor	8	
Shoe/boot maker	104	
Tailor	79	
Weaver	1	
Total	195	
Leather crafts		
Harness maker	25	
Saddler	33	
Tanner	1	
Total	59	
Food and tobacco		
Apothecary/druggist	41	
Baker	43	
Bottler	4	

(Table 5 continued)

Group	Number	Percent
Butcher	38	
Cigar/segar maker	12	
Confectioner/candy maker	28	
Miller	55	
Tobacconist	120	
Total	341	
Furniture		
Cabinet maker	52	
Upholsterer	8	
Total	60	
Forging/manufacturing crafts		
Blacksmith	88	
Bobbin manufacturer	1	
Brand cutter	1	
Car maker/builder	4	
Dyer	2	
Finisher	23	
Founder	3	
Gainer and finisher	1	
Gas fitter	6	
Gunsmith	12	
Machinist	87	
Mechanic	20	
Molder	29	
Pattern maker	5	
Plater	1	
Plow maker	5	
Rope maker	5	
Tinner/coppersmith	55	
Trimmer	1	
Total	349	
Printing and paper		
Bookbinder	6	
Editor	2	
Printer	62	
Total	70	

APPENDIX

(Table 5 continued)

Group	Number	Percent
Clocks/jewelry/pianos		
Engraver	2	
Jeweler	9	
Locksmith	1	
Piano maker	1	
Piano tuner	3	
Silver plater/smith	8	
Watchmaker	17	
Total	41	
Transportation/service		
Barber	2	
Cartman	16	
Civil engineer	3	
Daguerian	5	
Dentist	7	
Engine driver	8	
Florist	2	
Gardner	6	
Physician	63	
Plumber	4	
Surveyor	2	
Veterinary surgeon	1	
Wagoner	1	
Total	120	
Boiling crafts/containers		
Basket maker	2	
Box maker	6	
Cooper	14	
Jug manufacturer	1	
Potter	2	
Soap/tallow chandler	10	
Willow ware maker	1	
Total	6	
Grand total	1,927	

Source: Categories based on Howard B. Rock, *Artisans of the New Republic: The Tradesmen of New York City in the Age of Jefferson* (New York: New York University Press, 1979), 13.

TABLE 6 Skilled Middling White Artisans

Group/Title	Number	Percent
A. Persisting middling white artisans by occupational group (artisans enumerated in 1850 Petersburg census and persisting through 1860 census)		
Construction/woodworking crafts	73	39
Clothing crafts	21	11
Leather	5	3
Food/tobacco	26	14
Forging/manufacturing	22	12
Furniture	8	4
Printing/paper	4	2
Clocks/jewelry	4	2
Transportation/service	18	10
Boiling crafts/containers	6	3
Total	187	
B. Occupational distribution of persisting middling white artisans (artisans enumerated in 1850 Petersburg census and persisting through 1860 census)		
Bell gauger	1	
Apothecary/druggist	5	
Baker	1	
Blacksmith	5	
Bookbinder	1	
Bricklayer	5	
Butcher	2	
Cabinetmaker	8	
Carpenter	33	
Cartman	1	
Cigar maker	1	
Coach maker	11	
Confectioner	1	
Cooper	2	
Dyer/daguerreian	1	
Engineer	2	
Gunsmith	2	
Hatter	2	
Leather dealer	2	
Machinist	5	
Mechanic	2	
Miller	2	

(Table 6, continued)

Group/Title	Number	Percent
Painter	13	
Physician/M.D.	15	
Plasterer	2	
Plow maker	1	
Printer	3	
Saddle/harness maker	3	
Shoe/boot maker	12	
Silversmith	1	
Soap/tallow chandler	4	
Stabler	1	
Stone cutter/mason	6	
Surveyor	1	
Tailor	6	
Tinner	3	
Tobacco inspector	2	
Tobacconist	12	
Watchmaker/jeweler	3	
Weaver	1	
Wheelwright	3	
Total	187	

TABLE 7   Adult Free Workingmen by Nativity and Race, 1860

City	Number	*Percentage of Workingmen*			
		Southern-born white	Northern-born white	Foreign-born white	Free black
Richmond	4,929	39	8	39	14
Charleston	3,846	28	6	52	14
Mobile	4,552	19	14	64	3
Nashville	2,533	42	12	41	5
Petersburg	2,373	54	4	11	30
Lynchburg	661	62	4	20	14
Baton Rouge	529	35	11	47	7

Sources: Ira Berlin and Herbert G. Gutman, "Natives and Immigrants, Free Men and Slaves: Urban Workingmen in the Antebellum American South," *American Historical Review* 88 (December 1983): 1181; and Bureau of the Census, Population Schedules, Petersburg, Va., 1860.

TABLE 8   Free Workingmen, Skilled and Unskilled, 1860

City	Number	Percentage of Workingmen			
		Southern-born white	Northern-born white	Foreign-born white	Free black
A. Skilled free workingmen					
Richmond	3, 341	48	10	36	6
Charleston	2,413	38	6	40	16
Mobile	2,211	25	17	54	3
Nashville	1,522	46	17	33	4
Petersburg	1,581	68	7	11	14
Lynchburg	434	70	5	18	7
Baton Rouge	416	36	12	44	8
B. Unskilled free workingmen					
Richmond	1,588	20	4	46	30
Charleston	1,433	11	5	72	11
Mobile	2,341	14	12	69	4
Nashville	1,011	35	4	51	9
Petersburg	792	27	0.5	9	64
Lynchburg	227	46	2	25	27
Baton Rouge	113	34	5	57	4

Sources: Ira Berlin and Herbert G. Gutman, "Natives and Immigrants, Free Men and Slaves: Urban Workingmen in the Antebellum American South," American Historical Review 88 (December 1983): 1181; and Bureau of the Census, Population Schedules, Petersburg, Va., 1860.

TABLE 9   Petersburg Area Manufacturers, 1860

Trade	Number of firms	Men employed
A. Petersburg City		
Bookbinder/manufacturer	1	3
Cabinetmaker	1	12
Coach maker/wagoner	6	41
Confectionery	1	5
Copper/tinsmith	2	25
Cotton textile factory	2	140
Flour/grain mill	3	52
Foundry/ironworks	1	70
Fertilizer manufacturer	1	12
Pottery/stoneware	1	6
Saddle/harness maker	3	22
Shoe/boot manufacturer	3	20
Soap/candle maker	2	7
Stone/granite works	1	10
Tobacco factory	22	1,929
Total	50	2,354
B. Chesterfield County		
Blacksmith	6	8
Brick manufactory	2	40
Coal mine	4	483
Cooper	7	30
Cotton textile factory	5	441
Flour/grain mill	4	68
Foundry/ironworks	2	45
Millwright	1	3
Saw/grist mill/lumber	10	61
Shoe/boots	2	2
Stone quarry	1	18
Tobacco factory	2	145
Wheelwright	3	7
Total	49	1,351

Source: Bureau of the Census, 1860 Census, Schedule 5, Products of Industry during the Year Ending 1 June 1860, microfilm.

TABLE 10   Free Black Population, Selected Urban Areas in the South, 1850

City	Total population	Free black population	Percent of total free	Percent of total population
Baltimore, Md.	169,054	25,442	15.3	15
Charleston, S.C.	42,985	3,441	14.6	8
Louisville, Ky.	43,194	1,538	4	3.5
Mobile, Ala.	20,515	715	5.2	3.4
Nashville, Tenn.	10,165	511	6.2	5
New Orleans, La.	133,650	10,330	9	7.7
Norfolk, Va.	14,326	956	9.5	6
Petersburg, Va.	14,010	2,616	28.1	18.6
Richmond, Va.	27,570	2,369	13	8.5
Savannah, Ga.	15,312	686	7.5	4.4

Source: Bureau of the Census, *Statistical View of the United States: Compendium of the Seventh Census* (Washington, D.C.: Beverley Tucker, Senate Printer, 1854), 397–398.

TABLE 11   Skilled Free Black Workers

Group	Number	Percent
A. Distribution of skilled free black workers by occupational group		
Construction/woodworking crafts	128	44
Clothing crafts	26	9
Food and tobacco	16	6
Furniture	1	0.3
Forging/manufacturing	39	13
Transportation/service	68	23
Boiling crafts/containers	14	5
Total	292	100.3
B. Occupational breakdown of skilled free black workers		
Construction/woodworking crafts		
Carpenter	57	
Caulker	2	
Bricklayer	32	
Brickmaker/molder	8	

(Table 11, continued)

Group	Number	Percent
Painter	5	
Plasterer	4	
Sawyer	8	
Screwman	1	
Stone mason	6	
Wheelwright	2	
Whitewasher	3	
Total	128	
Clothing crafts		
Tailor	1	
Shoe/boot maker	25	
Total	26	
Food and tobacco		
Baker	1	
Butcher	5	
Candy maker	1	
Fisherman	2	
Miller	5	
Tobacconist	2	
Total	16	
Furniture crafts		
Upholsterer	1	
Total	1	
Forging/manufacturing crafts		
Blacksmith	36	
Finisher	1	
Machinist	1	
Tinner	1	
Total	39	
Transportation/service		
Barber	25	
Boatman	21	
Cartman/cartie	8	
Drayman	1	

(Table 11, continued)

Group	Number	Percent
Driver furniture wagon	1	
Gardener	6	
Wagoner	5	
Well digger	1	
Total	68	
Boiling crafts/containers		
Cooper	14	
Total	14	
Grand total	292	

Source: Categories based on Howard B. Rock, *Artisans of the New Republic: The Tradesmen of New York City in the Age of Jefferson* (New York: New York University Press, 1979), 13.

TABLE 12   Slaveholding Patterns of Petersburg Tobacconists, 1850

Business	Slaves owned
James Blankenship	14
William Cameron	13
James Chieves	51
David Dunlop	62
Dunlop & Tennant	30
Owen H. Hobson	37
Jones & Hudson	94
Robert Leslie	31
William Long	23
McEnery & McCulloch	22
Gilbert V. Rambaut	15
John Sturdivant	39
J. S. and J. D. Williams	36
Total	467

Source: Stephen E. Bradley, comp., *1850 Federal Census Dinwiddie County, Virginia and the City of Petersburg* (Keysville, Va.: Author, 1991), 129–142.

Bibliography

Primary Sources

Government Documents

Bradley, Stephen E. *The 1850 Federal Census Dinwiddie County, Virginia and the City of Petersburg.* Keysville, Va.: Author, 1991.

Tate, Joseph. *A Digest of the Laws of Virginia.* Richmond: Shepherd and Pollard, 1823.

U.S. Bureau of the Census. 1850 U.S. Census, Schedule 5, Products of Industry, Fiscal Year 1849–1850, microfilm.

———. 1860 Census, Schedule 5, Products of Industry during the Year Ending June 1, 1860, microfilm.

———. *Population of the United States in 1860: The Eighth Census.* Washington, D.C.: GPO, 1864.

———. Population Schedules of the Eighth Census of the United States, 1860, roll 1389, Virginia, Slave Schedules, vol. 2, microfilm.

———. Population Schedules of the Seventh Census of the United States, 1850, microfilm.

———. Records of the 1820 Census of Manufactures, roll 18, Schedules for Virginia, microfilm.

———. *Compendium of the Enumeration of the Inhabitants and Statistics of the United States, as Obtained at the Department of State, From the Returns of the Sixth Census.* Washington, D.C.: Thomas Allen, 1841.

———. *Statistical View of the United States, Compendium of the Seventh Census.* Washington, D.C.: Beverley Tucker, Senate Printer, 1854.

———. *The Seventh Census of the United States, 1850.* Washington, D.C.: Robert Armstrong, 1853.

———. *Statistics of the United States in 1860.* Washington, D.C.: GPO, 1866.

Virginia, *Acts of the General Assembly.* Richmond: Samuel Shepherd and others, 1824–1860.

Virginia, *Acts of the General Assembly of Virginia Relative to the Jurisdiction and Powers of the Town of Petersburg: To Which are Added, the Ordinances, Bye-laws, and Regulations of the Corporation.* Petersburg, Va.: Edward Pescud, 1824.

Virginia, *The Revised Code of the Laws of Virginia.* Richmond: Thomas Ritchie, 1819.

The War of the Rebellion: A Compilation of the Official Records of the Union and Confederate Armies. Washington, D.C.: GPO, 1880–1901.

Newspapers

American Constellation (Petersburg, Va.)
Daily Express (Petersburg, Va.)
Daily Southside Democrat (Petersburg, Va.)
Grant's Petersburg Progress
Intelligencer and Petersburg Commercial Advertiser
New York Tribune
Niles' Weekly Register (Baltimore)
Progress-Index (Petersburg, Va.)
Republican (Petersburg, Va.)
Richmond Daily Whig
Th' Time O' Day (Petersburg, Va.)

Manuscript Collections

LIBRARY OF VIRGINIA, RICHMOND, VA.

Legislative Petitions, 1810–1847.

Petersburg, Va. Hustings Court Minute Books, 1820–1867, microfilm.

Petersburg, Va. Hustings Court Will Books, 1–6, microfilm.

Virginia, Dept. of Taxation, Personal Property Tax List, City of Petersburg, 1820–1850, microfilm.

Virginia, Dept. of Taxation, Personal Property Tax List, City of Petersburg, 1851–1859.

VIRGINIA HISTORICAL SOCIETY, RICHMOND, VA.

Branch & Company, Richmond, Va., Records, 1837–1976.

Charles Friend Papers.

John Vaughan Wilcox Papers.

Petersburg Benevolent Mechanic Association, Petersburg, Va., Records, 1825–1836.

Richard Eppes Account Book, 1851–1861.

Richard Eppes, Diary, 12 March–30 September 1852.

Richard G. Dunn Papers.

Upper Appomattox Company Records.

"Virginia & N. Carolina French Burr Mill-Stone Manufactory," Broadside, 1836.

SPECIAL COLLECTIONS, VIRGINIA POLYTECHNIC INSTITUTE AND STATE
UNIVERSITY, BLACKSBURG, VA.

Norfolk and Western Railway Archives

VIRGINIA STATE UNIVERSITY, PETERSBURG, VA.

Colson/Hill Papers.

John K. Shore Papers, Receipts and Bills, 1844–1845, box 19, Colson-Hill Family Papers, 1834–1984.

SPECIAL COLLECTIONS, UNIVERSITY OF VIRGINIA, CHARLOTTESVILLE, VA.

Gillfield Baptist Church Records, microfilm.

Papers of John Herbert Claiborne, 1861–1905.

Petersburg Benevolent Mechanic Association Papers, 1825–1921, microfilm.

Published Sources

Brown, Henry Box. *Narrative of Henry Box Brown.* Boston: Brown & Stearns, 1849.

Bruce, H. C. *The New Man: Twenty-Nine Years a Slave, Twenty-Nine Years a Free Man.* York, Pa.: F. Amstadt & Sons, 1895.

Byrd, William. *Journey to the Land of Eden and other Papers by William Byrd.* New York: Vanguard, 1928.

Charter and By-Laws of the Petersburg Benevolent Mechanic Association . . . Revised October, 1900. Petersburg, Va.: Fenn & Owen, 1900.

Claiborne, John Herbert. *Seventy-Five Years in Old Virginia.* New York: Neale, 1904.

The Constitution of the Charleston Mechanic Society, Instituted at Charleston, South-Carolina, 1794. Charleston, S.C.: James and Williams, Printers, 1858.

Delano, Charles Anson. *The Man-Child Born of the Sun, and an Exposition of the Prophecies of Daniel and the Book of Revelation.* Petersburg, Va.: Author, 1858.

Fitzhugh, George. *Sociology for the South or the Failure of Free Society.* Richmond: A. Morris, 1854.

Harris, William Tell. *Remarks Made During a Tour of the United States of America in the Years 1817, 1818, and 1819.* London: Sherwood, Neely & Jones, 1821.

Historical Census Browser, University of Virginia, Geospatial and Statistical Data Center: http://fisher.lib.virginia.edu/collections/stats/histcensus/index.html (accessed 8 August 2006).

Hodgson, Adam. *Remarks During a Journey Through North America in the Years 1819, 1820, and 1821 in a Series of Letters.* 1823. Reprint, Westport, Conn.: Negro Universities Press, 1970.

Martin, Joseph. *A New and Comprehensive Gazetteer of Virginia, and the District of Columbia.* Charlottesville, Va.: Joseph Martin, Mosely & Tomkins, Printers, 1836.

Mendell, [Sarah], and [Charlotte] Hosmer. *Notes of Travel and Life.* New York: Authors, 1854.

Olmsted, Frederick Law. *The Slave States before the Civil War.* Edited by Harvey Wish. New York: Capricorn, 1959.

Petersburg Common Council. *The Charter and Laws of the City of Petersburg.* Petersburg, Va.: O. Ellyson, 1852.

Pickard, Kate E. R. *The Kidnapped and the Ransomed.* 1856. Reprint, n.p.: Negro Publication Society of America, 1941.

Second Annual Directory for the City of Petersburg. Compiled by W. Eugene Ferslew. Petersburg, Va.: George E. Ford, 1860.

Thomson's Mercantile and Professional Directory. Baltimore: William Thomson, 1851.

Secondary Sources

Articles and Chapters

Babcock, Robert H. "The Decline of Artisan Republicanism in Portland, Maine, 1825–1850." *New England Quarterly* 63 (1990): 3–34.

Berlin, Ira, and Herbert G. Gutman. "Natives and Immigrants, Free Men and Slaves: Urban Workingmen in the Antebellum American South." *American Historical Review* 88 (December 1983): 1175–1200.

Berry, Thomas S. "The Rise of Flour Milling in Richmond." *Virginia Magazine of History and Biography* 78 (1970): 387–408.

Bodenhorn, Howard. "Private Banking in Antebellum Virginia: Thomas Branch & Sons of Petersburg." *Business History Review* 71 (1997): 513–542.

Crofts, Daniel W. "Late Antebellum Virginia Reconsidered." *Virginia Magazine of History and Biography* 107 (1999): EBSCOhost.

Daniels, Christine. "'WANTED: A Blacksmith who Understands Plantation Work': Artisans in Maryland 1700–1810." *William and Mary Quarterly* 50 (3rd ser. October 1993): 743–767.

Downey, Tom. "Riparian Rights and Manufacturing in Antebellum South Carolina: William Gregg and the Origins of the 'Industrial Mind.'" *Journal of Southern History* 65 (February 1999): 77–108.

Ford, Lacy K., Jr. "Making the 'White Man's' Country White: Race, Slavery, and State-Building in the Jacksonian South." *Journal of the Early Republic* 19 (Winter 1999): 713–737.

Gillespie, Michele. "To Harden a Lady's Hand: Gender Politics, Racial Realities, and Women Millworkers in Antebellum Georgia." In *Neither Lady nor Slave: Working Women of the Old South,* edited by Susanna Delfino and Michele Gillespie. Chapel Hill: University of North Carolina Press, 2002.

Goldfield, David R. "Pursuing the American Urban Dream: Cities in the Old South." In *The City in Southern History: The Growth of Urban Civilization in the South,* edited by Blaine A. Brownwell and David R. Goldfield. Port Washington, N.Y.: Kennikat, 1977.

Green, Rodney D. "Industrial Transition in the Land of Chattel Slavery: Richmond, Virginia, 1820–60." *International Journal of Urban and Regional Research* 8, no. 2 (1984): 238–253.

Henderson, William D. "'A Great Deal of Enterprise': The Petersburg Cotton Mills in the Nineteenth Century." *Virginia Cavalcade* 30 (September 1981): 176–185.

Jackson, Luther P. "Free Negroes of Petersburg." *Journal of Negro History* 12 (1927): 365–388.

———. "Manumission in Certain Virginia Cities." *Journal of Negro History* 15 (1930): 278–314.

Rice, Philip Morrison. "The Know-Nothing Party in Virginia, 1854–1855." *Virginia Magazine of History and Biography* 55 (January 1947): 61–75.

Roediger, David R. "The Pursuit of Whiteness: Property, Terror, and Expansion, 1790–1860." *Journal of the Early Republic* 19 (Winter 1999): 579–600.

Rousey, Dennis C. "From Whence They Came to Savannah: The Origins of an Urban Population in the Old South." *Georgia Historical Quarterly* 79 (1995): 305–336.

Russo, Jean B. "Self-sufficiency and Local Exchange: Free Craftsmen in the Rural Chesapeake Economy." In *Colonial Chesapeake Society,* edited by Lois Green Carr, Philip D. Morgan, and Jean B. Russo. Chapel Hill: University of North Carolina Press for the Institute of Early American History and Culture, 1988.

Shade, William G. "Society and Politics in Antebellum Virginia's Southside." *Journal of Southern History* 53 (1987): 163–193.

Siegel, Fred. "Artisans and Immigrants in the Politics of Late Antebellum Georgia." *Civil War History* 27 (1984): 221–230.

Smith, James W. "The Role of Blacks in Petersburg's Carrying Trade and Service-Oriented Industry, 1800–1865." *Virginia Geographer* 16 (1984): 15–22.

Steffen, Charles G. "Changes in the Organization of Artisan Production in Baltimore, 1790–1820." *William and Mary Quarterly* 36 (3rd ser. 1979): 101–117.

Stewart, Peter C. "Railroads and Urban Rivalries in Antebellum Eastern Virginia." *Virginia Magazine of History and Biography* 81 (1973): 3–22.

Watkinson, James D. "Reluctant Scholars: Apprentices and the Petersburg (Virginia) Benevolent Mechanics' Association's School." *History of Education Quarterly* 36 (1996): 429–448.

Wyatt, Edward A. "Rise of Industry in Ante-Bellum Petersburg." *William and Mary Quarterly* 17 (2nd ser. January 1937): 1–36.

Books

Appleby, Joyce. *Capitalism and a New Social Order: The Republican Vision of the 1790s.* New York: New York University Press, 1984.

———. *Inheriting the Revolution: The First Generation of Americans.* Cambridge, Mass.: The Belknap Press of Harvard University Press, 2000.

Ayers, Edward L. *In the Presence of Mine Enemies: War in the Heart of America, 1859–1863.* New York: W. W. Norton, 2003.

Bateman, Fred, and Thomas Weiss. *A Deplorable Scarcity: The Failure of Industrialization in the Slave Economy.* Chapel Hill: University of North Carolina Press, 1981.

Berlin, Ira. *Slaves Without Masters: The Free Negro in the Antebellum South.* New York: Vintage, 1974.

———. *Generations of Captivity: A History of African-American Slaves.* Cambridge, Mass.: The Belknap Press of Harvard University Press, 2003.

Blassingame, John. *Black New Orleans, 1860–1880.* Chicago: University of Chicago Press, 1973.

Blumin, Stuart M. *The Emergence of the Middle Class: Social Experience in the American City, 1760–1900.* New York: Cambridge University Press, 1989.

Bourke, Paul, and Donald DeBats. *Washington County: Politics and Community in Antebellum America.* Baltimore: Johns Hopkins University Press, 1995.

Bridenbaugh, Carl. *The Colonial Craftsman.* Chicago: University of Chicago Press, 1950.

Bruce, Kathleen. *Virginia Iron Manufacture in the Slave Era.* New York: Century, 1930.

Cappon, Lester J. *Virginia Newspapers, 1821–1935: A Bibliography with Historical Introduction and Notes.* New York: D. Appleton-Century, 1936.

Clawson, Mary Ann. *Constructing Brotherhood: Class, Gender, and Fraternalism.* Princeton, N.J.: Princeton University Press, 1989.

Click, Patricia C. *The Spirit of the Times: Amusements in Nineteenth-Century Baltimore, Norfolk, and Richmond.* Charlottesville: University Press of Virginia, 1989.

Crofts, Daniel W. *Old Southampton: Politics and Society in a Virginia County, 1834–1869.* Charlottesville: University Press of Virginia, 1992.

Cronon, William. *Nature's Metropolis: Chicago and the Great West.* New York: W. W. Norton, 1991.

Crossick, Geoffrey, ed. *The Artisan and the European Town, 1500–1900.* Hants, U.K.: Scholar, 1997.

Crossick, Geoffrey, and Heinz-Gerhard Haupt. *Shopkeepers and Masters Artisans in Nineteenth-Century Europe.* London: Methuen, 1984.

Curry, Leonard P. *The Free Black in Urban America 1800–1850.* Chicago: University of Chicago Press, 1981.

Davis, Susan G. *Parades and Power: Street Theatre in Nineteenth-Century Philadelphia.* Philadelphia: Temple University Press, 1986.

Dew, Charles B. *Bond of Iron: Master and Slave at Buffalo Forge.* New York: W. W. Norton, 1994.

———. *Ironmaker to the Confederacy: Joseph R. Anderson and the Tredegar Iron Works.* New Haven: Yale University Press, 1966.

Dillon, Merton L. *Slavery Attacked: Southern Slaves and their Allies, 1619–1865.* Baton Rouge: Louisiana State University Press, 1990.

Faler, Paul G. *Mechanics and Manufacturers in the Early Industrial Revolution: Lynn Massachusetts 1780–1860.* Albany: State University of New York Press, 1981.

Fields, Barbara Jeanne. *Slavery and Freedom on the Middle Ground: Maryland during the Nineteenth Century.* New Haven: Yale University Press, 1985.

Fink, Leon. *Workingmen's Democracy: The Knights of Labor and American Politics.* Urbana: University of Illinois Press, 1983.

Fogel, Robert William, and Stanley L. Engerman. *Time On the Cross: The Economics of American Negro Slavery.* 1974. Reprint, New York: W. W. Norton, 1989.

Foner, Eric. *Free Soil, Free Labor, Free Men: The Ideology of the Republican Party Before the Civil War.* 1970. Reprint, New York: Oxford University Press, 1995.

Foner, Philip S., and Ronald L. Lewis. *Black Workers: A Documentary History from Colonial Times to the Present.* Philadelphia: Temple University Pres, 1989.

Franklin, John Hope. *The Free Negro in North Carolina, 1790–1860.* 1943. Reprint, New York: W. W. Norton, 1971.

Freehling, Alison Goodyear. *Drift Toward Dissolution: The Virginia Slavery Debate of 1831–1832.* Baton Rouge: Louisiana State University Press, 1982.

Freehling, William W. *The South vs. The South: How Anti-Confederate Southerners Shaped the Course of the Civil War.* New York: Oxford University Press, 2001.

Gallagher, Gary W. *The Confederate War.* Cambridge, Mass.: Harvard University Press, 1997.

Genovese, Eugene D. *The Political Economy of Slavery: Studies in the Economy and Society of the Slave South.* 1961. Reprint, New York: Vintage, 1967.

———. *Roll Jordan Roll: The World the Slaves Made.* New York: Vintage, 1974.

Gilje, Paul, ed. *Wages of Independence: Capitalism in the Early American Republic.* Madison, Wis.: Madison House, 1997.

Gilkeson, John S. *Middle-Class Providence, 1820–1940.* Princeton, N.J.: Princeton University Press, 1986.

Gillespie, Michele. *Free Labor in an Unfree World: White Artisans in Slaveholding Georgia, 1789–1860.* Athens: University of Georgia Press, 2000.

Gleeson, David T. *The Irish in the South, 1815–1877.* Chapel Hill: University of North Carolina Press, 2001.

Glickstein, Jonathan A. *Concepts of Free Labor in Antebellum America.* New Haven: Yale University Press, 1991.

Goldfield, David R. *Urban Growth in the Age of Sectionalism: Virginia, 1847–1861.* Baton Rouge: Louisiana State University Press, 1977.

Goldin, Claudia Dale. *Urban Slavery in the American South, 1820–1860: A Quantitative History.* Chicago: University of Chicago Press, 1976.

Gutman, Herbert G. *Work, Culture, and Society in Industrializing America: Essays in American Working-Class and Social History.* New York: Vintage, 1977.

Halttunen, Karen. *Confidence Men and Painted Women: A Study of Middle-class Culture in America, 1830–1870.* New Haven: Yale University Press, 1982.

Henderson, William D. *Petersburg in the Civil War: War at the Door.* Lynchburg, Va.: H. E. Howard, 1998.

———. *41st Virginia Infantry.* Lynchburg, Va.: H. E. Howard, 1986.

———. *12th Virginia Infantry.* 2nd ed. Lynchburg, Va.: H. E. Howard, 1984.

Hunter, Tera W. *To 'Joy My Freedom: Southern Black Women's Lives and Labors After the Civil War.* Cambridge, Mass.: Harvard University Press, 1997.

Huston, James L. *Calculating the Value of the Union: Slavery, Property Rights and the Economic Origins of the Civil War.* Chapel Hill: University of North Carolina Press, 2003.

Jackson, Luther Porter. *Free Negro Labor and Property Holding in Virginia, 1830–1860.* New York: D. Appleton-Century, 1942.

Johnson, Paul E. *A Shopkeeper's Millennium: Society and Revivals in Rochester, New York, 1815–1837.* New York: Hill and Wang, 1978.

Johnson, Whittington B. *Black Savannah, 1788–1864.* Fayetteville: University of Arkansas Press, 1996.

Jordan, Winthrop. *White Over Black: American Attitudes Toward the Negro, 1550–1812.* 1968. Reprint, Baltimore: Penguin, 1969.

Kimball, Gregg D. *American City, Southern Place: A Cultural History of Antebellum Richmond.* Athens: University of Georgia Press, 2000.

Lander, Ernest McPherson. *The Textile Industry in Antebellum South Carolina.* Baton Rouge: Louisiana State University Press, 1969.

Laurie, Bruce. *Working People of Philadelphia, 1800–1850.* Philadelphia: Temple University Press, 1980.

———. *Artisans into Workers: Labor in Nineteenth Century America.* New York: Noonday, 1989.

Lebsock, Suzanne. *The Free Women of Petersburg: Status and Culture in a Southern Town, 1784–1860.* New York: W. W. Norton, 1984.

Lewis, Johanna Miller. *Artisans in the North Carolina Backcountry.* Lexington: University Press of Kentucky, 1995.

Lewis, Ronald L. *Coal, Iron, and Slaves: Industrial Slavery in Maryland and Virginia, 1715–1865.* Westport, Conn.: Greenwood, 1979.

Link, William A. *Roots of Secession: Slavery and Politics in Antebellum Virginia.* Chapel Hill: University of North Carolina Press, 2003.

Litwack, Leon F. *North of Slavery: The Negro in the Free States, 1790–1860.* Chicago: University of Chicago Press, 1961.

McCardell, John, *The Idea of a Southern Nation: Southern Nationalists and Southern Nationalism, 1830–1860.* New York: W. W. Norton, 1979.

McCormick, Richard P. *The Second American Party System: Party Formation in the Jacksonian Era.* Chapel Hill: University of North Carolina Press, 1966.

McCurry, Stephanie. *Masters of Small Worlds: Yeoman Households, Gender Relations, and Political Culture of the Antebellum South Carolina Low Country.* New York: Oxford University Press, 1995.

McGaw, Judith A. *Most Wonderful Machine: Mechanization and Social Change in Berkshire Paper Making, 1801–1885.* Princeton, N.J.: Princeton University Press, 1987.

McKee, Stephenson, and Marianne McKee, eds. *Virginia in Maps: Four Centuries of Settlement, Growth, and Development.* Richmond, Library of Virginia, 2000.

McLaurin, Melton Alonza. *The Knights of Labor in the South.* Westport, Conn.: Greenwood, 1978.

McPherson, James M. *Battle Cry of Freedom: The Civil War Era.* New York: Ballantine, 1989.

Mitchell, Broadus. *William Gregg: Factory Master of the Old South.* 1928. Reprint, New York: Octagon, 1966.

Morgan, Lynda J. *Emancipation in Virginia's Tobacco Belt, 1850–1870.* Athens: University of Georgia Press, 1992.

Newman, Simon P. *Parades and the Politics of the Streets: Festive Culture in the Early American Republic.* Philadelphia: University of Pennsylvania Press, 1997.

Noe, Kenneth W. *Southwest Virginia's Railroad: Modernization and the Sectional Crisis.* Urbana: University of Illinois Press, 1994.

Oakes, James. *The Ruling Race: A History of American Slaveholders.* 1982. Reprint, New York: W. W. Norton, 1998.

Oates, Stephen B. *The Fires of Jubilee: Nat Turner's Fierce Rebellion.* New York: New American Library, 1976.

Olton, Charles S. *Artisans for Independence: Philadelphia Mechanics and the American Revolution.* Syracuse, N.Y.: Syracuse University Press, 1975.

Phillips, Christopher. *Freedom's Port: The African American Community of Baltimore, 1790–1860.* Urbana: University of Illinois Press, 1997.

Phillips, Ulrich B. *Life and Labor in the Old South.* Boston: Little, Brown, 1929.

Powers, Bernard E. *Black Charlestonians: A Social History, 1822–1885.* Fayetteville: University of Arkansas Press, 1994.

Prude, Jonathan. *The Coming of Industrial Order: Town and Factory Life in Rural Massachusetts, 1810–1860.* Cambridge: Cambridge University Press, 1983.

Quist, John W. *Restless Visionaries: The Social Roots of Antebellum Reform in Alabama and Michigan.* Baton Rouge: Louisiana State University Press, 1998.

Rilling, Donna J. *Making Houses, Crafting Capitalism: Builders in Philadelphia, 1790–1850.* Philadelphia: University of Pennsylvania Press, 2001.

Robert, Joseph Clarke. *The Tobacco Kingdom: Plantation, Market, and Factory in Virginia and North Carolina, 1800–1860.* 1938. Reprint, Gloucester, Mass.: Peter Smith, 1965.

Roberts, Bruce. *Plantation Homes of the James River.* Chapel Hill: University of North Carolina Press, 1990.

Robertson, William G. *The Battle of Old Men and Young Boys, June 9 1864.* Lynchburg, Va.: H. E. Howard, 1989.

Rock, Howard B. *Artisans of the New Republic: The Tradesmen of New York City in the Age of Jefferson.* New York: New York University Press, 1979.

Rock, Howard B., Paul A. Gilje, and Robert Asher, eds. *American Artisans: Crafting Social Identity, 1750–1850.* Baltimore: Johns Hopkins University Press, 1995.

Roediger, David R. *The Wages of Whiteness: Race and the Making of the American Working Class.* London: Verso, 1991.

Rorabaugh, W. J. *The Craft Apprentice: From Franklin to the Machine Age in America.* New York: Oxford University Press, 1986.

Ross, Steven J. *Workers on the Edge: Work, Leisure, and Politics in Industrializing Cincinnati, 1788–1890.* New York: Columbia University Press, 1985.

Scarborough, William Kauffman. *Masters of the Big House: Elite Slaveholders of the Mid-Nineteenth-Century South.* Baton Rouge: Louisiana State University Press, 2003.

Schultz, Ronald. *The Republic of Labor: Philadelphia Artisans and the Politics of Class, 1720–1830.* New York: Oxford University Press, 1993.

Scott, James G., and Edward A. Wyatt. *Petersburg's Story: A History.* Petersburg, Va.: Titmus Optical, 1960.

Sellers, Charles. *The Market Revolution: Jacksonian America, 1815–1846.* New York: Oxford University Press, 1991.

Shade, William G. *Democratizing the Old Dominion: Virginia and the Second Party System, 1824–1861.* Charlottesville: University Press of Virginia, 1996.

Shirley, Michael. *From Congregational Town to Industrial City: Culture and Social Change in a Southern Community.* New York: New York University Press, 1994.

Sidbury, James. *Ploughshares into Swords: Race, Rebellion, and Identity in Gabriel's Virginia, 1730–1810.* Cambridge: Cambridge University Press, 1997.

Siegel, Frederick F. *The Roots of Southern Distinctiveness: Tobacco and Society in Danville, Virginia, 1780–1865.* Chapel Hill: University of North Carolina Press, 1987.

Stampp, Kenneth M. *The Peculiar Institution: Slavery in the Ante-Bellum South.* New York: Vintage, 1956.

Starobin, Robert S. *Industrial Slavery in the Old South.* Oxford: Oxford University Press, 1970.

Steffen, Charles G. *The Mechanics of Baltimore: Workers and Politics in the Age of Revolution, 1763–1812.* Urbana: University of Illinois Press, 1984.

Stokes, Melvyn, and Stephen Conway, eds. *The Market Revolution in America: Social, Political, and Religious Expressions, 1800–1880.* Charlottesville: University Press of Virginia, 1996.

Striplin, E. F. Pat. *The Norfolk and Western: A History.* Roanoke, Va.: The Norfolk and Western Railway Company, 1981.

Sutton, William R. *Journeymen for Jesus: Evangelical Artisans Confront Capitalism in Jacksonian Baltimore.* University Park: Pennsylvania State University Press, 1998.

Sydnor, Charles S. *Gentlemen Freeholders: Political Practices in Washington's Virginia.* Chapel Hill: University of North Carolina Press, 1952.

———. *The Development of Southern Sectionalism, 1819–1848.* 1948. Reprint, Baton Rouge: Louisiana State University Press, 1968.

Tadman, Michael. *Speculators and Slaves: Masters, Traders, and Slaves in the Old South.* Madison: University of Wisconsin Press, 1989.

Takagi, Midori. *"Rearing Wolves to Our Own Destruction": Slavery in Richmond, Virginia, 1782–1865.* Charlottesville: University Press of Virginia, 1999.

Takaki, Ronald. *Iron Cages: Race and Culture in 19th-Century America.* Rev. ed. New York: Oxford University Press, 2000.

Taylor, George Rogers. *The Transportation Revolution, 1815–1860.* New York: Harper & Row, 1951.

Thernstrom, Stephen. *Poverty and Progress: Social Mobility in a Nineteenth Century City.* Cambridge, Mass.: Harvard University Press, 1964.

Thompson, E. P. *The Making of the English Working Class.* New York: Pantheon, 1964.

Tise, Larry E. *Proslavery: A History of the Defense of Slavery in America, 1701–1840*. Athens: University of Georgia Press, 1987.

Towers, Frank. *The Urban South and the Coming of the Civil War*. Charlottesville: University of Virginia Press, 2004.

Tripp, Steven Elliott. *Yankee Town, Southern City: Race and Class Relations in Civil War Lynchburg*. New York: New York University Press, 1997.

Trudeau, Noah Andre. *The Last Citadel: Petersburg, Virginia, June 1864–April 1865*. Boston: Little, Brown, 1991.

Wade, Richard C. *Slavery in the Cities: The South 1820–1860*. New York: Oxford University Press, 1964.

Waldstreicher, David. *In the Midst of Perpetual Fetes: The Making of American Nationalism, 1776–1820*. Chapel Hill: University of North Carolina Press for the Omohundro Institute of Early American History and Culture, 1997.

Wallace, Lee A. *A Guide to Virginia Military Organizations 1861–1865*. Rev. 2nd ed. Lynchburg, Va.: H. E. Howard, 1986.

Wells, Jonathan Daniel. *The Origins of the Southern Middle Class, 1800–1861*. Chapel Hill: University of North Carolina Press, 2004.

Wertenbaker, Thomas J. *Norfolk: Historic Southern Port*. 1931. Reprint, Durham, N.C.: Duke University Press, 1962.

Whitman, T. Stephen. *The Price of Freedom: Slavery and Manumission in Baltimore and Early National Maryland*. Lexington: University Press of Kentucky, 1997.

Wilentz, Sean. *Chants Democratic: New York City and the Rise of the American Working Class, 1788–1850*. New York: Oxford University Press, 1984.

Woodson, Carter G. *Free Negro Owners of Slaves in the United States in 1830*. New York: Negro Universities Press, 1924.

Wyatt, Edward A. *Along Petersburg Streets: Historic Sites and Buildings of Petersburg, Virginia*. Richmond: Dietz, 1943.

———. *Plantation Houses Around Petersburg in the Counties of Prince George, Chesterfield, and Dinwiddie, Virginia*. Petersburg, Va.: Reprinted from the Petersburg *Progress-Index*, 1955.

———. *Preliminary Checklist for Petersburg, 1786–1876*. Richmond: Virginia State Library, 1949.

Wyatt-Brown, Bertram. *Southern Honor: Ethics and Behavior in the Old South*. New York: Oxford University Press, 1982.

Theses and Dissertations

Edwards, Lucious. "Free Black Property Holders in Petersburg, Virginia: 1865–1874." M.A. thesis, Virginia State College, 1977.

Ferrari, Mary Catherine. "Artisans of the South: A Comparative Study of Norfolk, Charleston and Alexandria, 1763–1800." Ph.D. diss., College of William and Mary, 1992.

Gillespie, Michele K. "Artisans and Mechanics in the Political Economy of Georgia, 1790–1860." Ph.D. diss., Princeton University, 1990.

Hart, Emma. "Constructing a New World: Charleston's Artisans and the Transformation of the South Carolina Lowcountry, 1700–1800." Ph.D. diss., Johns Hopkins University, 2002.

Hartzell, Lawrence Leroy. "Black Life in Petersburg, 1870–1902." M.A. thesis, University of Virginia, 1985.

Kimball, Gregg David. "Place and Perception: Richmond in Late Antebellum America." Ph.D. diss., University of Virginia, 1997.

Kornblith, Gary J. "From Artisans to Businessmen: Master Mechanics in New England, 1789–1850." Ph.D. diss., Princeton University, 1983.

Russo, Jean Burrell. "Free Workers in a Plantation Economy: Talbot County, Maryland, 1690–1759." Ph.D. diss., Johns Hopkins University, 1983.

Steger, Werner H. "'United to Support, But Not Combined to Injure': Free Workers and Immigrants in Richmond, Virginia, during the Era of Sectionalism, 1847–1865." Ph.D. diss., George Washington University, 1999.

Index

Adams, George W., 167

Adams, Richard, 87, 101

Adkins, William, 144

African Americans (free): 4, 7, 13, 36, 68, 111–112, 131, 156–157, 168, 169, 173–174, 190–191, 195, 197, 201–202, 202–203, 211; as artisans, 127, 132, 135–136; as barbers, 136–138, 203; attempts to remove from Virginia, 107–108, 146–147; benevolent aid of, 133–134, 154–155; businesses owned by, 132–133, 134, 143, 203; carrying trade and, 133, 208; and competition with white labor, 106–108, 112, 128, 135, 152–153, 185–186, 192, 194; importance to the economy, 34, 130, 145; in the North, 9, 141, 191–192; legal rights and restrictions of, 130–131, 138, 139–141, 202; and mulattoes, 128, 136, 137–138, 140; occupations of, 98, 129, 132–133, 134, 136–138, 139, 140, 142, 160, 202; Petersburg population of, 33–34, 127–128, 129–130, 215; slave ownership by, 146–150; unskilled, 98, 127–128, 132

African Baptist Church, 146

Albright, Isaac, 151

Alley, H. T., 76

Alley, Martin, 87

Alley, Thomas, 63

American Colonization Society, 46

American Constellation (Petersburg), 78

Apothecaries, 73, 94, 163, 204, 217, 221, 224

Appomattox Canal, 21–22, 27, 199, 207

Appomattox Iron Works, 32

Appomattox Manor, 15, 28, 84–85

Appomattox River, 1, 12, 21–22, 25, 31, 51, 58, 84, 85, 113, 132, 135, 165, 172, 208, 212

Apprentices: 47, 49–50, 51, 52, 66, 75, 76, 77, 101, 110, 141, 148, 178, 183, 201; African American,

81, 134, 142, 143, 144; bound to factories, 81; and changes in the apprenticeship system, 76–81; female, 81; in print shops, 79–80; poor relief and, 80–81

Archer, Alfred, 111

Archer, Allen, 47, 64, 167, 184

Archer, Fletcher H., 204

Archer Rifles (Company K, Twelfth Va. Infantry), 204, 205

Armory Works (Richmond, Va.), 164

Army Medical Corps, 207

Army of Northern Virginia, 205

Artisans: downward mobility of, 8, 186–188; European, 82; Fourth of July and, 176, 183–184; immigrant, 71, 95–96, 97–104; investment in industry and internal improvements, 57–60; involvement in local politics, 48, 54–56, 104–106, 109, 182, 210; northern, 86–87, 99, 178, 188–189, 197; occupations of, 37–38, 41, 43; persistence rates of, 86–91; producer ideology of, 48–49; property ownership of, 88–89; racially mixed workshops of, 142–143, 150, 202; and relationship to the hinterland, 10, 38, 81–86, 145; republicanism of, 2, 49, 66, 107, 112, 176–181, 185–186, 200; slavery and, 9–10, 92–96, 109, 147–149, 176–177, 190–191; upward mobility of, 8, 40, 56–60, 180–182. *See also* Apprentices; Journeymen

Artisanal societies, 8, 40. *See also* Petersburg Benevolent Mechanic Society (PBMA); Petersburg Mechanic Association (PMA)

Athens, Ga., 97

Atkinson, Jedediah T., 48

Atwill, Major John D., 74

Augusta County, Va., 6

245

McCracken, Davy, 99
McCreay, John, 148
McEnery, Henry O., 19
McFarland, James, Jr., 59, 60
Mechanical Association of Cincinnati (Ohio), 141
Mechanical Society of Philadelphia (Pa.), 39
Mechanics. *See* Artisans
Mechanics and Apprentices' Library, 49–51
Mechanics' Association (Providence, R.I.), 50
Mechanics' Association of Charleston (S.C.), 193
Mechanics' Hall (Petersburg), 86, 111
Mechanics' Institute (N.Y.), 50
Mechanics' Lyceum, 110
Mechanics Manufacturing Company, 26, 59–60
Mechanics Savings Society, 59–60
Mechanization, 18, 67, 187, 188
Mendell, Sarah, 12, 36
Merchant's Manufacturing Company, 25
Middle class: 8, 9, 111, 145, 179; artisans mov-
   ing into, 2, 37, 41, 43–45, 49, 65, 68–69, 187,
   197, 200; in the North, 40, 203; in the South,
   69–70, 93, 96
Middling artisans: 45, 52, 60, 62, 68–71, 88–89,
   104–108, 135, 185, 201; compared to Peters-
   burg Benevolent Mechanical Association mem-
   bers, 56, 72, 74–76, 86, 89–90, 179; occupations
   of, 71–74; organizations of, 109–112, 185–186;
   persistence rates of, 86–88, 92; slaveholding by,
   89, 93–96, 196
Militia, artisans and, 70, 91, 94, 100, 143, 182, 184,
   191, 200, 204, 205
Miller, Charles, 100
Millers, 41, 43, 64, 73, 76, 90, 95, 136, 173, 217,
   219, 222, 224, 229
Minetree, James, 111
Minnis, George W., 87
Mobile, Ala., 97
Moody, Alexander, 104
Moore, Joseph L., 47
Morgan, William, 57
Morris, William, 137
Morrison, John, 104
Mowberry, William, 151
Mulattoes. *See* African Americans
Mumford, Nancy, 146
Murphy, James T., 77

Nashville, Tenn., 97
Neal, John M., 46
New Orleans, La., 102, 104, 142, 146, 169
New York Mechanics' Mutual Protection Associa-
   tion, 39
Newsom, George F., 88, 89
Newsome, Richard, 151–152
Niles' Weekly Register (Baltimore, Md.), 22, 58
Noah Walker & Company, 209
Norfolk, Va., 28, 30, 204, 205
Norfolk and Petersburg Railroad, 30, 58, 212
North Carolina, 5, 13, 16, 27, 28, 53, 208
Nott, Josiah, 195

Oakes, James, 45, 47, 93, 196
Odd Fellows, 41, 153, 154
Order of United American Mechanics, 103
Osborne, Charles F., 47, 59, 159
Overseers of the poor, 66, 77, 143, 144, 158

Painters, 63, 78–79, 83, 85, 89, 110, 136, 137, 196,
   207, 219, 225, 229
Panic of 1837, 53, 62
Panic of 1857, 71, 110, 128, 153, 157, 185, 192, 194,
   202
Parades, July Fourth, 176, 184
Parham, Arthur, 148
Parham, William, 143
Patterson, John H., 143, 212
Patton, James C., 84
Paul, D'Arcy, 53, 111
Payne, John H., 79
Peace, George, 100
Pearman, Silas, 89
Penman, Robert, 78, 101, 110
Perkinson, Daniel, 84
Pescud, Edward, 58, 76
Petersburg: demographics of, 14, 32–36, 71,
   127–128, 131; economy during the Civil War,
   11, 204, 209–210, 211–212; immigrants in,
   98–100; siege of, 211–212
Petersburg Benevolent Mechanic Association
   (PBMA); 8, 36, 37, 50, 66, 68, 70, 75–76, 111,
   143, 161, 179–182; membership and occupations
   of, 41–43, 45; mutual aid provided, 44, 61–64;
   persistence rates as compared to nonmembers,